DISCARDED

# Thai
## Phrase Book
## &
## Dictionary

**Berlitz Publishing**
New York     Munich     Singapore

Contacting the Editors
Every effort has been made to provide accurate information in this publication, but changes are inevitable. The publisher cannot be responsible for any resulting loss, inconvenience or injury. We would appreciate it if readers would call our attention to any errors or outdated information. We also welcome your suggestions; if you come across a relevant expression not in our phrase book, please contact us:
Berlitz Publishing, 193 Morris Avenue, Springfield, NJ 07081, USA. E-mail: comments@berlitzbooks.com

First Printing: October 2008
Printed in Singapore

Publishing Director: Sheryl Olinsky Borg
Senior Editor/Project Manager: Lorraine Sova
Editorial: Dr. Yuphaphann Hoonchamlong, Dr. Chatchawadee Saralamba,
Dr. Sompong Witayasakpan
Composition: Datagrafix, Inc.
Cover Design: Claudia Petrilli
Interior Design: Derrick Lim, Juergen Bartz
Production Manager: Elizabeth Gaynor
Cover Photo: © Nicholas Pitt/Digital Vision/Photolibrary.com
Interior Photos: p. 14 © Studio Fourteen/Brand X Pictures/age fotostock; p. 18 © Charles Taylor, 2008. Used under license from Shutterstock, Inc.; p. 26 © Pixtal/age fotostock; p. 40 © Corbis/fotosearch.com; p. 50 © Purestock/Alamy; p. 55 © Dan Peretz, 2008. Used under license from Shutterstock, Inc.; p. 68 © Paul Clarke, 2008. Used under license from Shutterstock, Inc.; p. 84 © ImageDJ/Alamy; p. 87 © Netflis/2003-2007 Shutterstock, Inc.; p. 103 © Image Source Pink/Alamy; p. 107 © BananaStock Ltd./; p. 112 © Daniel Thistlethwaite/PictureQuest; p. 113 © Travelwide / Alamy; p. 116 © Jason Maehl 2008. Used under license from Shutterstock, Inc.; p. 120, 126 © 2007-2008 Jupiterimages Corporation; p. 139 © Jupiterimages/Brand X/Corbis; p. 142 © Stockbyte/Fotosearch.com; p. 145 © Corbis/2006 Jupiterimages Corporation; p. 146 © David McKee/2003-2007 Shutterstock, Inc.; p. 148, 152, 167 © 2007 Jupiterimages Corporation

# *Contents*

## *Survival*

# Food

# People

# *Fun*

# *Special Needs*

## Resources

## Dictionary

# *Pronunciation*

This section is designed to make you familiar with the sounds of Thai using our simplified phonetic transcription. You'll find the pronunciation of the Thai letters and sounds explained below, together with their "imitated" equivalents. This system is used throughout the phrase book; simply read the pronunciation as if it were English, noting any special rules below.

## Consonants

 Consonants are considerably easier to pronounce in Thai than vowels since all but a few have English equivalents. The consonants producing the same sound are grouped together. The sounds you will find as initial consonants of syllables are as follows.

| Letter(s) | Approximate Pronunciation | Symbol | Example | Pronunciation |
|---|---|---|---|---|
| ก | g as in gas | g | กิน | gihn |
| ข, ค, ฆ | k as in king | k | ค้า, ขาย, ฆ่า | kár, kǐe, kâr |
| จ | j as in jet | j | จาน | jarn |
| ง | ng as in singer | ng | งาน | ngarn |
| ฉ, ช | ch as in cheese | ch | ฉัน, ช้าง | cháhn, chárng |
| ซ, ศ, ษ, ส | s as in sun | s | ซ้าย, ศาล, ภาษา, สิบ | síe, sǎrn, par·sǎr, sìhp |
| ญ, ย | y as in year | y | ใหญ่, เย็น | yì, yehn |
| ด, ฎ | d as in dog | d | ดอกไม้, ฎกา | dòrk·mí, chah·dar |
| ต, ฏ | t as in star (sharp t) | dt[1] | เต่า ปฏัก | dtòu, bpà·dtàhk |

7

| Letter(s) | Approximate Pronunciation | Symbol | Example | Pronunciation |
|---|---|---|---|---|
| ฐ, ฑ, ฒ, ถ, ธ | t as in tan | t | ฐาน, ทหาร, ผู้เฒ่า, ถนน, ธรรมชาติ | tărn, tah·hărn, pôo·tôu, tah·nŏn, tahm·mah·chârt |
| ณ, น | n as in new | n | เณร, น้ำ | nen, nárm |
| บ | b as in band | b | บอก | bòrk |
| ป | p as in speak (sharp p) | bp[2] | ไป | bpi |
| ผ, พ, ภ | p as in pen | p | ผึ้ง, เพื่อน, รูปภาพ | pûeng, pûean, rôop·pârp[3] |
| ฝ, ฟ | f as in fun | f | ฝน, สีฟ้า | fŏn, sĕe·fár |
| ม | m as in man | m | แม่ | mâe |
| ร | r as in run | r | รถยนต์ | rót·yon |
| ล, ฬ | l as in love | l | ลิง, นาฬิกา | lihng, nar·lih·gar |
| ว | w as in work | w | วัน | wahn |
| ห, ฮ | h as in happy | h | แห้ง, นกฮูก | hâeng, nók·hôok |
| อ | o as in on | o | อ่อน | òrn |

[1] A combination of two letters, *d* and *t*, are used here to indicate the sharp sound *t* in order to differentiate this sound from the normal sound of *t*.

[2] Similarly, *b* and *p* are used to indicate the sharp sound *p*.

[3] As final consonants of syllables, the letters *p,t* and *k* are pronounced as the sharp sounds *p*, *t* and *k*.

# Vowels

In Thai, each vowel is pronounced with either a short or a long duration; try to mimic these durations when speaking Thai, as that they indicate different meanings. Following are the approximate pronunciation of short and long vowels.

| Letter[1] | Sound Duration | Approximate Pronunciation | Symbol | Example | Pronunciation |
|---|---|---|---|---|---|
| -ะ, -ั- | short | a as in about | ah | จะ, รัก | jah, ráhk |
| -า- | long | ar as in cart, without pronouncing the r | ar | ขา | kǎr |
| -ิ | short | i as in pit | ih | บิน | bihn |
| -ี | long | ee as in bee | ee | ปีก | bpèek |
| -ึ | short | u as in put + e as in exam | ue | ลึก | lúek |
| -ื | long | u as in put + e as in exam, with the e sound lengthened | uee | กลางคืน | glarng·kueen |
| -ุ | short | u as in put | uh | ขุด | kùht |
| -ู | long | oo as in root | oo | พูด | pôot |
| เ-ะ, เ-็ | short | e as in get | eh | เตะ, เล็ก | dtèh, léhk |
| เ- | long | e as in bed with the e sound lengthened | e | เพลง | pleng |
| แ-ะ, แ-็ | short | a as in match | a | แกะ, แข็งแรง | gà, kǎng·raeng |
| แ- | long | a as in band | ae | สีแดง | sěe·daeng |

[1] The dash (-) indicates the position of the consonant in relation to the vowel or vowel cluster.

9

| Letter | Sound Duration | Approximate Pronunciation | Symbol | Example | Pronunciation |
|--------|------|--------------------------|--------|---------|---------------|
| โ-ะ | short | o as in no with a short duration | o | โต๊ะ | dtó |
| โ- | long | oe as in toe | oe | โรงเรียน | roeng·rean |
| เ-าะ | short | o as in spot | oh | เกาะ | gòh |
| -อ- | long | or as in worn, without pronouncing the r | or | รอ, ทอง | ror, torng |
| เ-ีย | long | ea as in spear | ea | เปลี่ยน | bplèan |
| เ-ือ | long | like ue + a sound | uea | มะเขือเทศ | máh·kŭea·têt |
| -ัว, -ว- | long | oar as in boar without pronouncing the r | oar | กลัว, สวม | gloar, sŏarm |
| เ-ิ, เ-อ | long | er as in per without pronouncing the rer | er | เดิน, เจอ | dern, jer |
| -ำ | short | a as in about + m | ahm | ทำ | tahm |
| -้ำ | long | a as in cart + m | arm | น้ำ | nárm |
| ไ-, ใ- | short | i as in bicycle | i | ไป, ใหม่ | bpi, mì |
| -าย | long | ie as in pie | ie | สาย | sĭe |
| เ-า | short | ou as in count | ou | เขา | kŏu |
| -าว | long | ow as in how | ow | ขาว | kŏw |

Two Thai letters, อ and ว, function as both consonants and vowels. When they are used as consonants they will always be initial consonants in a syllable and take an initial sound as listed in the consonant table. But when they are used as vowels their sounds will be as follows:

– อ has an or sound as in torn and can be in the middle or at the end of a syllable.

– ว has an oar sound as in boar and will always be in the middle of a syllable.

## Tones

Thai is a tonal language. The phonetic transcriptions in this phrase book include the following tone marks:

| Tone | Pitch | Symbol |
| --- | --- | --- |
| mid tone | normal speaking with the voice at a steady pitch | no mark |
| high tone | pitched slightly higher than normal | ´ |
| low tone | pitched slightly lower than normal | ` |
| falling tone | pitched high and falling sharply | ^ |
| rising tone | pitched low and rising sharply | ˇ |

Here are examples of how tone changes the meaning of a word:

| Thai Script | Pronunciation | Tone | Meaning |
| --- | --- | --- | --- |
| คา | kar | mid tone | to dangle |
| ข่า | kàr | low tone | galanga (a cooking spice) |
| ฆ่า | kâr | falling tone | to kill |
| ค้า | kár | high tone | to trade |
| ขา | kǎr | rising tone | a leg |

Standard Thai, sometimes called Central Thai or Siamese, part of the Tai family of languages, is a tonal language with a highly complex orthographic system. Written Thai does not use space to mark word boundary: "thaileavesnospacebetweenwords". And, though punctuation marks exist, they are generally not used in writing.

Standard Thai is the official language of Thailand, though it has several different forms, which are used in special social situations, especially in informal, formal, religious and royal contexts.

# *How to Use This Book*

These essential phrases can also be heard on the audio CD.

Sometimes you see two alternatives in italics, separated by a slash. Choose the one that's right for your situation.

## Essential

| | |
|---|---|
| I'm on *vacation* *[holiday]*/*business*. | ผม♂/ฉัน♀ มา *เที่ยว*/*ธุระ* pŏm♂/cháhn♀ mar *têaw*/*túh•ráh* |
| I'm going to... | ผม♂/ฉัน♀ จะไปที่... pŏm♂/cháhn♀ jah bpi têe... |
| I'm staying at the... Hotel. | ผม♂/ฉัน♀ พักอยู่ที่โรงแรม... pŏm♂/cháhn♀ páhk yòo têe roeng•raem... |

## You May See...

| | |
|---|---|
| ขาเข้า kăr kôu | arrivals |
| ขาออก kăr òrk | departures |
| ที่รับกระเป๋า têe ráhp grah•bpŏu | baggage claim |

## Finding Lodging

| | |
|---|---|
| Can you recommend...? | ช่วยแนะนำ...ให้หน่อยได้ไหม? chôary ná•nahm... hî nòhy dîe mí |
| – a hotel | – โรงแรม roeng•raem |
| – a hostel | – ที่พักเยาวชน têe páhk you•wah•chon |
| – a campsite | – ที่ตั้งแค็มป์ têe dtâhng káem |

Words you may see are shown in *You May See* boxes.

Any of the words or phrases preceded by dashes can be plugged into the sentence above.

Thai phrases appear in red.

Read the simplified pronunciation as if it were English. For more on pronunciation, see page 7.

## Relationships

| | |
|---|---|
| How old are you? | คุณอายุเท่าไหร่? kuhn ar·yúh tôu·rì |
| I'm... | ผม ♂/ฉัน ♀ อายุ... pǒm ♂/cháhn ♀ ar·yúh... |

▶ For numbers, see page 165.

When different gender forms apply, the masculine form is followed by ♂; feminine by ♀.

| | |
|---|---|
| Are you married? | คุณแต่งงานแล้วหรือยัง? rúe yahng |
| I'm... | ผม ♂/ฉัน ♀... pǒm ♂/c... |
| – single/in a relationship | – ยังโสด/มีแฟนแล้ว yahng sòet/mee faen láew |
| – engaged/married | – มีศูหมั้นแล้ว/แต่งงานแล้ว mee kôo·mâhn láew/ dtàng·ngarn láew |
| – divorced/separated | – หย่าแล้ว/แยกกันอยู่ yàr láew/yâek gahn yòo |
| – widowed | – เป็นหม้าย bpehn mîe |

The arrow indicates a cross reference where you'll find related phrases.

Information boxes contain relevant country, culture and language tips.

*i* Rather than shaking hands, in Thailand it is polite to greet people with a ไหว้ **wîe** ("wai", Thai gesture of greeting).

## You May Hear...

| | |
|---|---|
| ผม ♂/ฉัน ♀ พูดภาษาอังกฤษได้ นิดหน่อย pǒm ♂/ cháhn ♀ pôot par·sǎr ahng·grìht dîe níht·nòhy | I only speak a little English. |
| ผม ♂/ฉัน ♀ พูดภาษาอังกฤษไม่ได้ pǒm ♂/cháhn ♀ pôot par·sǎr ahng·grìht mî dîe | I don't speak English |

Expressions you may hear are shown in *You May Hear* boxes.

Color-coded side bars identify each section of the book.

# ▼ Survival

# Arrival and Departure

## Essential

| | |
|---|---|
| I'm on *vacation* [*holiday*]/business. | ผม ♂/ฉัน ♀ มา *เที่ยว/ธุระ* pŏm ♂/cháhn ♀ mar têaw/túh·ráh |
| I'm going to… | ผม ♂/ฉัน ♀ จะไปที่… pŏm ♂/cháhn ♀ jah bpi têe… |
| I'm staying at the… Hotel. | ผม ♂/ฉัน ♀ พักอยู่ที่โรงแรม… pŏm ♂/cháhn ♀ páhk yòo têe roeng·raem… |

## You May Hear…

| | |
|---|---|
| ขอดูพาสปอร์ตหน่อย kŏr doo páns·sah·bpòrt nòhy | Your passport, please. |
| จุดประสงค์ในการมาครั้งนี้คืออะไร? jùht·bprah·sŏng ni garn mar kráhng née kuee ah·ri | What's the purpose of your visit? |
| คุณพักที่ไหน? kuhn páhk têe·nĭ | Where are you staying? |
| คุณจะอยู่ที่นี่นานเท่าไหร่? kuhn jah yòo têe·nêe narn tôu·rì | How long are you staying? |
| คุณมาที่นี่กับใคร? kuhn mar têe·nêe gàhp kri | Who are you here with? |

## Passport Control and Customs

| | |
|---|---|
| I'm just passing through. | ผม ♂/ฉัน ♀ แค่แวะผ่านเท่านั้น pŏm ♂/cháhn ♀ kâe wá pàrn tôu·náhn |
| I'd like to declare… | ผม ♂/ฉัน ♀ มี…ที่ต้องการแสดง pŏm ♂/cháhn ♀ mee…têe dtôhng·garn sah·daeng |
| I have nothing to declare. | ผม ♂/ฉัน ♀ ไม่มีสิ่งของต้องแสดง pŏm ♂/cháhn ♀ mî mee sìhng·kŏrng dtôrng sah·daeng |

## You May Hear...

มีอะไรจะแสดงไหม? mee ah·ri jah sah·daeng mí — Anything to declare?

คุณจะต้องจ่ายภาษีสำหรับสิ่งนี้ kuhn jah dtôrng jìe par·sĕe săhm·ràhp sìhng née — You must pay duty on this.

ช่วยเปิดกระเป๋าใบนี้หน่อย chôary bpèrt grah·bpŏu bi née nòhy — Open this luggage.

## You May See...

ศุลกากร sĭhn·lah·gar·gorn — customs

สินค้าปลอดภาษี sĭhn·kár bplòrt par·sĕe — duty-free goods

จุดตรวจหนังสือเดินทาง jùht dtròart năhng·sŭee dern·tarng — passport control

ตำรวจ dtahm·ròart — police

# *Money and Banking*

## Essential

| | |
|---|---|
| Where's...? | ...อยู่ที่ไหน? ...yòo têe·nĭ |
| – the ATM | – ตู้เอทีเอ็ม dtôo e·tee·ehm |
| – the bank | – ธนาคาร tah·nar·karn |
| – the currency exchange office | – ที่รับแลกเงิน têe ráhp lâek ngern |
| When does the bank *open/close*? | ธนาคาร *เปิด/ปิด* เมื่อไหร่? tah·nar·karn *bpèrt/bpiht* mûea·rì |

I'd like to change *dollars/pounds* into baht.

ผม♂/ฉัน♀ อยากแลกเงินดอลลาร์/ปอนด์เป็นเงินบาท pŏm♂/cháhn♀ yàrk lâek ngern *dohn·lâr/bporn* bpehn ngern bàrt

I'd like to cash traveler's checks [cheques].

ผม♂/ฉัน♀ อยากขึ้นเงินเช็คเดินทาง pŏm♂/cháhn♀ yàrk kûen·ngern chéhk dern·tarng

## ATM, Bank and Currency Exchange

I'd like to...

ผม♂/ฉัน♀ อยากจะ... pŏm♂/cháhn♀ yàrk jah...

– change money

– แลกเงิน lâek ngern

– change *dollars/ pounds* into baht

– แลกเงินดอลลาร์/ปอนด์เป็นเงินบาท lâek ngern *dohn·lâr/bporn* bpehn ngern bàrt

– cash *traveler's checks [cheques]/ Eurocheques*

– ขึ้นเงิน เช็คเดินทาง/ยูโรเช็ค kûen·ngern *chéhk dern·tarng/yoo·roe chéhk*

– get a cash advance

– เบิกเงินสดล่วงหน้า bèrk ngern·sòt lôarng nâr

What's the exchange *rate/fee*?

อัตรา/ค่าธรรมเนียม แลกเปลี่ยนเท่าไหร่? àht·dtrar/kâr·tahm·neam lâek·bplèan tôu·rì

I think there's a mistake.

ผม♂/ฉัน♀ คิดว่ามีอะไรผิดพลาด pŏm♂/cháhn♀ kíht wâr mee ah·ri pìht·plârt

I lost my traveler's checks [cheques].

ผม♂/ฉัน♀ ทำเช็คเดินทางหาย pŏm♂/cháhn♀ tahm chéhk dern·tarng hĭe

My card...

บัตรของผม♂/ฉัน♀... bàht kŏhng pŏm♂/cháhn♀...

– was lost

– หาย hĭe

– was stolen

– ถูกขโมย tòok kah·moey

– doesn't work

– ใช้ไม่ได้ chí mî dîe

The ATM ate my card.

ตู้เอทีเอ็มกินบัตรของผม♂/ฉัน♀ ไป dtôo e·tee·ehm gihn bàht kŏhng pŏm♂/cháhn♀ bpi

Cash can be obtained from ATMs throughout Thailand, though some machines may be unreliable. Some debit cards and most major credit cards are accepted. Be sure to confirm this with your card-issuing bank. Also, know whether your PIN is compatible with Thai machines, which usually expect a four-digit, numeric code. ATMs usually offer good rates, though there may be some hidden fees.

Currency exchange offices and banks are an option for exchanging currency. Banks across the country are generally open Monday to Friday 8:30 a.m. to 3:30 p.m.

## You May See...

| | |
|---|---|
| สอดบัตรที่นี่ sòrt bàht têe•nêe | insert card here |
| ยกเลิก yók•lêrk | cancel |
| รหัส ra•hàht | PIN |
| ถอน tŏrn | withdrawal |
| ใบบันทึกรายการ bi bahn•túek rie•garn | receipt |

*i* Thai currency is the บาท **bàrt** (baht), divided into สตางค์ **sah-dtarng** (satang).

Coins: 25 and 50 satang; 1, 2, 5, and 10 baht.

Bills: 20 (green bill), 50 (blue bill), 100 (red bill), 500 (purple bill) and 1000 (gray bill) baht.

# *Transportation*

## Essential

| | |
|---|---|
| How do I get to town? | ผม♂/ฉัน♀ จะเข้าเมืองยังไง? pŏm♂/cháhn♀ jah kôu mueang yahng•ngi |
| Where's…? | …อยู่ที่ไหน? …yòo têe•nǐ |
| – the airport | – สนามบิน sah•nǎrm•bihn |
| – the train [railway] station | – สถานีรถไฟ sah•tǎr•nee rót•fi |
| – the bus station | – สถานีขนส่ง sah•tǎr•nee kǒn•sòng |
| – the subway [underground] station | – สถานีรถไฟใต้ดิน sah•tǎr•nee rót•fi tîe dihn |
| – the skytrain station | – สถานีรถไฟฟ้า sah•tǎr•nee rót•fi•fár |
| How far is it? | มันอยู่ไกลแค่ไหน? mahn yòo gli kâe nǐ |
| Where do I buy a ticket? | ผม♂/ฉัน♀ จะซื้อตั๋วได้ที่ไหน? pŏm♂/cháhn♀ jah súea dtŏar đîe têe•nǐ |
| A *one-way/round-trip [return]* ticket to… | ตั๋ว *เที่ยวเดียว/ไปกลับ ไป*… dtŏar *têaw deaw/ bpi glàhp* bpi… |
| How much? | เท่าไหร่? tôu•rì |
| Is there a discount? | มีส่วนลดไหม? mee sòarn•lót mí |

| Which…? | …ไหน? …nǎi |
| – gate | – ประตู bprah·dtoo |
| – line | – แถว tǎew |
| – platform | – ชานชาลา charn·char·lar |
| Where can I get a taxi? | ผม♂/ฉัน♀ จะเรียกแท็กซี่ได้ที่ไหน? pǒm♂/cháhn♀ jah rêark ták·sêe dîe têe·nǎi |
| Take me to this address. | พาผม♂/ฉัน♀ ไปส่งที่ที่อยู่นี้ด้วย par pǒm♂/cháhn♀ bpi sòng têe têe·yòo née dôary |
| Where's the car rental [hire]? | ผม♂/ฉัน♀ จะเช่ารถได้ที่ไหน? pǒm♂/cháhn♀ jah chôu rót dîe têe·nǎi |
| Can I have a map? | ผม♂/ฉัน♀ ขอแผนที่หน่อยได้ไหม? pǒm♂/cháhn♀ kǒr pǎen·têe nòhy dî mí |

## Ticketing

| When's…to Bangkok? | …ไปกรุงเทพออกเมื่อไหร่? …bpi gruhng·têp òrk mûea·ri |
| – the (first) bus | – รถบัส (เที่ยวแรก) rót báhs (têaw râek) |
| – the (next) flight | – เที่ยวบิน (เที่ยวต่อไป) têaw bihn (têaw dtòr·bpi) |
| – the (last) train | – รถไฟ (ขบวนสุดท้าย) rót·fi (kah·boarn sùht·tíe) |
| Is there…trip? | มีเที่ยว…ไหม? mee têaw…mí |
| – an earlier | – เร็วกว่านี้ rehw gwàr née |
| – a later | – หลังจากนี้ lǎhng jàrk née |
| – a cheaper | – ถูกกว่านี้ tòok gwàr née |
| Where do I buy a ticket? | ผม♂/ฉัน♀ จะซื้อตั๋วได้ที่ไหน? pǒm♂/cháhn♀ jah súee dtǒar dîe têe·nǎi |
| *One ticket/Two tickets*, please. | ขอซื้อตั๋ว หนึ่ง/สอง ใบ kǒr súee dtǒar *nùeng/sǒrng* bi |

| For *today/tomorrow*. | สำหรับ วันนี้/พรุ่งนี้ săhm·ràhp *wahn·née/ prûhng·née* |
|---|---|

▶ For days, see page 168.

▶ For time, see page 167.

| ...ticket. | ตั๋ว... dtŏar... |
|---|---|
| – A one-way | – เที่ยว เดียว têaw deaw |
| – A round-trip [return] | – ไปกลับ bpi glàhp |
| – A first class | – ชั้นหนึ่ง cháhn nùeng |
| – A business class | – ชั้นธุรกิจ cháhn túh·rá·gìht |
| – An economy class | – ชั้นประหยัด cháhn bprah·yàht |
| How much? | เท่าไหร่? tôu·rì |
| Is there...discount? | มีส่วนลดสำหรับ... ไหม? mee sòarn·lót săhm·ràhp...mí |
| – a child | – เด็ก dèhk |
| – a student | – นักศึกษา náhk·sùek·săr |
| – a senior citizen | – ผู้สูงอายุ pôo·sŏong·ar·yúh |
| – a tourist | – นักท่องเที่ยว náhk·tôhng·têaw |
| I have an e-ticket. | ผม♂/ฉัน♀ มีตั๋วอิเล็กทรอนิกส์ pŏm♂/cháhn♀ mee dtŏar ee·léhk·tror·nìhk |
| Can I buy a ticket on the *bus/train*? | ผม♂/ฉัน♀ จะซื้อตั๋วบน *รถบัส/รถไฟ* ได้ไหม? pŏm♂/cháhn♀ jah súee dtŏar bon *rót báhs/ rót·fi* dî mí |
| I'd like to...my reservation. | ผม♂/ฉัน♀ อยากจะ...การจองตั๋ว pŏm♂/ cháhn♀ yàrk jah...garn jorng·dtŏar |
| – cancel | – ยกเลิก yók·lêrk |
| – change | – เปลี่ยนแปลง bplèan·bplaeng |
| – confirm | – ยืนยัน yueen·yahn |

# Plane

## Getting to the Airport

| | |
|---|---|
| How much is a taxi to the airport? | ค่าแท็กซี่ไปสนามบินเท่าไหร่? kâr ták·sêe bpi sah·nǎrm·bihn tôu·rì |
| To…Airport, please. | ไปสนามบิน… bpi sah·nǎrm·bihn… |
| My airline is… | ผม♂/ฉัน♀ ไปสายการบิน… pǒm♂/cháhn♀ bpi sǐe·garn·bihn… |
| My flight leaves at… | เครื่องของผม♂/ฉัน♀ จะออกเวลา… krûeang kǒhng pǒm♂/cháhn♀ jah òrk we·lar… |
| I'm in a rush. | ผม♂/ฉัน♀ ต้องรีบไป pǒm♂/cháhn♀ dtôhng rêep bpi |

▶ For time, see page 167.

| | |
|---|---|
| Can you take an alternate route? | คุณไปทางอื่นได้ไหม? kuhn bpi tarng ùeen dî mí |
| Can you drive *faster/slower*? | คุณช่วยขับ *เร็วขึ้น/ช้าลง* หน่อยได้ไหม? kuhn chôary kàhp *rehw kûen/chár long* nòhy dî mí |

## You May Hear…

| | |
|---|---|
| คุณเดินทางด้วยสายการบินอะไร? kuhn dern·tarng dôary sǐe·garn·bihn ah·ri | What airline are you flying? |
| ในประเทศหรือระหว่างประเทศ? ni bprah·têt rǔee rah·wàrng bprah·têt | Domestic or international? |
| เทอร์มินอลไหน? ter·mih·nôrn ní | What terminal? |

## You May See…

| | |
|---|---|
| ขาเข้า kǎr kôu | arrivals |
| ขาออก kǎr òrk | departures |

| | | |
|---|---|---|
| ที่รับกระเป๋า têe ráhp grah·bpǒu | | baggage claim |
| รักษาความปลอดภัย ráhk·sǎr kwarm bplòrt·pi | | security |
| เช็คอิน chéhk ihn | | check-in |
| เช็คอินด้วยตั๋วอิเล็กทรอนิกส์ chéhk ihn dôary dtǒar ee·léhk·tror·nìhk | | e-ticket check-in |
| ประตูทางออกขึ้นเครื่อง bprah·dtoo tarng·òrk kûen krûeang | | departure gates |

## Check-in and Boarding

| | |
|---|---|
| Where's check-in? | เคาน์เตอร์เช็คอินอยู่ที่ไหน? kóu·têr chéhk ihn yòo têe·nǐ |
| My name is… | ผม♂/ฉัน♀ ชื่อ… pǒm♂/cháhn♀ chûee… |
| I'm going to… | ผม♂/ฉัน♀ จะไป… pǒm♂/cháhn♀ jah bpi… |
| I have… | ผม♂/ฉัน♀ มี… pǒm♂/cháhn♀ mee… |
| – one suitcase | – กระเป๋าหนึ่งใบ grah·bpǒu nùeng bi |
| – two suitcases | – กระเป๋าสองใบ grah·bpǒu sǒrng bi |
| – one carry-on [piece of hand luggage] | – กระเป๋าถือขึ้นเครื่องหนึ่งใบ grah·bpǒu tǔee kûen krûeang nùeng bi |
| How much luggage is allowed? | อนุญาตให้นำสัมภาระไปได้เท่า ไหร่? àh·núh·yârt hî nahm sǎhm·par·ráh bpi dîe tôu·rì |
| Which *terminal/gate*? | เทอร์มินอล/ประตู ไหน? ter·mih·nôrn/bprah·dtoo nǐ |
| I'd like *a window/an aisle* seat. | ผม♂/ฉัน♀ อยากได้ที่นั่ง ริมหน้าต่าง/ริมทางเดิน pǒm♂/cháhn♀ yàrk dîe têe·nâhng *rihm nâr·dtàrng/rihm tarng dern* |
| When do we *leave/arrive*? | เราจะ ออก/ถึง เมื่อไหร่? rou jah *òrk/tǔeng* mûea·rì |
| Is the flight delayed? | เที่ยวบินล่าช้าหรือเปล่า? têaw bihn lâr·chár rúe·bplòw |
| How late? | ช้าแค่ไหน? chár kâe nǐ |

## You May Hear…

คนต่อไป! kon dtòr·bpi

Next!

ขอดู หนังสือเดินทาง/ตั๋ว หน่อย kŏr doo nǎhng·sǔee dern·tarng/dtŏar nòhy

Your *passport/ticket*, please.

คุณมีสัมภาระที่จะเช็คขึ้นเครื่อง ไหม? kuhn mee sǎhm·par·ráh têe jah chéhk kûen krûeang mí

Are you checking any luggage?

สัมภาระของคุณน้ำหนักเกิน sǎhm·par·ráh kŏhng kuhn nárm·nàhk gern

You have excess luggage.

กระเป๋าใบนั้นใหญ่เกินกว่าที่ จะอนุญาตให้ถือขึ้นเครื่อง grah·bpŏu bi náhn yì gern gwàr têe jah ah·núh·yârt hî tǔee kûen krûeang

That's too large for a carry-on [to carry on board].

ขึ้นเครื่องได้… kûen krûeang dîe…

Now boarding…

### Luggage

| | |
|---|---|
| Where *is/are*…? | …อยู่ที่ไหน? …yòo têe·nǐ |
| – the luggage carts [trolleys] | – รถเข็นสัมภาระ rót kěhn sǎhm·par·ráh |
| – the luggage lockers | – ตู้เก็บสัมภาระ dtôo gèhp sǎhm·par·ráh |
| – the baggage claim | – ที่รับกระเป๋า têe ráhp grah·bpŏu |
| My luggage has been *lost/stolen*. | กระเป๋าของผม♂/ฉัน♀ หาย/ถูกขโมย grah·bpŏu kŏhng pŏm♂/cháhn♀ *hǐe/ tòok kah·moey* |
| My suitcase is damaged. | กระเป๋าของผม♂/ฉัน♀ เสียหาย grah·bpŏu kŏhng pŏm♂/cháhn♀ sěa·hǐe |

### Finding Your Way

| | |
|---|---|
| Where *is/are*…? | …อยู่ที่ไหน? …yòo têe·nǐ |
| – the car rental [hire] | – รถเช่า rót chôu |

| – the exit | – ทางออก tarng òrk |
|---|---|
| – the phones | – โทรศัพท์ toe·rah·sàhp |
| – the taxis | – รถแท็กซี่ rót ták·sêe |
| Is there...into town? | มี...เข้าเมืองไหม? mee...kôu mueang mí |
| – a bus | – รถเมล์ rót·me |
| – a train | – รถไฟ rót·fi |
| – a subway [underground] | – รถไฟใต้ดิน rót·fi tîe·dihn |
| – a skytrain | – รถไฟฟ้า rót fi·fár |

## Train

| Where's the train [railway] station? | สถานีรถไฟอยู่ที่ไหน? sah·tăr·nee rót·fi yòo têe·nǐ |
|---|---|
| How far is it? | อยู่ไกลแค่ไหน? yòo gli kâe nǐ |
| Where *is/are*...? | ...อยู่ที่ไหน? ...yòo têe·nǐ |
| – the ticket office | – ที่ขายตั๋ว têe kǐe dtŏar |
| – the information desk | – ประชาสัมพันธ์ bprah·char·săhm·pahn |
| – the luggage lockers | – ตู้เก็บสัมภาระ dtôo gèhp săhm·par·ráh |
| – the platforms | – ชานชาลา charn·char·lar |

▶ For directions, see page 35.

▶ For ticketing, see page 20.

## You May See...

| ชานชาลา charn·char·lar | platforms |
|---|---|
| ประชาสัมพันธ์ bprah·char·săhm·pahn | information |

| แผนกสำรองที่นั่ง pah·nàek săhm·rorng têe·nâhng | reservations |
| ขาเข้า kăr kôu | arrivals |
| ขาออก kăr òrk | departures |

## Questions

| Can I have a schedule [timetable]? | มีตารางเดินรถไหม? mee dtar·rarng dern rót mí |
| How long is the trip? | ใช้เวลาเดินทางเท่าไหร่? chí we·lar dern·tarng tôu·rì |
| Is it a direct train? | เป็นรถไฟสายตรงหรือเปล่า? bpehn rót·fi sĭe dtrong rúe·bplòw |
| Do I have to change trains? | ผม♂/ฉัน♀ จะต้องเปลี่ยนรถหรือเปล่า? pŏm♂/ cháhn♀ jah dtôhng plèan rót rúe·bplòw |
| Is the train on time? | รถไฟมาตรงเวลาไหม? rót·fi mar dtrong we·lar mí |

| ไปไหน? bpi nǐ | Where to? |
| ตั๋วกี่ใบ? dtŏar gèe bi | How many tickets? |

The Thai train network connects towns across the mainland and the peninsula. Though travel by train may be somewhat slow, it is inexpensive and a great way to enjoy the scenery. You should be aware, though, that in some towns, the station is some distance from the city center, so double check before you start making plans. There are a variety of train options, differentiated by speed. Express trains are the fastest. Trains also have first, second and third class cars, as well as sleepers, which are all priced accordingly.

## Departures

| | |
|---|---|
| Which track [platform] to…? | ชานชาลาไหนที่จะไป…? charn·char·lar nǐ têe jah bpi… |
| Is this the track [platform] train to…? | ชานชาลานี้เป็นรถไฟที่จะไป…ใช่ไหม? charn·char·lar née bpehn rót·fi têe jah bpi…chî·mí |
| Where is track [platform]…? | ชานชาลา…อยู่ที่ไหน? charn·char·lar…yòo têe·nǐ |
| Where do I change for…? | ผม♂/ฉัน♀ จะเปลี่ยนรถไฟไป…ได้ที่ไหน? pǒm♂/cháhn♀ jah bplèan rót·fi bpi…dîe têe·nǐ |

## Boarding

| | |
|---|---|
| Can I *sit here/open the window*? | ผม♂/ฉัน♀ *นั่งตรงนี้/เปิดหน้าต่าง*ได้ไหม? pǒm♂/cháhn♀ *nâhng dtrong née/bpèrt nâr·dtàrng* dî mí |
| That's my seat. | ตรงนั้นเป็นที่นั่งของผม♂/ฉัน♀ dtrong náhn bpehn têe·nâhng kǒhng pǒm♂/cháhn♀ |
| Here's my reservation. | นี่คือที่ผม♂/ฉัน♀ จองไว้ née kuee têe têe pǒm♂/cháhn♀ jorng wí |

## You May Hear...

| | |
|---|---|
| คุณจะต้องเปลี่ยนรถที่... kuhn jah dtôhng plèan rót têe... | You have to change at... |
| สถานีต่อไป... sah·tăr·nee dtòr·bpi... | Next stop... |

## Bus

| | |
|---|---|
| Where's the bus station? | สถานีขนส่งอยู่ที่ไหน? sah·tăr·nee kŏn·sòng yòo têe·nĭ |
| How far is it? | อยู่ไกลแค่ไหน? yòo gli kâe nĭ |
| How do I get to...? | ผม♂/ฉัน♀ จะไป...ได้ยังไง? pŏm♂/cháhn♀ jah bpi...dîe yahng·ngi |
| Is this the bus to...? | นี่เป็นรถที่จะไป...ใช่ไหม? nêe bpehn rót têe jah bpi...chî·mí |
| Please tell me when to get off. | ช่วยบอกให้ผม♂/ฉัน♀ รู้ด้วยเมื่อไปถึง chôary bòrk hî pŏm♂/cháhn♀ róo dôary mûea bpi tŭeng |
| Do I have to change buses? | ผม♂/ฉัน♀ จะต้องเปลี่ยนรถหรือเปล่า? pŏm♂/cháhn♀ jah dtôhng plèan rót rúe·bplòw |
| How many stops to...? | ไป...ประมาณกี่ป้าย? bpi...bprah·marn gèe bpîe |
| Stop here, please! | จอดด้วย! jòrt dôary |

▶ For ticketing, see page 20.

 Both the Thai government and private companies offer bus service. Prices between the two are competitive and rates are usually based on distance. Bus travel is common and usually packed at rush hour in the bigger cities. Buying round-trip tickets will often get you a discount.

28

## You May See...

| | |
|---|---|
| ป้ายรถเมล์ bpîe rót·me | bus stop |
| ทางขึ้น/ทางลง tarng kûen/tarng long | enter/exit |

## Subway [Underground] and Skytrain

| | |
|---|---|
| Where's the *subway/ skytrain* station? | สถานี *รถไฟใต้ดิน/รถไฟฟ้า* อยู่ที่ไหน? sah·tăr·nee rót·fi tîe·dihn/rót·fi·fár yòo têe·nĭ |
| A map, please. | ขอแผนที่หน่อย kŏr păen·têe nòhy |
| Which line for...? | สายไหนไปที่...? sĭe nĭ bpi têe... |
| Which direction? | ไปทางไหน? bpi tarng nĭ |
| Do I have to transfer [change]? | ผม♂/ฉัน♀ ต้องเปลี่ยนขบวนไหม? pŏm♂/ cháhn♀ dtôrng plèan kah·boarn mí |
| Is this the *subway [train]/skytrain* to...? | *รถไฟใต้ดิน/รถไฟฟ้า* ขบวนนี้ไป...ใช่ไหม? rót·fi tîe dihn/rót·fi·fár kah·boarn née bpi...chî·mí |
| How many stops to...? | ไป...ประมาณกี่ป้าย? bpi...bprah·marn gèe bpîe |
| Where are we? | เราอยู่ที่ไหน? rou yòo têe·nĭ |

▶For ticketing, see page 20.

Bangkok has its own skytrain and subway services that offer the fastest and most convenient way to travel within the city center. The skytrain, known as บีทีเอส (BTS), currently has two lines: the Sukhumvit Line and the Silom Line. Both routes cover the city center and its commercial and tourist areas. The subway (MRT) currently has only one line that runs mostly north-south along the eastern part of Bangkok. Both the skytrain and the subway operate from 6 a.m. until midnight daily. Though subway and skytrain lines intersect at some stations, the ticketing system is separate at present. However, the plan for common ticketing between BTS skytrain and MRT is now in progress. Both services offer a discounted-fare smart card, which can be refilled with credit at the ticket office. For shorter stays, you can buy either a 1-day BTS pass, or a 1-day or 3-day MRT pass valid for unlimited travel within those periods. MRT also offers a 30-day unlimited ride pass.

## Boat and Ferry

| | |
|---|---|
| When is the ferry to…? | เรือข้ามฟากไป…ออกเมื่อไหร่? ruea kârm fârk bpi…òrk mûea·rì |
| Where are the life jackets? | เสื้อชูชีพอยู่ที่ไหน? sûea choo·chêep yòo têe·nǐ |

▶ For ticketing, see page 20.

### You May See...

| | |
|---|---|
| เรือชูชีพ reua choo·chêep | life boat |
| เสื้อชูชีพ sûea choo·chêep | life jacket |

Boat travel in Thailand may offer some of your trip's most unforgettable experiences, since it is a unique method of transportation, which allows you to see the city from another perspective. Service is convenient and usually functions regularly between sunrise to sunset. One of the most popular routes in Bangkok is along the Chao Phraya river.

## Bicycle and Motorcycle

| | |
|---|---|
| I'd like to rent [hire]… | ผม♂/ฉัน♀ อยากจะเช่า… pǒm♂/cháhn♀ yàrk jah chôu… |
| – a bicycle | – จักรยาน jàhk·grah·yarn |

| | |
|---|---|
| – a moped | – จักรยานมอเตอร์ไซค์ jàhk·grah·yarn mor·dter·si |
| – a motorcycle | – มอเตอร์ไซค์ mor·dter·si |
| How much per *day/ week*? | ค่าเช่าวัน/อาทิตย์ ละเท่าไหร่? kâr·chôu *wahn/ ar·tíht* lah tôu·ri |
| Can I have a *helmet/ lock*? | ผม♂/ฉัน♀ ขอ *หมวกกันน็อค/กุญแจล็อค* ด้วยได้ไหม? pŏm♂/chán♀ kŏr *mòark·gahn·nóhk/guhn·jae lóhk* dôary dî mí |

## Taxi

| | |
|---|---|
| Where can I get a taxi? | ผม♂/ฉัน♀ จะ เรียกแท็กซี่ได้ที่ไหน? pŏm♂/ chán♀ jah rêak ták·sêe dîe têe·ní |
| Do you have the number for a taxi? | คุณมีเบอร์โทรเรียกแท็กซี่ไหม? kuhn mee ber toe rêak ták·sêe mí |
| I'd like a taxi *now/in an hour*. | ผม♂/ฉัน♀ ต้องการแท็กซี่ *เดี๋ยวนี้/ภายใน หนึ่ง ชั่วโมง* pŏm♂/chán♀ dtôhng·garn ták·sêe *dĕaw née/pie·ni nùeng chôar·moeng* |
| Pick me up at… | รับผม♂/ฉัน♀ ที่… ráhp pŏm♂/chán♀ têe… |
| I'm going to… | ผม♂/ฉัน♀ จะไปที่… pŏm♂/chán♀ jah bpi têe… |
| – this address | – ที่อยู่นี้ têe·yòo née |
| – the airport | – สนามบิน sah·nărm·bihn |
| – the train [railway] station | – สถานีรถไฟ sah·tăr·nee rót·fi |
| I'm late. | ผม♂/ฉัน♀ สายแล้ว pŏm♂/chán♀ sǐe láew |
| Can you drive *faster/ slower*? | คุณช่วยขับ *เร็วขึ้น/ช้าลง* หน่อยได้ไหม? kuhn chôary kàhp *rehw kûen/chár long* nòhy dî mí |
| *Stop/Wait* here. | *จอด/รอ* ตรงนี้ *jòrt/ror* dtôhng·née |
| How much? | เท่าไหร่? tôu·rì |
| Can I have a receipt? | ขอใบเสร็จด้วยได้ไหม? kŏr bi·sèht dôary dî mí |

| You said it would cost… | คุณบอกว่ามันแค่... kuhn bòrk wâr mahn kê… |
| Keep the change. | ไม่ต้องทอน mî dtôhng torn |

| ไปไหน? bpi nǎi | Where to? |
| ที่อยู่อะไร? têe·yòo ah·ri | What's the address? |
| มีค่าบริการ ช่วงกลางคืน/สนามบิน เพิ่มด้วย mee kâr bor·rih·garn *chôarng glarng·kueen/ sah·nǎrm·bihn* pêrm dôary | There's a *nighttime/ airport* surcharge. |

Taxis can be hailed in the street. Just look for the Taxi Meter sign for car taxis, since metered taxis are cheaper than non-metered taxis. Motorcycle taxis are also an option, if you're game. Fares are all-inclusive, so tipping is not necessary, but you may round up, if you like. When you take a taxi outside of Bangkok, the fare may have to be negotiated before the start of the trip.

ตุ๊ก ตุ๊ก **dtúhk·dtúhk** (three-wheeled taxi), both motorized and man-powered, is an alternative to taking taxis. These are not metered, so you should negotiate the fare. Tipping is generally not necessary, though you may choose to round-up the fare.

You'll also find that, especially in rural areas, you also have the option of สองแถว **sǒrng tǎew** that is actually a truck with two benches in the back. Like for the three-wheeled taxi, you should negotiate the fare with the driver before starting off.

# Car

## Car Rental [Hire]

| | |
|---|---|
| Where's the car rental [hire]? | บริการรถเช่าอยู่ที่ไหน? bor·rih·garn rót chôu yòo têe·nî |
| I'd like… | ผม♂/ฉัน♀ อยากได้… pŏm♂/cháhn♀ yàrk dîe… |
| – an automatic/ a manual | – รถ เกียร์อัตโนมัติ/เกียร์ธรรมดา rót gea àht·dtah·noe·máht/gea tahm·mah·dar |
| – a car with air conditioning | – รถที่มีแอร์ rót têe mee ae |
| – a car seat | – รถที่มีเบาะสำหรับเด็ก rót têe mee bòh sǎhm·ràhp dèhk |
| How much…? | …เท่าไหร่? …tôu·rì |
| – per *day/week* | –วัน/สัปดาห์ ละ wahn/sàhp·dar lah |
| – for…days | – สำหรับ…วัน sǎhm·ràhp…wahn |
| – per kilometer | – กิโลเมตร ละ gih·loe·mét lah |
| – for unlimited mileage | – แบบไม่จำกัดระยะทาง bàep mî jahm·gàht rah·yáh·tarng |
| – with insurance | – รวมประกัน roarm bprah·gahn |
| Are there any discounts? | มีส่วนลดไหม? mee sòarn·lót mí |

---

*i* Thai driving is much less tame than at home and Americans must adapt to the fact that traffic drives on the left side of the road. Though car rental is cheap by Western standards, renting a car without a chauffeur is generally discouraged. Privately-hired excursion drivers are customarily tipped.

### Gas [Petrol] Station

| | |
|---|---|
| Where's the gas [petrol] station? | ปั๊มน้ำมันอยู่ที่ไหน? bpáhm·náhm·mahn yòo têe·nǐ |
| Fill it up. | เติมเต็มถัง dterm dtehm tǎhng |
| ...baht, please. | ...บาท ...bàrt |
| I'll pay *in cash/by credit card*. | ผม♂/ฉัน♀ จะจ่ายด้วย เงินสด/บัตรเครดิต pǒm♂/ cháhn♀ jah jìe dôary *ngern·sòt/bàht·kre·dìht* |

▶For numbers, see page 165.

## You May See...

| | |
|---|---|
| เบนซิน ben·sihn | gas [petrol] |
| ดีเซล dee·sen | diesel |
| แก๊สโซฮอล์ gáes·soe·horn | gasohol* |

### Asking Directions

| | |
|---|---|
| Is this the way to...? | ทางนี้ไป...ใช่ไหม? tarng née bpi...chî·mí |
| How far is it to...? | ไป...อีกไกลไหม? bpi...èek gli mí |
| Where's...? | ...อยู่ที่ไหน? ...yòo têe·nǐ |
| – ...Street | – ถนน... tah·nǒn... |
| – this address | – ที่อยู่นี้ têe·yòo née |
| – the highway [motorway] | – ทางหลวง tarng·lǒarng |
| Can you show me on the map? | คุณช่วยชี้ในแผนที่ให้หน่อยได้ไหม? kuhn chôary chée ni pǎen·têe hî nòhy dî mí |
| I'm lost. | ผม♂/ฉัน♀ หลงทาง pǒm♂/cháhn♀ lǒng tarng |

*Gasohol is a mixture of gasoline and ethanol.

## You May Hear...

| | |
|---|---|
| ตรงไป dtrong bpi | straight ahead |
| ซ้าย síe | left |
| ขวา kwǎr | right |
| ตรง/เลย หัวมุม *dtrong/lery* hǒar·muhm | *on/around* the corner |
| ด้านตรงข้าม dârn dtrong·kârm | opposite |
| ด้านหลัง dârn lǎhng | behind |
| ติดกับ dtìht gàhp | next to |
| หลังจาก lǎhng·jàrk | after |
| ทิศเหนือ/ทิศใต้ tíht nǔea/tíht dtîe | north/south |
| ทิศตะวันออก/ทิศตะวันตก tíht dtah·wahn·òrk/tíht dtah·wahn·dtòk | east/west |
| ตรงไฟแดง dtrong fi·daeng | at the traffic light |
| ตรงสี่แยก dtrong sèe·yâek | at the intersection |

## You May See...

| | |
|---|---|
| หยุด yùht | stop |
| ให้ทาง hî tarng | yield |
| ห้ามเข้า hârm kôu | no entry |
| ห้ามจอด hârm jòrt | no parking |

| | | |
|---|---|---|
|  หยุดตรวจ yùht dtròart | police check point |
|  ห้ามแซง hârm saeng | no passing |
|  ห้ามกลับรถ hârm glàhp rót | no u-turn |

## Parking

| | |
|---|---|
| Can I park here? | ผม♂/ฉัน♀ จอดรถตรงนี้ได้ไหม? pŏm♂/cháhn♀ jòrt rót dtrong•née dî mí |
| Where's...? | ...อยู่ที่ไหน? ...yòo têe•nǐ |
| – the parking garage | – อาคารจอดรถ ar•karn jòrt rót |
| – the parking lot [car park] | – ลานจอดรถ larn jòrt rót |
| – the parking meter | – มิเตอร์จอดรถ míh•dtêr jòrt rót |
| How much...? | ...เท่าไหร่? ...tôu•rì |
| – per hour | – ชั่วโมงละ chôar•moeng lah |
| – per day | – วันละ wahn lah |
| – overnight | – คืนละ kueen lah |

## Breakdown and Repairs

| | |
|---|---|
| My car *broke down/ won't start.* | รถของผม♂/ฉัน♀ *เสีย/สตาร์ทไม่ติด* rót kŏhng pŏm♂/cháhn♀ *sěa/sah•dtárt mî dtit* |
| Can you fix it (today)? | คุณซ่อม (วันนี้) ได้ไหม? kuhn sôhm (wahn•née) dîe mí |
| When will it be ready? | จะเสร็จเมื่อไหร่? jah sèht mûea•rì |
| How much? | เท่าไหร่? tôu•rì |

#### Accidents

| | |
|---|---|
| There was an accident. | มีอุบัติเหตุ mee uh·bàht·tìh·hèt |
| Call *an ambulance/ the police.* | เรียก *รถพยาบาล/ตำรวจ* ให้หน่อย rêak *rót pah·yar·barn/dtahm·ròart* hî nòhy |

# Accommodations

## Essential

| | |
|---|---|
| Can you recommend a hotel? | ช่วยแนะนำโรงแรมให้หน่อยได้ไหม? chôary ná·nahm roeng·raem hî nòhy dî mí |
| I have a reservation. | ผม♂/ฉัน♀ จองห้องไว้ pŏm♂/cháhn♀ jorng hôhng wí |
| My name is... | ผม♂/ฉัน♀ ชื่อ... pŏm♂/cháhn♀ chûee... |
| Do you have a room...? | คุณมีห้อง...ไหม? kuhn mee hôhng...mí |
| – for *one/two* | – สำหรับ *คนเดียว/สองคน* săhm·ràhp *kon deaw/sŏrng kon* |
| – with a bathroom | – ที่มีห้องน้ำ têe mee hôhng nárm |
| – with air conditioning | – ที่มีแอร์ têe mee ae |
| For... | สำหรับ... săhm·ràhp... |
| – tonight | – คืนนี้ kueen née |
| – two nights | – สองคืน sŏrng kueen |
| – one week | – หนึ่งสัปดาห์ nùeng sàhp·dar |
| How much? | เท่าไหร่? tôu·rì |
| Is there anything cheaper? | มีอะไรที่ถูกกว่านี้ไหม? mee ah·ri têe tòok gwàr née mí |

| When's check-out? | ต้องเช็คเอาท์กี่โมง? dtôrng chéhk-ou gèe moeng |
| Can I leave this in the safe? | ผม♂/ฉัน♀ จะฝากของไว้ในเซฟได้ไหม? pŏm♂/cháhn♀ jah fàrk kŏrng wí ni sép dî mí |
| Can I leave my bags? | ผม♂/ฉัน♀ จะฝากกระเป๋าไว้ได้ไหม? pŏm♂/cháhn♀ jah fàrk grah-bpŏu wí dî mí |
| Can I have *my bill/ a receipt*? | ขอ *บิล/ใบเสร็จ* ด้วยได้ไหม? kŏr *bihn/bi-sèht* dôary dî mí |
| I'll pay *in cash/by credit card*. | ผม♂/ฉัน♀ จะจ่ายด้วย *เงินสด/บัตรเครดิต* pŏm♂/cháhn♀ jah jìe dôary *ngern-sòt/ bàht-kre-dìht* |

In Thailand, there are many types of accommodations available, ranging from extreme luxury to the bare essentials. Various western hotel chains offer high-end accommodations throughout the country; Amari and Dusit are top-level Thai-owned chains. You can also find many moderately-priced hotels that offer very good value for the money. Budget travelers wil have their pick of inexpensive hotels, guestrooms and hostels.

If you didn't reserve any accommodations before your trip, visit the local Tourist Information Office (Tourism Authority of Thailand, TAT) for recommendations on places to stay.

▶ For useful websites, see page 172.

## Finding Lodging

| Can you recommend...? | ช่วยแนะนำ...ให้หน่อยได้ไหม? chôary ná-nahm...hî nòhy dîe mí |
| – a hotel | – โรงแรม roeng-raem |
| – a hostel | – ที่พักเยาวชน têe páhk you-wah-chon |

| | |
|---|---|
| – a guesthouse | – เกสต์เฮ้าส์ gét·hóus |
| – a campsite | – ที่ตั้งแค้มป์ têe dtâhng káem |
| What is it near? | มันอยู่ใกล้กับอะไร? mahn yòo glî gàhp ah·ri |
| How do I get there? | ผม♂/ฉัน♀ จะไปที่นั่นได้ยังไง? pŏm♂/cháhn♀ jah bpi têe nâhn dîe yahng·ngi |

## At the Hotel

| | |
|---|---|
| I have a reservation. | ผม♂/ฉัน♂ จองห้องไว้ pŏm♂/cháhn♀ jorng hôhng wí |
| My name is… | ผม♂/ฉัน♀ ชื่อ… pŏm♂/cháhn♀ chûee… |
| Do you have a room…? | คุณมีห้อง…ไหม? kuhn mee hôhng…mí |
| – for *one/two* | – สำหรับ *คนเดียว/สองคน* sǎhm·ràhp *kon deaw/ sŏrng kon* |
| – with a *bathroom [toilet]/shower* | – ที่มี *ห้องน้ำ/ห้องอาบน้ำ* têe mee *hôhng nárm/ hôhng àrp·nárm* |
| – with air conditioning | – ที่มีแอร์ têe mee ae |
| – that's handicapped [disabled] accessible | – ที่มีทางเข้าออกสำหรับคนพิการ têe mee tarng kôu òrk sǎhm·ràhp kon píh·garn |
| – on the ground floor | – ที่อยู่ชั้นล่าง têe·yòo cháhn lârng |
| – that's *smoking/ non-smoking* | – ที่ *สูบบุหรี่ได้/ห้ามสูบบุหรี่* têe *sòop buh·rèe dîe/hârm sòop buh·rèe* |
| For… | สำหรับ… sǎhm·ràhp… |
| – tonight | – คืนนี้ kueen née |
| – two nights | – สองคืน sŏrng kueen |
| – a week | – หนึ่งสัปดาห์ nùeng sàhp·dar |

▶ For numbers, see page 165.

| Do you have…? | คุณมี…ไหม? kuhn mee…mí |
|---|---|
| – a computer | – คอมพิวเตอร์ kohm·pihw·dtêr |
| – an elevator [a lift] | – ลิฟต์ líhp |
| – (wireless) internet service | – บริการอินเตอร์เน็ต (ไร้สาย) bor·rih·garn ihn·dter·nèht (rí sǐe) |
| – room service | – รูมเซอร์วิส room ser·wìht |
| Do you have…? | คุณมี…ไหม? kuhn mee…mí |
| – a TV | – โทรทัศน์ toe·rah·táht |
| – a pool | – สระว่ายน้ำ sàh wîe·nárm |
| – a gym | – ห้องออกกำลังกาย hôhng òrk·gahm·lahng·gie |
| I need… | ผม♂/ฉัน♀ ต้องการ… pǒm♂/cháhn♀ dtôhng·garn… |
| – an extra bed | – เตียงเสริม dteang sěrm |
| – a cot | – เตียงพับ dteang·páhp |
| – a crib | – เปลเด็ก bple dèhk |

## You May Hear...

| | |
|---|---|
| ขอดู พาสปอร์ต/บัตรเครดิต หน่อย kŏr doo *párs·sah·bpòrt/bàht·kre·dìht* nòhy | Your *passport/credit card*, please. |
| กรุณากรอกเอกสารนี้ gah·rúh·nar gròrk èk·gah·sărn née | Fill out this form. |
| เซ็นชื่อตรงนี้ sehn chûee dtrong née | Sign here. |

### Price

| | |
|---|---|
| How much per *night/ week*? | วัน/สัปดาห์ ละเท่าไหร่? *wahn/sàhp·dar* lah tôu·rì |
| Does that include *breakfast/sales tax [VAT]*? | รวม อาหารเช้า/ภาษี ด้วยไหม? roarm *ar·hărn chóu/par·sĕe* dôary mí |
| Are there any discounts? | มีส่วนลดไหม? mee sòarn·lót mí |

### Decisions

| | |
|---|---|
| Can I see the room? | ผม♂/ฉัน♀ ขอดูห้องก่อนได้ไหม? pŏm♂/ cháhn♀ kŏr doo hôhng gòrn dî mí |
| I'd like...room. | ผม♂/ฉัน♀ อยากได้ห้องที่... pŏm♂/cháhn♀ yàrk dîe hôhng têe... |
| – a better | – ดีกว่านี้ dee gwàr née |
| – a bigger | – ใหญ่กว่านี้ yì gwàr née |
| – a cheaper | – ถูกกว่านี้ tòok gwàr née |
| – a quieter | – เงียบกว่านี้ ngêap gwàr née |
| I'll take it. | ผม♂/ฉัน♀ เอาห้องนี้ pŏm♂/cháhn♀ ou hôhng née |
| No, I won't take it. | ผม♂/ฉัน♀ ไม่เอาห้องนี้ pŏm♂/cháhn♀ mî ou hôhng née |

## Questions

| | |
|---|---|
| Where's…? | …อยู่ที่ไหน? …yòo têe·nǐ |
| – the bar | – บาร์ bar |
| – the restroom [toilet] | – ห้องน้ำ hôhng·nárm |
| – the elevator [lift] | – ลิฟต์ líhp |
| – the pool | – สระว่ายน้ำ sàh wîe·nárm |
| Can I have…? | ผม♂/ฉัน♀ ขอ…หน่อยได้ไหม? pǒm♂/ cháhn♀ kǒr…nòhy dî mí |
| – a blanket | – ผ้าห่ม pâr·hòm |
| – an iron | – เตารีด dtou·rêet |
| – the *room key/ key card* | – กุญแจห้อง/คีย์การ์ด guhn·jae hôhng/kee·gárt |
| – a pillow | – หมอน mǒrn |
| – soap | – สบู่ sah·bòo |
| – toilet paper | – กระดาษชำระ grah·dàrt chahm·ráh |
| – a towel | – ผ้าเช็ดตัว pâr·chéht·dtoar |
| Do you have an adapter for this? | คุณมีปลั๊กแปลงไฟฟ้าสำหรับนี้ไหม? kuhn mee bpláhk bplaeng fi·fár sǎhm·ràhp nêe mí |
| How do I turn on the lights? | ผม♂/ฉัน♀ จะเปิดไฟยังไง? pǒm♂/cháhn♀ jah bpèrt fi yahng·ngi |
| Can you wake me at…? | ช่วยปลุกผม♂/ฉัน♀ เวลา…ได้ไหม? chôary bplùhk pǒm♂/cháhn♀ we·lar…dî mí |
| When does breakfast *start/end*? | อาหารเช้าจะ *เริ่ม/หยุด* เสิร์ฟเมื่อไหร่? ar·hǎrn chóu jah *rêrm/yùht* sèrp mûea·rì |
| Can I leave this in the safe? | ผม♂/ฉัน♀ จะฝากของไว้ในเซฟได้ไหม? pǒm♂/ cháhn♀ jah fàrk kǒrng wí ni sép dî mí |

| | |
|---|---|
| Can I have my things from the safe? | ผม♂/ฉัน♀ จะขอของที่ฝากไว้ในเซฟได้ไหม? pŏm♂/cháhn♀ jah kŏr kŏrng têe fàrk wí ni sép dî mí |
| Is there *mail [post]/ a message* for me? | มี *จดหมาย/ข้อความ* ถึงผม♂/ฉัน♀ ไหม? mee *jòt·mǐe/kôr·kwarm* tǔeng pŏm♂/cháhn♀ mí |

## You May See...

| | |
|---|---|
| ห้องน้ำ hôhng·nárm | restroom [toilet] |
| ห้องอาบน้ำ hôhng àrp·nárm | shower |
| ประตูหนีไฟ bprah·dtoo něe fi | fire door |
| ทางออก(ฉุกเฉิน) tarng òrk (chùhk·chěrn) | (emergency) exit |

### Problems

| | |
|---|---|
| There's a problem. | ผม♂/ฉัน♀ มีปัญหา pŏm♂/cháhn♀ mee pahn·hǎr |
| I lost my *key/key card*. | ผม♂/ฉัน♀ ทำ *กุญแจ/คีย์การ์ด* หาย pŏm♂/cháhn♀ tahm *guhn·jae/kee·gárt* hǐe |
| I'm locked out of the room. | ผม♂/ฉัน♀ เข้าห้องไม่ได้ pŏm♂/cháhn♀ kôu hôhng mî dîe |
| There's no *hot water/toilet paper*. | ไม่มีน้ำร้อน/กระดาษชำระ mî mee *nárm rórn/ grah·dàrt chahm·ráh* |
| The room is dirty. | ห้องสกปรก hôhng sòk·grah·bpròk |
| There are bugs in the room. | มีแมลงในห้อง mee mah·laeng ni hôhng |
| The...doesn't work. | ...ไม่ทำงาน ...mî tahm·ngarn |
| Can you fix...? | คุณช่วยซ่อม...ให้หน่อยได้ไหม? kuhn chôary sôhm...hî nòhy dî mí |
| – the air conditioning | – แอร์ ae |

| Can you fix...? | คุณช่วยซ่อม...ให้หน่อยได้ไหม? kuhn chôary sôhm...hî nòhy dî mí |
| --- | --- |
| – the fan | – พัดลม páht·lom |
| – the heat [heating] | – เครื่องทำความร้อน krûeang tahm kwarm·rórn |
| – the light | – หลอดไฟ lòrt·fi |
| – the TV | – โทรทัศน์ toe·rah·táht |
| – the toilet | – โถส้วม tŏe·sôarm |
| I'd like another room. | ผม♂/ฉัน♀ อยากจะเปลี่ยนห้อง pŏm♂/cháhn♀ yàrk·jah bplèan hôhng |

## Check-out

| When's check-out? | ต้องเช็คเอาท์กี่โมง? dtôrng chéhk·ou gèe moeng |
| --- | --- |
| Can I leave my bags here until...? | ผม♂/ฉัน♀ จะฝากกระเป๋าไว้ที่นี่ถึง...ได้ไหม? pŏm♂/cháhn♀ jah fàrk grah·bpŏu wí têe·nêe tŭeng...dî mí |
| Can I have an itemized bill/ a receipt? | ผม♂/ฉัน♀ ขอบิลแยกตามรายการ/ใบเสร็จได้ไหม? pŏm♂/cháhn♀ kŏr bihn yâek dtarm rie·garn/bi·sèht dî mí |
| I think there's a mistake. | ผม♂/ฉัน♀ คิดว่ามีอะไรผิดซักอย่าง pŏm♂/cháhn♀ kíht wâr mee ah·ri piht sáhk yàrng |
| I'll pay in cash/by credit card. | ผม♂/ฉัน♀ จะจ่ายด้วย เงินสด/บัตรเครดิต pŏm♂/cháhn♀ jah jìe dôary ngern·sòt/bàht·kre·diht |

## Renting

| I reserved an apartment/a room. | ผม♂/ฉัน♀ จอง อพาร์ตเมนต์/ห้องไว้ pŏm♂/cháhn♀ jorng ah·párt·méhn/hôhng wí |
| --- | --- |
| My name is... | ผม♂/ฉัน♀ ชื่อ... pŏm♂/cháhn♀ chûee... |
| Can I have the key/ key card? | ผม♂/ฉัน♀ ขอกุญแจ/คีย์การ์ดหน่อย pŏm♂/cháhn♀ kŏr guhn·jae hôhng/kee·gárt nòhy |
| Are there...? | มี...ไหม? mee...mí |

| | |
|---|---|
| – dishes | – ถ้วยชาม tôary·charm |
| – pillows | – หมอน mŏrn |
| – sheets | – ผ้าปูที่นอน pâr bpoo têe·norn |
| – towels | – ผ้าเช็ดตัว pâr·chéht·dtoar |
| – utensils | – เครื่องใช้ krûeang·chí |
| When do I put out the *trash [rubbish]/ recycling*? | ผม ♂/ฉัน ♀ จะทิ้ง *ขยะ/ขยะรีไซเคิล* ได้เมื่อไหร่? pŏm ♂/cháhn ♀ jah tíhng *kah·yàh/ kah·yàh ree·si·kêrn* dîe mûea·rì |
| …is broken. | …เสีย …sĕa |
| How does…work? | …ใช้งานยังไง? …chí ngarn yahng·ngi |
| – the air conditioner | – แอร์ ae |
| – the dishwasher | – เครื่องล้างจาน krûeang lárng·jarn |
| – the freezer | – ตู้แช่แข็ง dtôo·châe·kăeng |
| – the heater | – เครื่องทำน้ำร้อน krûeang tahm náhm·rórn |
| – the microwave | – ไมโครเวฟ mi·kroe·wef |
| – the refrigerator | – ตู้เย็น dtôo·yehn |
| – the stove | – เตา dtou |
| – the washing machine | – เครื่องซักผ้า krûeang·sáhk·pâr |

## Household Items

| | |
|---|---|
| I need… | ผม ♂/ฉัน ♀ ต้องการ… pŏm ♂/cháhn ♀ dtôhng·garn… |
| – an adapter | – ปลั๊กแปลงไฟฟ้า bpláhk bplaeng fi·fár |
| – aluminum [kitchen] foil | – กระดาษฟอยล์ grah·dàrt fory |
| – a bottle opener | – ที่เปิดขวด têe·bpèrt·kòart |
| – a broom | – ไม้กวาด míe·gwàrt |

| I need... | ผม ♂/ฉัน ♀ ต้องการ... pŏm ♂/cháhn ♀ dtôhng·garn... |
|---|---|
| – a can opener | – ที่เปิดกระป๋อง têe bpèrt grah·bpŏhng |
| – cleaning supplies | – อุปกรณ์ทำความสะอาด ùhp·bpah·gorn tahm kwarm sah·àrt |
| – a corkscrew | – ที่เปิดจุกก๊อก têe bpèrt jùhk·góhk |
| – detergent | – ผงซักฟอก pŏng·sáhk·fôrk |
| – dishwashing liquid | – น้ำยาล้างจาน náhm·yar lárng·jarn |
| – garbage [rubbish] bags | – ถุงใส่ขยะ tŭhng sì kah·yàh |
| – a lightbulb | – หลอดไฟ lòrt·fi |
| – matches | – ไม้ขีด míe·kèet |
| – napkins | – กระดาษเช็ดปาก grah·dàrt chéht bpàrk |
| – paper towels | – กระดาษเช็ดมือ grah·dàrt chéht muee |
| – plastic wrap [cling film] | – ฟิล์มถนอมอาหาร feem tah·nŏrm ar·hăhn |
| – a plunger | – ที่ดูดส้วม têe dòot sôarm |
| – scissors | – กรรไกร gahn·gri |

▶ For dishes and utensils, see page 64.

▶ For oven temperatures, see page 171.

## Hostel

| Is there a bed available? | มีเตียงว่างไหม? mee dteang wârng mí |
|---|---|
| Can I have...? | ขอ...ได้ไหม? kŏr...dî mí |
| – a *single/double* room | – ห้องเดี่ยว/ห้องคู่ hôhng dèaw/hôhng kôo |
| – a blanket | – ผ้าห่ม pâr·hòm |
| – a pillow | – หมอน mŏrn |

| | |
|---|---|
| – sheets | – ผ้าปูที่นอน pâr bpoo têe·norn |
| – a towel | – ผ้าเช็ดตัว pâr chéht·dtoar |
| Do you have lockers? | มีล็อคเกอร์ไหม? mee lóhk·gêr mí |
| When do you lock up? | คุณปิดกี่โมง? kuhn bpìht gèe moeng |
| Do I need a membership card? | ผม♂/ฉัน♀ ต้องแสดงบัตรสมาชิกหรือเปล่า? pŏm♂/cháhn♀ dtôrng sah·daeng bàht sah·mar·chíhk rúe·bplòw |

## Camping

| | |
|---|---|
| Can I camp here? | ผม♂/ฉัน♀ ตั้งแค้มป์ตรงนี้ได้ไหม? pŏm♂/cháhn♀ dtâhng káem dtrong·née dîe mí |
| Where's the campsite? | ที่ตั้งแค้มป์อยู่ตรงไหน? têe dtâhng káem yòo dtrong nĭ |
| What is the charge per *day/week*? | *วัน/สัปดาห์* ละเท่าไหร่? *wahn/sàhp·dar* lah tôu·rì |
| Are there…? | มี…ไหม? mee…mí |
| – cooking facilities | – ที่ทำอาหาร têe tahm ar·hărn |
| – electric outlets | – ปลั๊กไฟ bpláhk·fi |
| – laundry facilities | – ที่ซักผ้า têe sáhk·pâr |
| Are there…? | มี…ไหม? mee…mí |
| – showers | – ห้องอาบน้ำ hôhng àrp·nárm |
| – tents for rent [hire] | – เต็นท์ให้เช่า dtéhn hî chôu |

▶ For household items, see page 45.

▶ For dishes and utensils, see page 64.

# *Internet and Communications*

## Essential

| | |
|---|---|
| Where's an internet cafe? | อินเตอร์เน็ตคาเฟ่อยู่ที่ไหน? ihn·dter·nèht kar·fê yòo têe·nǐ |
| Can I *access the internet*/*check e-mail* here? | ผม♂/ฉัน♀ ใช้อินเตอร์เน็ต/เช็คอีเมล ที่นี่ได้ไหม? pǒm♂/cháhn♀ chí ihn·dter·nèht/chéhk ee·mew têe·nêe dî mí |
| How much per *hour*/*half hour*? | ชั่วโมงละ/ครึ่งชั่วโมง เท่าไหร่? chôar·moeng lah/krûeng chôar·moeng tôu·rì |
| How do I *connect*/*log on*? | ผม♂/ฉัน♀ จะ เชื่อมต่อ/เข้าระบบได้ยังไง? pǒm♂/cháhn♀ jah chûeam·dtòr/kôu rah·bòp dî yahng·ngi |
| A phone card, please. | ขอซื้อบัตรโทรศัพท์หน่อย kǒr súee bàht toe·rah·sàhp nòhy |
| Can I have your phone number? | ผม♂/ฉัน♀ ขอเบอร์โทรศัพท์คุณหน่อยได้ไหม? pǒm♂/cháhn♀ kǒr ber toe·rah·sàhp kuhn nòhy dî mí |
| Here's my *number*/*e-mail*. | นี่ เบอร์โทรศัพท์/อีเมล ของผม♂/ฉัน♀ nêe ber toe·rah·sàhp/ee·mew kǒhng pǒm♂/cháhn♀ |
| Call me. | โทรหาผม♂/ฉัน♀ นะ toe hǎr pǒm♂/cháhn♀ náh |
| E-mail me. | อีเมล์หาผม♂/ฉัน♀ นะ ee·mew hǎr pǒm♂/cháhn♀ náh |
| Hello. This is… | ฮัลโหล นี่… hahn·lǒe nêe… |
| Can I speak to…? | ขอพูดกับคุณ… kǒr pôot gàhp kuhn… |
| Can you repeat that? | พูดอีกทีได้ไหม? pôot èek tee dî mí |
| I'll call back later. | ผม♂/ฉัน♀ จะโทรกลับมาใหม่ pǒm♂/cháhn♀ jah toe glàhp mar mì |
| Bye. | สวัสดี sah·wàht·dee |

| Where's the post office? | ที่ทำการไปรษณีย์อยู่ที่ไหน? têe·tahm·garn bpri·sah·nee yòo têe·nĭ |
|---|---|
| I'd like to send this to… | ผม♂/ฉัน♀ อยากจะส่งของนี้ไปที่… pŏm♂/ chán♀ yàrk jah sòng kŏrng née bpi têe… |

## Computer, Internet and E-mail

| Where's an internet cafe? | อินเตอร์เน็ตคาเฟ่อยู่ที่ไหน? ihn·dter·nèht kar·fê yòo têe·nĭ |
|---|---|
| Does it have wireless internet? | มีอินเตอร์เน็ตไร้สายไหม? mee ihn·dter·nèht rí sĭe mí |
| How do I turn the computer *on/off*? | ผม♂/ฉัน♀ จะ *เปิดเครื่อง/ปิดเครื่องคอมพิวเตอร์* ยังไง? pŏm♂/chán♀ jah *bpert krûeang/bpìht krûeang* kohm·pihw·dtêr yahng·ngi |
| How much per *hour/ half hour*? | *ชั่วโมงละ/ครึ่งชั่วโมง* เท่าไหร่? *chôar·moeng lah/ krûeng chôar·moeng* tôu·rì |
| How do I…? | ผม♂/ฉัน♀ จะ…ได้ยังไง? pŏm♂/chán♀ jah…dîe yahng·ngi |
| – connect/disconnect | – เชื่อมต่อ/ตัดการเชื่อมต่อ chûeam·dtòr/dtàht garn chûeam·dtòr |
| – log *on/off* | – เข้าระบบ/ออกจากระบบ kôu rah·bòp/òrk jàrk rah·bòp |
| – type this symbol | – พิมพ์สัญลักษณ์นี้ pihm săhn·yah·láhk née |
| What's your e-mail? | ขออีเมล์ของคุณหน่อยได้ไหม? kŏr ee·mew kuhn nòhy dî mí |
| My e-mail is… | อีเมล์ของผม♂/ฉัน♀ คือ… ee·mew kŏhng pŏm♂/chán♀ kuee… |

## You May See…

| | |
|---|---|
| ปิด bpìht | close |
| ลบ lóp | delete |
| อีเมล์ ee·mew | e-mail |
| ออก òrk | exit |
| ตัวช่วย dtoar·chôary | help |
| อินเตอร์เน็ต ihn·dter·nèht | internet |
| เปิด bpèrt | open |
| ปริ๊นต์ bpríhn | print |
| บันทึก bahn·túek | save |
| ส่ง sòng | send |
| ชื่อผู้ใช้/รหัส chûee pôo·chí/rah·hàht | username/password |
| อินเตอร์เน็ตไร้สาย ihn·dter·nèht rí sǐe | wireless internet |

i Internet service in Thailand is widespread. You can find internet cafes throughout Bangkok, at tourist attractions and even in small towns. Many areas, especially business districts, have hotspots; pre-registration may be required.

## Phone

| | |
|---|---|
| A *phone card/prepaid phone*, please. | ขอซื้อ บัตรโทรศัพท์/บัตรเติมเงินหน่อย kŏr súee bàht toe·rah·sàhp/bàht dterm ngern nòhy |
| How much? | เท่าไหร่? tôu·rì |
| Can I *recharge/buy minutes* for this phone? | ผม♂/ฉัน♀ จะ เติมเงิน/เพิ่มเวลา ในโทรศัพท์นี้ได้ ไหม? pŏm♂/chán♀ jah dterm ngern/pêrm we·lar ni toe·rah·sàhp née dîe mí |
| Where's the pay phone? | ตู้โทรศัพท์อยู่ที่ไหน? dtôo toe·rah·sàhp yòo têe·nî |
| My phone doesn't work here. | โทรศัพท์ของผม♂/ฉัน♀ ใช้ไม่ได้ที่นี่ toe·rah·sàhp kŏhng pŏm♂/chán♀ chí mî dîe têe·nêe |
| What's the *area/country* code for...? | รหัส พื้นที่/ประเทศ ของ...รหัสอะ ไร? rah·hàht púeen·têe/bprah·têt kŏhng...rah·hàht ah·ri |
| What's the number for Information? | เบอร์โทรศัพท์ของประชาสัมพันธ์เบอร์อะไร? ber toe·rah·sàhp kŏrng bprach·char·sǎhm·pahn ber ah·ri |
| I'd like the number for... | ผม♂/ฉัน♀ ต้องการเบอร์โทรศัพท์ของ... pŏm♂/chán♀ dtôhng·garn ber toe·rah·sàhp kŏhng... |
| I'd like to call collect [reverse the charges]. | ผม♂/ฉัน♀ ต้องการ โทรเก็บเงินปลายทาง pŏm♂/chán♀ dtôhng·garn toe gèhp ngern bplie tarng |
| Can I have your number? | ผม♂/ฉัน♀ ขอเบอร์โทรศัพท์ของคุณหน่อยได้ ไหม? pŏm♂/chán♀ kŏr ber toe·rah·sàhp kŏhng kuhn nòhy dî mí |
| Here's my number. | นี่เบอร์โทรศัพท์ของผม♂/ฉัน♀ nêe ber toe·rah·sàhp kŏhng pŏm♂/chán♀ |

| Please call me. | ช่วยโทรมาหาผม♂/ฉัน♀ หน่อย chôary toe mar hăr pŏm♂/cháhn♀ nòhy |
| Please text me. | ช่วยส่งข้อความมาหาผม♂/ฉัน♀ หน่อย chôary sòng kôr•kwarm mar hăr pŏm ♂/cháhn♀ nòhy |
| I'll call you. | ผม♂/ฉัน♀ จะโทรหาคุณ pŏm ♂/cháhn♀ jah toe hăr kuhn |
| I'll text you. | ผม♂/ฉัน♀ จะส่งข้อความถึงคุณ pŏm♂/cháhn♀ jah sòng kôr•kwarm tŭeng kuhn |

▶ For numbers, see page 165.

## On the Phone

| Hello. This is… | ฮัลโหล นี่… hahn•lŏe nêe… |
| Can I speak to…? | ขอพูดกับคุณ…ได้ไหม? kŏr pôot gàhp kuhn…dî mí |
| Extension… | ต่อหมายเลข… dtòr mĭe•lêk… |
| Speak *louder/more slowly*, please. | ช่วยพูด *ดังขึ้น/ช้าลง* หน่อยได้ไหม chôary pôot *dahng kêuhn/chár long* nòhy dî mí |
| Can you repeat that? | พูดอีกทีได้ไหม? pôot èek tee dî mí |

| | |
|---|---|
| I'll call back later. | ผม♂/ฉัน♀ จะโทรกลับมาใหม่ pŏm♂/cháhn♀ jah toe glàhp mar mì |
| Bye. | สวัสดี sah·wàht·dee |

## You May Hear…

| | |
|---|---|
| ใครโทรมา? kri toe mar | Who's calling? |
| รอสักครู่ ror sáhk krôo | Hold on. |
| เขา/เธอ *ไม่อยู่/ติดสายอยู่* kóu/ter *mî yòo/ dtiht·sĭe yòo* | He/She is *not here/ on another line*. |
| จะให้ เขา/เธอ โทรกลับไหม? jah hî kóu/ter toe glàhp mí | Can he/she call you back? |
| เบอร์โทรศัพท์ของคุณเบอร์อะไร? ber toe·rah·sàhp kŏhng kuhn ber ah·ri | What's your number? |

## Fax

| | |
|---|---|
| Can I *send/receive* a fax here? | ผม♂/ฉัน♀ *ส่ง/รับ*แฟ็กซ์ที่นี่ได้ไหม? pŏm♂/ cháhn♀ *sòng/ráhp* fàk têe·nêe dî mí |
| What's the fax number? | แฟ็กซ์เบอร์อะไร? fàk ber ah·ri |
| Please fax this to… | กรุณาแฟ็กซ์อันนี้ไปที่… gah·rúh·nar fàk àhn née bpi têe… |

---

In Thailand, public phones are yellow and accept prepaid phone cards, which can be bought in convenience stores. Public phones are frequently found in major areas, but you may have a harder time finding one in the countryside.

To call the U.S. or Canada from Thailand, dial 00 + 1 + area code + phone number. To call the U.K., dial 00 + 44 + area code (minus the first 0) + phone number.

## Post Office

| | |
|---|---|
| Where's the *post office/mailbox [postbox]*? | ที่ทำการ ไปรษณีย์/ตู้ ไปรษณีย์ อยู่ที่ไหน? têe tahm garn bpri·sah·nee/dtôo bpri·sah·nee yòo têe·nî |
| A stamp for this *postcard/letter* to… | ขอซื้อแสตมป์สำหรับส่งจดหมาย/โปสการ์ด นี้ไปที่… kŏr súee sah·dtaem săhm·ràp sòng jòt·mĭe/bpóet·sah·gárt née bpi têe… |
| How much? | เท่าไหร่? tôu·rì |
| Send this package *by airmail/express*. | ช่วยส่งพัสดุนี้ทาง ไปรษณีย์อากาศ/อีเอ็มเอส chôary sòng páht·sah·dùh née tarng bpri·sah·nee ar·gàrt/ee·ehm·ét |
| A receipt, please. | ขอใบเสร็จด้วย kŏr bi·sèht dôary |

## You May Hear…

| | |
|---|---|
| กรอกข้อความในใบศุลกากรด้วย gròrk kôr·kwarm ni bi sŭhn·lah·gar·gorn dôary | Fill out the customs declaration form. |
| มูลค่าของเท่าไหร่? moon·lah·kâr kŏrng tôu·rì | What's the value? |
| มีอะไรอยู่ในนี้? mee ah·ri yòo ni née | What's inside? |

 Most Thai post offices are open from approximately 8 a.m. to 4 p.m. and provide the typical range of services, including phone services. The central service in Bangkok, the General Post Office, located on Charoen Krung Road, is open 24 hours a day.

# ▼ Food

# Eating Out

## Essential

| | |
|---|---|
| Can you recommend a good *restaurant/ bar*? | คุณช่วยแนะนำ *ร้านอาหาร/บาร์* ดีๆให้หน่อยได้ไหม? kuhn chôary ná·nahm *rárn ar·hărn/bar* dee dee hî nòhy dî mí |
| Is there *a traditional Thai/an inexpensive* restaurant nearby? | มี *ร้านอาหารไทย/ร้านที่ราคา ไม่แพง* ใกล้ๆแถวนี้ไหม? mee *rárn ar·hărn ti/rárn têe rar·kar mî paeng* glî glî tăew née mí |
| A table for…, please. | ขอโต๊ะสำหรับ…คน kǒr dtó sǎhm·ràhp…kon |
| Can we sit…? | ขอนั่งตรง…ได้ไหม? kǒr nâhng dtrong…dî mí |
| – here/there | – นี่/นั่น née/náhn |
| – outside | – ด้านนอก dârn nôrk |
| – in a non-smoking area | – บริเวณห้ามสูบบุหรี่ bor·rih·wen hârm sòop bu·rèe |
| I'm waiting for someone. | ผม♂/ฉัน♀ กำลังรอเพื่อนอยู่ pǒm♂/cháhn♀ gahm·lahng ror pûean yòo |
| Where's the restroom [toilet]? | ห้องน้ำไปทางไหน? hôhng·nárm bpi tarng nǐ |
| A menu, please. | ขอเมนูหน่อย kǒr me·noo nòhy |
| What do you recommend? | มีอะไรแนะนำบ้าง? mee ah·ri ná·nahm bârng |
| I'd like… | ผม♂/ฉัน♀ อยากได้… pǒm♂/cháhn♀ yàrk dîe… |
| Some more…, please. | ขอ…เพิ่มอีกหน่อย kǒr…pêrm èek nòhy |
| Enjoy your meal! | ทานให้อร่อย! tarn hî ah·ròhy |
| The check [bill], please. | เช็คบิลด้วย chéhk bihn dôary |

| Is service included? | รวมค่าบริการแล้วหรือยัง? roarm kâr bor·rih·garn láew rúe yahng |
| Can I pay by credit card? | ผม♂/ฉัน♀ จ่ายด้วยบัตรเครดิตได้ไหม? pŏm♂/ cháhn♀ jie dôary bàht kre·dìht dî mí |
| Can I have a receipt? | ผม♂/ฉัน♀ ขอใบเสร็จด้วยได้ไหม? pŏm♂/ cháhn♀ kŏr bi·sèht dôary dî mí |
| Thank you! | ขอบคุณ! kòrp·kuhn |

## Restaurant Types

| Can you recommend…? | คุณช่วยแนะนำ…ให้หน่อยได้ไหม? kuhn chôary ná·nahm…hî nòhy dî mí |
| – a restaurant | – ร้านอาหาร rárn ar·hărn |
| – a bar | – บาร์ bar |
| – a cafe | – ร้านกาแฟ rárn gar·fae |
| – a fast-food place | – ร้านอาหารฟาสต์ฟู้ด rárn ar·hărn fárt·fóot |

## Reservations and Questions

| I'd like to reserve a table… | ผม♂/ฉัน♀ อยากจะจองโต๊ะ… pŏm♂/cháhn♀ yàrk jah jorng dtó… |
| – for two | – สำหรับสองคน săhm·ràhp sŏrng kon |
| – for this evening | – สำหรับเย็นนี้ săhm·ràhp yehn née |
| – for tomorrow at… | – สำหรับพรุ่งนี้ตอน… săhm·ràhp prûhng née dtorn… |
| A table for two, please. | ขอโต๊ะสำหรับสองที่ kŏr dtó săhm·ràhp sŏrng têe |
| We have a reservation. | เราจองไว้แล้ว rou jorng wí láew |
| My name is… | ผม♂/ฉัน♀ ชื่อ… pŏm♂/cháhn♀ chûee… |

| Can we sit...? | ขอนั่งตรง...ได้ไหม? kŏr nâhng dtrong...dî mí |
| – here/there | – นี่/นั่น née/náhn |
| – outside | – ด้านนอก dârn nôrk |
| – in a non-smoking area | – บริเวณห้ามสูบบุหรี่ bor·rih·wen hârm sòop bu·rèe |
| – by the window | – ริมหน้าต่าง rihm nâr·dtàrng |
| Where's the restroom [toilet]? | ห้องน้ำไปทางไหน? hôhng·nárm bpi tarng nǐ |

## You May Hear...

| คุณจะสั่งอาหารเลยไหม? kuhn jah sàhng ar·hǎrn lery mí | Are you ready to order? |
| ผม♂/ฉัน♀ อยากจะแนะนำ... pŏm♂/cháhn♀ yàrk jah ná·nahm... | I recommend... |
| ทานให้อร่อย tarn hî ah·ròhy | Enjoy your meal. |

## Ordering

| Waiter/Waitress! | บ๋อย/คุณ! bŏhy/kuhn |
| We're ready to order. | เราต้องการสั่งอาหาร rou dtôhng·garn sàhng ar·hǎrn |
| The wine list, please. | ขอรายการไวน์หน่อย kŏr rie·garn wie nòhy |
| I'd like... | ผม♂/ฉัน♀ อยากได้... pŏm♂/cháhn♀ yàrk dîe... |
| – a bottle of... | – ...หนึ่งขวด ...nùeng kòart |
| – a carafe of... | – ...หนึ่งเหยือก ...nùeng yùeek |
| – a glass of... | – ...หนึ่งแก้ว ...nùeng gâew |

▶ For alcoholic and non-alcoholic drinks, see page 81.

| The menu, please. | ขอเมนูหน่อย kŏr me·noo nòhy |

| Do you have...? | คุณมี... ไหม? kuhn mee...mí |
| – a menu in English | – เมนูเป็นภาษาอังกฤษ me·noo bpehn par·săr ahng·griht |
| – a fixed-price menu | – เมนูอาหารชุด me·noo ar·hărn chúht |
| – a children's menu | – เมนูสำหรับเด็ก me·noo săhm·ràhp dèhk |
| What do you recommend? | มีอะไรแนะนำบ้าง? mee ah·ri ná·nahm bârng |
| What's this? | นี่อะไร? nêe ah·ri |
| Is it spicy? | เผ็ดไหม? pèht mí |
| Without..., please. | ไม่ใส่...นะ mî sì...náh |
| It's to go [take away]. | ใส่ห่อไปกินที่บ้าน sì hòr bpi gin têe bârn |

## You May See...

| ราคาตายตัว rar·kar dtie·dtoar | fixed-price |
| เมนูพิเศษวันนี้ me·noo píh·sèt wahn·née | menu of the day |
| (ไม่)รวมค่าบริการ (mî) roarm kăr bor·rihgarn | service (not) included |
| พิเศษ píh·sèt | specials |

## Cooking Methods

| baked | อบ òp |
| boiled | ต้ม dtôm |
| breaded | ชุบขนมปัง chúhp kah·nŏm·bpahng |
| diced | หั่น hàhn |
| fileted | แล่ lâe |
| deep-fried | ทอด tôrt |
| stir-fried | ผัด pàht |
| grilled | ปิ้ง/ย่าง bpîhng/yârng |

| poached | เคี่ยว kêaw |
| roasted | อบ òp |
| sautéed | ผัด pàht |
| smoked | รมควัน rom kwahn |
| steamed | นึ่ง nûeng |
| stewed | ตุ๋น dtŭhn |
| stuffed | ยัดไส้ yáht sî |

## Special Requirements

| I'm diabetic. | ผม♂/ฉัน♀ เป็น โรคเบาหวาน pŏm♂/cháhn♀ bpehn rôek bou•wărn |
| I'm… | ผม♂/ฉัน♀ กิน… pŏm♂/cháhn♀ kihn… |
| – lactose intolerant | – นมไม่ได้ nom mî dîe |
| – vegetarian | – มังสวิรัติ mahng•sàh•wíh•ráht |
| – vegan | – เจ je |
| I'm allergic to… | ผม♂/ฉัน♀ แพ้… pŏm♂/cháhn♀ páe… |
| I can't eat… | ผม♂/ฉัน♀ กิน…ไม่ได้ pŏm♂/cháhn♀ gihn…mî dîe |
| – dairy | – นม nom |
| – gluten | – สารกลูเตน sărn gloo•dtêhn |
| – nuts | – ถั่ว tòar |
| – pork | – เนื้อหมู núea mŏo |
| Is it *halal/kosher*? | อันนี้เป็นอาหาร ฮาลาล/โคเชอร์ หรือเปล่า? ahn née bpehn ar•hărn *har•larn/koe•chêr* rúe•bplòw |

## Dining with Kids

| Do you have children's portions? | คุณมีขนาดสำหรับเด็กหรือเปล่า? kuhn mee kah•nàrt săhm•ràhp dèhk rúe•bplòw |

| A *highchair/child's seat*, please. | ขอ *เก้าอี้เด็ก/ที่นั่งเด็ก* หน่อย kŏr *gôu·êe dèhk/ têe·nâhng dèhk* nòhy |
| Where can I *feed/ change* the baby? | ผม ♂/ฉัน ♀ จะ *ให้นม/เปลี่ยนผ้าอ้อม* เด็กได้ที่ไหน? pŏm ♂/chán ♀ jah *hî nom/ bplèan pâr·ôrm* dèhk dîe têe·nî |
| Can you warm this? | ช่วยอุ่นนี่ให้หน่อยได้ไหม? chôary ùhn nêe hî nòhy dîe mí |

▶ For travel with children, see page 142.

## Complaints

| How much longer will our food be? | อีกนานไหมกว่าอาหารจะมา? èek narn mí gwàr ar·hărn jah mar |
| We can't wait any longer. | เรารอต่อไปไม่ไหวแล้ว rou ror dtòr bpi mî wǐ láew |
| We're leaving. | เราจะกลับแล้ว rou jah glahp láew |
| I didn't order this. | ผม ♂/ฉัน ♀ ไม่ได้สั่งอันนี้ pŏm ♂/chán ♀ mî dî sàhng ahn née |
| I ordered… | ผม ♂/ฉัน ♀ สั่ง… pŏm ♂/chán ♀ sàhng… |
| I can't eat this. | ผม ♂/ฉัน ♀ กินอันนี้ไม่ได้ pŏm ♂/chán ♀ gihn ahn née mî dîe |
| This isn't *clean/fresh*. | อันนี้ไม่ *สะอาด/สด* ahn née mî *sah·àrt/sòt* |

## Paying

| The check [bill], please. | เช็คบิลด้วย chéhk bihn dôary |
| Separate checks [bills], please. | แยกบิลด้วย yâek bihn dôary |
| It's all together. | รวมบิลเลย roarm bihn lery |
| Is service included? | รวมค่าบริการแล้วหรือยัง? roarm kâr bor·rih·garn láew rúe yahng |
| What's this amount for? | อันนี้ค่าอะไร? ahn née kâr ah·ri |

| I didn't have that. I had… | ผม♂/ฉัน♀ ไม่ได้สั่งอันนี้ ผม♂/ฉัน♀ สั่ง… pǒm♂/cháhn♀ mî dî sàhng ahn née pǒm♂/cháhn♀ sàhng… |
|---|---|
| Can I have *a receipt/ an itemized bill*? | ผม♂/ฉัน♀ ขอ ใบเสร็จ/บิลแยกตามรายการ ได้ไหม? pǒm♂/cháhn♀ kǒr *bi·sèht/bihn yâek dtarm rie·garn* dîe mí |
| That was delicious! | อาหารอร่อยมาก! ar·hǎrn ah·ròhy mârk |

---

*i* A 10% service charge is usually included in the restaurant bill. When locals tip, they typically just leave behind some loose change. Tipping is not customary at food shops or roadside stands.

## Market

| Where are the *carts [trolleys]/baskets*? | รถเข็น/ตะกร้า อยู่ที่ไหน? *rót kěhn/dtah·grâr* yòo têe·nǐ |
|---|---|
| Where is…? | …อยู่ที่ไหน? …yòo têe·nǐ |

▶ For food items, see page 86.

| I'd like some of *that/this*. | ผม♂/ฉัน♀ ขอ อันนี้/อันนั้น pǒm♂/cháhn♀ kǒr *ahn née/ahn náhn* |
|---|---|
| Can I taste it? | ขอชิมหน่อยได้ไหม? kǒr chihm nòhy dî mí |
| I'd like… | ผม♂/ฉัน♀ ขอ… pǒm♂/cháhn♀ kǒr… |
| – a *kilo/half-kilo* of… | – …หนึ่งกิโล/ครึ่งกิโล …nùeng gih·loe/krûeng gih·loe |
| – a liter of… | – …หนึ่งลิตร …nùeng líht |
| – a piece of… | – …หนึ่งชิ้น …nùeng chíhn |
| – a slice of… | – …หนึ่งชิ้น …nùeng chíhn |
| *More/Less*. | มากกว่า/น้อยกว่า *mârk gwàr/nóry gwàr* |
| How much? | เท่าไหร่? tôu·rì |

| Where do I pay? | ผม♂/ฉัน♀ จะจ่ายเงินได้ที่ไหน? pŏm♂/cháhn♀ jah jìe ngern dîe têe·nǐ |
| A bag, please. | ขอถุงหน่อย kŏr tŭhng nòhy |
| I'm being helped. | ผม♂/ฉัน♀ มีคนช่วยแล้ว pŏm♂/cháhn♀ mee kon chôary láew |

▶For conversion tables, see page 170.

In Thailand, there are several large, international supermarkets in existence, as well as Thai chains. You will also find many small shops and, of course, markets. Seafood is typically fresh and abundant. The meat selection is quality controlled by the government.

## You May Hear...

| มีอะไรให้ช่วยไหม? mee ah·ri hî chôary mí | Can I help you? |
| คุณต้องการอะไร? kun dtôhng·garn ah·ri | What would you like? |
| รับอะไรอีกไหม? ráhp ah·ri èek mí | Anything else? |
| อันนั้น...บาท ahn náhn...bàrt | That's...baht. |

## You May See...

| ควรรับประทานก่อน... koarn ráh·bprah·tarn gòrn... | best if used by... |
| เก็บไว้ในตู้เย็น gèhp wí ni dtôo·yehn | keep refrigerated |
| จำหน่ายภายใน... jahm·nìe pie ni... | sell by... |
| สำหรับคนที่กินมังสวิรัติ sǎhm·ràhp kon têe gihn mahng·sà·wíh·ráht | suitable for vegetarians |

63

# Dishes, Utensils and Kitchen Tools

| | |
|---|---|
| bottle opener | ที่เปิดขวด têe bpèrt kòart |
| bowl | ชาม charm |
| can opener | ที่เปิดกระป๋อง têe bpèrt grah·bpǒhng |
| corkscrew | ที่เปิดจุกก๊อก têe bpèrt jùhk·góhk |
| cup | ถ้วย tôary |
| fork | ส้อม sôhm |
| frying pan | กระทะ grah·táh |
| glass | แก้วน้ำ gâew nárm |
| (steak) knife | มีด (สเต๊ก) mêet (sah·dték) |
| measuring *cup/ spoon* | ถ้วย/ช้อน ตวง *tôary/chórn* dtoarng |
| napkin | กระดาษเช็ดปาก grah·dàrt chéht bpàrk |
| plate | จาน jarn |
| pot | หม้อ môr |
| spatula | ตะหลิว dtah·lǐhw |
| spoon | ช้อน chórn |

## Meals

Food in Thailand is usually eaten with a fork and spoon, though Chinese-style noodle dishes are often eaten with chopsticks. Knives at the table are not necessary since food is cut into bite-sized chunks during cooking. It is common for the whole table to share several main dishes. While this is a great opportunity for you to try many new recipes at once, put only a spoonful at a time on your plate. In Thailand, it is impolite to fill your plate with food.

## Breakfast ────────────────────

| | |
|---|---|
| apple juice | น้ำแอปเปิ้ล nárm áep·bpêrn |
| bacon | เบคอน be·kôhn |
| bread | ขนมปัง kah·nŏm·bpahng |
| butter | เนย nery |
| (cold/hot) cereal | ซีเรียล (เย็น/ร้อน) see·rêal (yehn/rórn) |
| cheese | เนยแข็ง nery·kăng |
| coffee/tea… | กาแฟ/ชา… gar·fae/char… |
| – black | – ดำ dahm |
| – decaf | – ชนิดไม่มีคาเฟอีน chah·níht mî mee kar·fe·een |
| – with milk | – ใส่นม sì nom |
| – with sugar | – ใส่น้ำตาล sì náhm·dtarn |
| – with artificial sweetener | – ใส่น้ำตาลเทียม sì náhm·dtarn team |
| …eggs | ไข่… kì… |
| – *hard-/soft*-boiled | – ต้มสุก/ลวก dtôm sùhk/lôark |
| – fried | – ดาว dow |
| – scrambled | – คน kon |
| fruit juice | น้ำผลไม้ nárm pŏn·lah·mí |
| jam/jelly | แยม/เยลลี่ yaem/yen·lêe |
| milk | นม nom |
| muffin | มัฟฟิน máhp·fîhn |
| oatmeal | ข้าวโอ๊ต kôw·óet |
| omelet | ไข่เจียว kì·jeaw |
| orange juice | น้ำส้ม nárm sôm |
| pineapple juice | น้ำสับปะรด nárm sàhp·bpah·rót |

| | |
|---|---|
| rice porridge with *pork/chicken* | โจ๊ก *หมู/ไก่* jóek *mŏo/gì* |
| rice soup with… | ข้าวต้ม… kôw dtôm… |
| – chicken | – ไก่ gì |
| – pork | – หมู mŏo |
| – shrimp [prawn] | – กุ้ง gûhng |
| roll | ขนมปังก้อน kah·nŏm·bpahng gôrn |
| sausage | ไส้กรอก sî·gròrk |
| toast | ขนมปังปิ้ง kah·nŏm·bpahng bpîhng |
| yogurt | โยเกิร์ต yoe·gèrt |

## Appetizers [Starters]

| | |
|---|---|
| deep-fried bread with ground [minced] *pork/shrimp [prawn]* | ขนมปังหน้า *หมู/กุ้ง* kah·nŏm·bpahng nâr *mŏo/gûhng* |
| deep-fried, crispy wanton | เกี๊ยวทอด géaw tôrt |
| deep-fried pastry cup with ground [minced] pork | กระทงทอง grah·tong·torng |
| deep-fried, spicy fishcake | ทอดมันปลา tôrt·mahn bplar |
| deep-fried spring roll | เปาะเปี๊ยะทอด bpoh·bpéa tôrt |
| fresh spring roll | เปาะเปี๊ยะสด bpoh·bpéa sòt |
| grilled squid | ปลาหมึกย่าง bplar·mùek yârng |
| …satay | สะเต๊ะ… sah·dtéh… |
| – beef | – เนื้อ núea |

| | |
|---|---|
| I'd like… | ผม♂/ฉัน♀ ขอ…pŏm♂/cháhn♀ kŏr… |
| More…, please. | ขอ…เพิ่มหน่อย kŏr…pêrm nòhy |

| | |
|---|---|
| – chicken | ไก่ gì |
| – pork | หมู mŏo |
| shrimp [prawn] rice cracker | ข้าวเกรียบกุ้ง kôw·grèap gûhng |
| spicy pork sausage salad | แหนมสด năem·sòt |
| spicy northeastern sausage | ไส้กรอกอีสาน sî·gròrk ee·sărn |
| stuffed chicken wing | ปีกไก่ยัดไส้ bpèek·gì yáht sî |

 Thai food is highly regional, however น้ำปลา **náhm-bplar** (fish sauce) is one ingredient common to dishes across the country. Lemongrass, curry, cilantro and chili, the latter being responsible for a good deal of the spiciness of Thai cuisine, are also quite common.

## Fish and Seafood

| | |
|---|---|
| baby clam | หอยลาย hŏry·lie |
| black-banded kingfish (similar to mackerel) | ปลาสำลี bplar săhm·lee |
| catfish | ปลาดุก bplar·dùhk |
| clam | หอยกาบ hŏry·garp |
| crab | ปู bpoo |
| deep-fried, spicy fishcake | ทอดมันปลา tôrt·mahn bplar |
| featherback (freshwater fish) | ปลากราย bplar grie |

| | |
|---|---|
| With/Without… | ใส่/ไม่ใส่… sì/mî sì… |
| I can't have… | ผม♂/ฉัน♀ กิน…ไม่ได้ pŏm♂/cháhn♀ gihn…mî dîe |

| | |
|---|---|
| fried fish topped with sweet, sour and spicy sauce | ปลาสามรส bplar sărm•rót |
| gourami (freshwater fish) | ปลาสลิด bplar sah•lìht |
| grouper | ปลาเก๋า bplar gŏu |
| lobster | กุ้งมังกร gûhng mahng•gorn |
| mackerel | ปลาทู bplar too |
| mussels | หอยแมลงภู่ hŏry mah•laeng pôo |
| octopus | ปลาหมึกยักษ์ bplar•mùek yáhk |
| oyster | หอยนางรม hŏry narng•rom |
| pomfret (a deep-sea fish) | ปลาจาระเม็ด bplar jar•ráh•méht |
| red snapper | ปลากะพงแดง bplar grah•pong daeng |
| rock lobster | กั้ง gâhng |
| salmon | ปลาแซลมอน bplar san•môrn |
| sea bass | ปลากะพงขาว bplar grah•pong kŏw |
| seafood | อาหารทะเล ar•hărn tah•le |

| | |
|---|---|
| I'd like… | ผม♂/ฉัน♀ ขอ… pŏm♂/cháhn♀ kŏr… |
| More…, please. | ขอ…เพิ่มหน่อย kŏr…pêrm nòhy |

| | |
|---|---|
| snakehead (a freshwater fish) | ปลาช่อน bplar chôrn |
| shrimp [prawn] | กุ้ง gûhng |
| squid | ปลาหมึก bplar•mùek |
| steamed pomfret with plum pickles | ปลาจะระเม็ดนึ่งบ๊วย bplar jar•ráh•méht nûeng bóary |
| steamed seafood curry | ห่อหมกทะเล hòr mòk tah•le |
| sweet and sour fish | ปลาเปรี้ยวหวาน bplar bprêaw•wǎrn |
| tuna | ปลาทูน่า bplar too•nâr |

## Meat and Poultry

| | |
|---|---|
| beef | เนื้อวัว núea woar |
| capon | ไก่ตอน gì dtorn |
| chicken | ไก่ gì |
| crispy roast pork | หมูกรอบ mǒo gròrp |
| duck | เป็ด bpèht |
| (smoked) ham | หมูแฮม (รมควัน) mǒo•ham (rom•kwahn) |
| liver | ตับ dtàhp |
| meatballs | ลูกชิ้นเนื้อ look•chíhn núea |
| oxtail | หางวัว hǎrng woar |
| pork | เนื้อหมู núea mǒo |
| red roast pork | หมูแดง mǒo•daeng |
| roast beef | เนื้ออบ núea òp |
| sausage | ไส้กรอก sî gròrk |
| sirloin | เนื้อสันนอก núea sǎhn nôrk |

| | |
|---|---|
| With/Without… | ใส่/ไม่ใส่… sì/mî sì… |
| I can't have… | ผม♂/ฉัน♀ กิน…ไม่ได้ pǒm♂/cháhn♀ gihn…mî dîe |

| steak | สเต็ก sah·dték |
| suckling pig | หมูหัน mǒo·hǎhn |
| tenderloin | เนื้อสันใน núea sǎhn ni |
| tongue | ลิ้น líhn |

▶ For meat and poultry stir-fry dishes, see page 73.

| rare | ไม่ค่อยสุก mî·kôhy sùhk |
| medium | สุกปานกลาง sùhk bparn·glarng |
| well-done | สุกมาก sùhk mârk |

## Soup

| chicken and coconut milk soup flavored with galanga | ต้มข่าไก่ dtôm·kàr gì |
| chicken soup | ซุปไก่ súhp gì |
| clear soup with... | แกงจืด... gaeng·jùeet... |
| – Chinese glass noodles, pork and vegetables | – วุ้นเส้น wúhn·sêhn |
| – fish balls | – ลูกชิ้นปลา lôok·chíhn bplar |
| – pickled vegetables | – เกี้ยมฉ่าย géam·chìe |
| – seaweed | – สาหร่ายทะเล sǎr·rìe tah·le |
| – tofu and ground pork | – เต้าหู้หมูสับ dtôu·hôo mǒo sàhp |
| clear soup with mixed vegetables, pumpkin and shrimp [prawn] | แกงเลียง gaeng·leang |

| I'd like... | ผม♂/ฉัน♀ ขอ... pǒm♂/cháhn♀ kǒr... |
| More..., please. | ขอ...เพิ่มหน่อยkǒr...pêrm nòhy |

| | |
|---|---|
| clear soup with pork ribs and mixed vegetables | ต้มจับฉ่าย dtôm jàhp·chìe |
| egg noodle soup | บะหมี่น้ำ bàh·mèe nárm |
| hot and sour soup | ต้มยำ dtôm·yahm |
| hot and sour soup with dried fish and spices | ต้มโคล้งปลาย่าง dtôm·klóeng bplar·yârng |

## Curry Dishes

| | |
|---|---|
| hot and sour curry with snakehead (fish) and mixed vegetables | แกงส้มปลาช่อน gaeng·sôm bplar·chôrn |
| hot and sour curry with fish and water mimosa (type of watercress) | แกงส้มผักกระเฉด gaeng·sôm pàhk·grah·chèt |
| green curry with... | แกงเขียวหวาน... gaeng kěaw·wǎrn... |
| Indian-style curry with... | แกงมัสมั่น... gaeng máht·sah·màhn... |
| mild red curry with... | พะแนง... pah·naeng... |
| spicy red curry with... | แกงเผ็ด... gaeng·pèht... |
| – beef | – เนื้อ núea |
| – chicken | – ไก่ gì |
| – pork | – หมู mǒo |

## Rice and Noodle Dishes

| | |
|---|---|
| Chinese glass noodle | วุ้นเส้น wúhn·sêhn |
| egg noodle | บะหมี่ bàh·mèe |
| With/Without... | ใส่/ไม่ใส่... sì/mî sì... |
| I can't have... | ผม ♂/ฉัน ♀ กิน...ไม่ได้ pǒm ♂/cháhn ♀ gihn...mî dîe |

| | |
|---|---|
| egg noodle in spicy curry with *chicken/ beef* | ข้าวซอย ไก่/เนื้อ kôw•sory *gì/núea* |
| fermented rice noodle | เส้นขนมจีน sêhn kah•nǒm•jeen |
| fried noodles topped with thickened sauce and vegetables | ก๋วยเตี๋ยวราดหน้า gǒary•těaw rârt nâr |
| fried rice... | ข้าวผัด... kôw•pàht... |
| – American-style | – อเมริกัน ah•me•rih•gahn |
| – with crab | – ปู bpoo |
| – with pork | – หมู mǒo |
| – with shrimp [prawn] | – กุ้ง gûhng |
| pasta | เส้นพาสต้า sêhn párs•dtâr |
| rice vermicelli | เส้นหมี่ sêhn•mèe |
| rice with... | ข้าว... kôw... |
| – curry | – ราดแกง rârt gaeng |
| – fermented shrimp paste | – คลุกกะปิ klúhk gah•bpìh |
| – roast duck | – หน้าเป็ด nâr bpèht |
| – roast pork | – หมูแดง mǒo•daeng |
| – steamed chicken | – มันไก่ mahn gì |
| – stewed leg of pork | – ขาหมู kǎr•mǒo |
| stir-fried rice noodle in soy sauce with Chinese kale and *chicken/pork* | ผัดซีอิ๊ว ไก่/หมู pàht•see•íhw *gì/mǒo* |

| | |
|---|---|
| I'd like... | ผม♂/ฉัน♀ ขอ... pǒm♂/cháhn♀ kǒr... |
| More..., please. | ขอ...เพิ่มหน่อย kǒr...pêrm nòhy |

| | |
|---|---|
| stir-fried rice noodle with shrimp, tofu, peanuts (pad thai) | ผัดไทย pàht·ti |
| short, clear noodle | เส้นเซี่ยงไฮ้ sêhn sêang·hí |
| short, rolled rice noodle | เส้นก๋วยจั๊บ sêhn gǒary·jáhp |

> *i*
>
> Thailand is the largest exporter of rice in the world, so it is no surprise that rice is a staple at every meal. Jasmine rice is the most common type of rice grown in Thailand. Sticky rice, a particularly starchy variety, is commonly eaten in the North and Northeast, an area heavily influenced by the cuisine and culture of Laos. Though rice is generally the accompaniment to a dish, noodles comprise a dish all their own. Pad Thai is a popular stir-fried noodle recipe.

## Spicy Salads and Stir-fry Dishes

| | |
|---|---|
| spicy deep-fried catfish salad | ยำปลาดุกฟู yahm bplar·dùhk foo |
| spicy deep-fried gourami salad | ยำปลาสลิด yahm bplar·sah·liht |
| spicy beef salad | ยำเนื้อย่าง yam núea yârng |
| spicy ground [minced] *chicken/duck* salad | ลาบ *ไก่/เป็ด* lârp *gì/bpèht* |
| spicy papaya salad | ส้มตำ sôm·dtahm |
| spicy sausage salad | ยำหมูยอ yahm mǒo·yor |
| spicy seafood salad | ยำทะเล yahm tah·le |

| | |
|---|---|
| With/Without… | ใส่/ไม่ใส่… si/mî sì… |
| I can't have… | ผม♂/ฉัน♀ กิน…ไม่ได้ pǒm♂/cháhn♀ gihn…mî dîe |

| | |
|---|---|
| stir-fried, spicy...with holy basil leaves | ...ผัดกะเพรา ...pàht grah·prou |
| stir-fried...with chili | ...ผัดพริก ...pàht·príhk |
| stir-fried...with ginger | ...ผัดขิง ...pàht·kǐhng |
| – beef | – เนื้อ núea |
| – chicken | – ไก่ gì |
| – pork | – หมู mǒo |
| stir-fried beef with oyster sauce | เนื้อผัดน้ำมันหอย núea pàht náhm·mahn·hǒry |
| stir-fried chicken with cashew nuts | ไก่ผัดเม็ดมะม่วงหิมพานต์ gì pàht méht·mah·môarng·hǐhm·mah·parn |
| stir-fried crispy pork with Chinese kale | ผัดคะน้าหมูกรอบ pàht kah·nár mǒo·gròrp |

## Vegetarian Dishes

| | |
|---|---|
| clear soup with tofu and napa cabbage | แกงจืดเต้าหู้กับผักกาดขาว gaeng·jùeet dtôu·hôo gàhp pàhk·gàrt·kǒw |
| deep-fried bean curd | เต้าหู้ทอด dtôu·hôo tôrt |
| deep-fried, battered vegetables | ผักชุบแป้งทอด pàhk chúhp·bpâeng tôrt |
| fresh salad with peanut sauce | สลัดแขก sah·làht kàek |
| mushroom soup | ซุปเห็ด súhp hèht |
| red vegetable curry | แกงเผ็ดเจ gaeng·pèht je |
| spicy noodle salad | ยำวุ้นเส้นเจ yahm wúhn·sêhn je |
| spicy salad of ground [minced] mushrooms | ลาบเห็ด lârp·hèht |

| | |
|---|---|
| I'd like... | ผม♂/ฉัน♀ ขอ... pǒm♂/chǎhn♀ kǒr... |
| More..., please. | ขอ...เพิ่มหน่อย kǒr...pêrm nòhy |

| stir-fried eggplant | ผัดมะเขือยาว pàht mah·kŭea·yow |
|---|---|
| stir-fried mixed vegetables | ผัดผักรวมมิตรเจ pàht pàk roarm·míht je |
| stir-fried mushrooms, basil and baby corn | ผัดกะเพราเห็ดกับข้าวโพดอ่อน pàht grah·prou hèht gàhp kôw·pôet·òrn |
| stir-fried rice noodle in soy sauce with Chinese kale | ผัดซีอิ๊วเจ pàht see·ihw je |
| stir-fried rice noodle with peanut, bean curd and radish | ผัดไทยเจ pàht·ti je |
| stir-fried snow peas with baby corn | ผัดถั่วลันเตากับข้าวโพดอ่อน pàht tòar lahn·dtou gàhp kôw·pôet·òrn |
| stir-fried water spinach leaves | ผัดผักบุ้ง pàht pàhk·bûhng |
| sweet and sour fried vegetables | ผัดเปรี้ยวหวานเจ pàht bprêaw·wărn je |
| vegetarian spring rolls | เปาะเปี๊ยะเจ bpòr·bpéa je |

## Vegetables and Staples

| aniseed | โป๊ยกั๊ก bpóey·gáhk |
|---|---|
| aromatic ginger | กระชาย grah·chie |
| asparagus (tip) | (ยอด) หน่อไม้ฝรั่ง (yôrt) nòr·mí fah·ràhng |
| baby corn | ข้าวโพดอ่อน kôw pôet òrn |
| bay leaf | ใบกระวาน bi grah·warn |
| bean | ถั่ว tòar |
| beansprout | ถั่วงอก tòar·ngôrk |

| With/Without… | ใส่/ไม่ใส่… sì/mî sì… |
|---|---|
| I can't have… | ผม ♂/ฉัน ♀ กิน… ไม่ได้ pŏm ♂/cháhn ♀ gihn…mî dîe |

| bitter gourd | มะระ mah·ráh |
|---|---|
| broccoli | บร็อคโคลี่ bróhk·koe·lêe |
| cabbage | กะหล่ำปลี gah·làhm bplee |
| caraway | ยี่หร่า yêe·ràr |
| carrot | แคร็อท kae·ròht |
| cauliflower | กะหล่ำดอก gah·làhm dòrk |
| celery | คื่นช่ายฝรั่ง kûen·chîe fah·ràhng |
| chili | พริก príhk |
| cashew nut | เม็ดมะม่วงหิมพานต์ méht máh·môarng·hǐhm·mah·parn |
| cilantro [coriander] | ผักชี pàhk·chee |
| corn | ข้าวโพด kôw·pôet |
| cucumber | แตงกวา dtaeng·gwar |
| eggplant [aubergine] | มะเขือยาว mah·kǔea yow |
| galanga | ข่า kàr |
| garlic | กระเทียม grah·team |
| ginger | ขิง kǐhng |
| green bean | ถั่วแขก tòar kàek |
| green onion | ต้นหอม dtôn·hǒrm |
| holy basil | กะเพรา grah·prou |
| lemongrass | ตะไคร้ dtah·krí |
| lentils | ถั่วแขก tòar kàek |
| lettuce | ผักกาดหอม pàhk·gàrt hǒrm |
| long bean | ถั่วฝักยาว tòar fàhk·yow |
| mint | สะระแหน่ sah·rah·nàe |
| mushroom | เห็ด hèht |
| napa cabbage | ผักกาดขาว pàhk·gàrt kǒw |

| | |
|---|---|
| nutmeg | ลูกจันทน์ lôok·jahn |
| okra [ladies' fingers] | กระเจี๊ยบ grah·jéap |
| olive | มะกอก mah·gòrk |
| onion | หอมหัวใหญ่ hǒrm hǒar yì |
| parsley | ผักชีฝรั่ง pahk·chee fah·ràhng |
| peanut | ถั่วลิสง tòar·lih·sǒng |
| pepper (seasoning) | พริกไทย príhk·ti |
| (green/red) pepper | พริกหยวก (เขียว/แดง) príhk·yòark (kěaw/daeng) |
| potato | มันฝรั่ง mahn fah·rahng |
| pumpkin | ฟักทอง fáhk·torng |
| rice | ข้าว kôw |
| sesame | งา ngar |
| shallot | หอมแดง hǒrm·daeng |
| snow pea | ถั่วลันเตา tòar lahn·dtou |
| spinach | ผักโขม pàhk·kǒem |
| sweet basil | โหระพา hǒe·rah·par |
| sweet corn | ข้าวโพดหวาน kôw·pôet wǎrn |
| sweet potato | มันเทศ mahn·têt |
| tofu | เต้าหู้ dtôu·hôo |
| tomato | มะเขือเทศ mah·kǔea·têt |
| vegetable | ผัก pàhk |
| water mimosa | ผักกระเฉด pàhk grah·chèt |
| water spinach | ผักบุ้ง pàhk·bûhng |

## Fruit

| | |
|---|---|
| apple | แอปเปิ้ล áep·bpêrn |
| banana | กล้วย glôary |
| blueberry | บลูเบอรี่ bloo·ber·rêe |
| cherry | เชอรี่ cher·rêe |
| coconut | มะพร้าว mah·prów |
| custard apple | น้อยหน่า nóry·nàr |
| date | อินทผาลัม ihn·tah·pǎr·lahm |
| dragon fruit | แก้วมังกร gâew·mahng·gorn |
| dried fruit | ผลไม้แห้ง pǒn·lah·mí hâeng |
| durian | ทุเรียน túh·rean |
| fruit | ผลไม้ pǒn·lah·míe |
| grape | องุ่น ah·ngùhn |
| guava | ฝรั่ง fah·ràhng |
| jackfruit | ขนุน kah·nǔhn |
| langsat | ลางสาด larng·sàrt |
| lemon | มะนาวเหลือง mah·now lǔeang |
| lime | มะนาว mah·now |
| longan | ลำไย lahm·yi |
| lychee | ลิ้นจี่ líhn·jèe |
| mango | มะม่วง mah·môarng |
| mangosteen | มังคุด mahng·kúht |
| melon | แตงไทย dtaeng·ti |

| | |
|---|---|
| I'd like… | ผม♂/ฉัน♀ ขอ… pǒm♂/cháhn♀ kǒr… |
| More…, please. | ขอ…เพิ่มหน่อย kǒr…pêrm nòhy |

| orange | ส้ม sôm |
|--------|---------|
| papaya | มะละกอ mah·lah·gor |
| peach | ลูกท้อ lôok·tór |
| pear | สาลี่ săr·lêe |
| pineapple | สับปะรด sàhp·bpah·rót |
| plums | ลูกไหน lôok·năi |
| pomelo | ส้มโอ sôm·oe |
| prunes | ลูกพรุน lôok·pruhn |
| raisins | ลูกเกด lôok·gèt |
| rambutan | เงาะ ngóh |
| rose apple | ชมพู่ chom·pôo |
| sapodilla | ละมุด lah·múht |
| strawberry | สตรอเบอร์รี่ sah·dtror·ber·rêe |
| tangerine | ส้มจีน sôm·jeen |
| watermelon | แตงโม dtaeng·moe |

Exotic, tropical fruit is abundant year-round in Thailand. Some, like durian—a large fruit with a soft, yellow flesh—are available fresh, frozen, dried and even as fruit chips. Jackfruit is a sweet, golden fruit, frequently served with fruit punch or ice cream. Langsat and longan grow in bunches, and the fruit can be enjoyed by pressing or peeling off the skin. Mangosteen, with its reddish-purple skin, is often enjoyed fresh or as a juice. The pomelo is a large, grapefruit-like treat, peeled and eaten like an orange. Rambutan is a red fruit with a prickly exterior. Sapodilla, an oval-shaped fruit with yellow-brown skin, is peeled and eaten fresh.

| With/Without… | ใส่/ไม่ใส่… sì/mî sì… |
|---------------|----------------------|
| I can't have… | ผม♂/ฉัน♀ กิน…ไม่ได้ pŏm♂/cháhn♀ gihn…mî dîe |

## Dessert

| | |
|---|---|
| bananas in coconut milk | กล้วยบวชชี glôary bòart-chee |
| caramelized bananas | กล้วยเชื่อม glôary chûeam |
| egg custard | สังขยา săhng-kah-yăr |
| egg yolks with flour and syrup | ทองหยิบ torng-yìhp |
| jellied water chestnuts in coconut milk | ทับทิมกรอบ táhp-tihm-gròrp |
| layered sweet coconut cream pancakes | ขนมชั้น kah-nŏm-cháhn |
| mixed fresh fruit | ผลไม้รวม pŏn-lah-mí roarm |
| mung bean coconut custard | ขนมหม้อแกง kah-nŏm môr-gaeng |
| mung bean rice crepe | ถั่วแปบ tòar-bpàep |
| pandanus-scented rice noodles in coconut milk | ลอดช่องน้ำกะทิ lôrt-chôhng náhm-gah-tí |
| *pumpkin/taro stewed in coconut milk* | ฟักทอง/เผือก บวด *fáhk-torng/pèuak* bòart |
| sticky rice in coconut milk | ข้าวเหนียวเปียก kôw-nĕaw bpèak |
| sticky rice with banana or taro in banana leaves | ข้าวต้มมัด kôw-dtôm-máht |
| sticky rice with coconut cream and *egg custard/mango* | ข้าวเหนียวสังขยา/*มะม่วง* kôw-nĕaw *săhng-kah-yăr/mah-môarng* |

| | |
|---|---|
| I'd like… | ผม♂/ฉัน♀ ขอ… pŏm♂/cháhn♀ kŏr… |
| More…, please. | ขอ…เพิ่มหน่อย kŏr…pêrm nòhy |

| | |
|---|---|
| sweet bean threads in coconut milk | ซ่าหริ่ม sâr·rìhm |
| sweet coconut milk jelly | วุ้นกะทิ wúhn gah·tí |
| tapioca and beans in coconut milk | สาคูถั่วดำ sǎr·koo tòar·dahm |
| taro balls and eggs in coconut milk | บัวลอยไข่หวาน boar·lory kì·wǎrn |
| thread of egg yolk dropped in syrup | ฝอยทอง fǒry·torng |

# *Drinks*

## Essential

| | |
|---|---|
| The *wine list/drink menu*, please. | ขอเมนู*ไวน์/เครื่องดื่ม* หน่อย kǒr me·noo *wie/ krûeang dùeem* nòhy |
| What do you recommend? | มีอะไรแนะนำบ้าง? mee ah·ri ná·nahm bârng |
| I'd like a *bottle/glass* of *white/red* wine. | ผม♂/ฉัน♀ ขอไวน์ *ขาว/แดง* หนึ่งขวด/ แก้ว pǒm♂/cháhn♀ kǒr wie *kǒw/daeng* nùeng *kòart/gâew* |
| The house wine, please. | ขอเฮ้าส์ไวน์ kǒr hóus·wie |
| Another *bottle/glass*, please. | ขอเพิ่มอีก *ขวด/แก้ว* kǒr pérm èek *kòart/gâew* |

| | |
|---|---|
| With/Without… | ใส่/ไม่ใส่… sì/mî sì… |
| I can't have… | ผม♂/ฉัน♀ กิน…ไม่ได้ pǒm♂/cháhn♀ gihn…mî dîe |

| | |
|---|---|
| I'd like a local beer. | ผม♂/ฉัน♀ ขอเบียร์ไทย pǒm♂/cháhn♀ kǒr bea ti |
| Can I buy you a drink? | ผม♂/ฉัน♀ ขอเลี้ยงเครื่องดื่มคุณได้ไหม? pǒm♂/cháhn♀ kǒr léang krûeang·dùeem kuhn dî mí |
| A *coffee/tea*, please. | ขอ *กาแฟ/ชา* หนึ่งที่ kǒr *gar·fae/char* nùeng têe |
| Black. | ดำ dahm |
| With… | ใส่... sì… |
| – milk | – นม nom |
| – sugar | – น้ำตาล náhm·dtarn |
| – artificial sweetener | – น้ำตาลเทียม náhm·dtarn team |
| …, please. | ขอ... kǒr… |
| – Juice | – น้ำผลไม้ nárm pǒn·lah·mí |
| – Soda | – น้ำอัดลม nárm àht·lom |
| – *Sparkling/Still* water | – น้ำ *โซดา/เปล่า* nárm *soe·dar/bplòw* |
| Is the water safe to drink? | น้ำนี้ดื่มได้ไหม? nárm née dùeem dîe mí |

## Non-alcoholic Drinks

| | |
|---|---|
| apple juice | น้ำแอปเปิ้ล nárm áp·bpêrn |
| boiled water | น้ำต้มสุก nárm dtôm sùhk |
| chrysanthemum tea | น้ำเก๊กฮวย nárm géhk·hoary |
| Chinese tea | ชาจีน char jeen |
| (hot/iced) chocolate | ช็อกโกแล็ต (ร้อน/เย็น) chóhk·goe·lát (rórn/yehn) |
| (hot/iced) coffee | กาแฟ (ร้อน/เย็น) gar·fae (rórn/yehn) |
| fruit juice | น้ำผลไม้ nárm pǒn·lah·míe |

| | |
|---|---|
| ginger tea | น้ำขิง nárm kǐhng |
| herbal tea | ชาสมุนไพร char sah·mǔhn·pri |
| juice | น้ำผลไม้ nárm pǒn·lah·míe |
| longan tea | น้ำลำไย nárm lahm·yi |
| lemonade | น้ำมะนาว nárm mah·now |
| lemongrass tea | น้ำตะไคร้ nárm dtah·krí |
| lime juice | น้ำมะนาว nárm mah·now |
| milk | นม nom |
| milkshake | มิลค์เชค míw·chék |
| mineral water | น้ำแร่ nárm râe |
| mocha | ม็อคค่า móhk·kâr |
| orange juice | น้ำส้ม nárm sôm |
| roselle tea | น้ำกระเจี๊ยบ nárm grah·jéap |
| smoothie (drink) | น้ำ (ผลไม้) ปั่น nárm (pǒn·lah·mí) bpàhn |
| soda | น้ำอัดลม nárm àht·lom |
| (hot/iced) tea | ชา (ร้อน/เย็น) char (rórn/yehn) |
| tomato juice | น้ำมะเขือเทศ nárm mah·kǔea·têt |
| tonic water | น้ำโทนิค nárm toe·nìhk |
| water | น้ำ nárm |
| young coconut juice | น้ำมะพร้าวอ่อน nárm mah·prów·òrn |

*i* Curiously enough, Red Bull energy drinks are originally Thai. The Thai version, กระทิงแดง **grah·tihng·daeng** (Red Bull), however, is very sweet and non-carbonated. It is even more caffeinated than the western Red Bull, so watch out, and is also sold in bottles rather than cans. Another typical drink is Thai iced tea. The use of tamarind seed lends the drink its distinctive orange color. Strong, but sweet, it is usually served with condensed milk. As a general rule, do not drink the tap water in Thailand.

## You May Hear…

| | |
|---|---|
| คุณจะดื่มอะไรไหม? kuhn jah dùeem ah·ri mí | Can I get you a drink? |
| ใส่นมหรือน้ำตาลไหม? sì nom rŭee náhm·dtarn mí | With milk or sugar? |
| น้ำโซดา หรือ น้ำเปล่า? nárm soe·dar rŭee nárm bplòw | Sparkling or still water? |

# Aperitifs, Cocktails and Liqueurs

| brandy | บรั่นดี bah·ràhn·dee |
| cognac | คอนยัค korn·yàhk |
| gin | ยิน yihn |
| liqueur | เหล้าหวาน lôu wǎrn |
| rum | เหล้ารัม lôu rahm |
| scotch | เหล้าสก็อตช์ lôu sah·góht |
| tequila | เตกีล่า dte·gee·lâr |
| vermouth | เวอมัธ wer·máht |
| vodka | ว็อดก้า wóht·gâr |
| whisky | วิสกี้ wíht·sah·gêe |

## Beer

| beer | เบียร์ bea |
| canned/bottled | กระป๋อง/ขวด grah·bpǒhng/kòart |
| dark/light | ดำ/ไลท์ dahm/lí |
| draft [draught] | สด sòt |
| local/imported | ไทย/นำเข้า ti/nahm·kôu |
| non-alcoholic | ไม่มีแอลกอฮอล์ mî mee ael·gor·hor |

## Wine

| champagne | แชมเปญ chaem·bpen |
| dessert wine | ดิเสิร์ทไวน์ dih·sèrt wie |
| dry/sweet | ดราย/สวีท drie/sah·wèet |
| house/table | เฮ้าส์ไวน์/เทเบิลไวน์ hóus·wie/te·bêrn wie |
| red/white | แดง/ขาว daeng/kǒw |

| sparkling wine | สปาร์กลิ่งไวน์ sah•bpárk•lîhng wie |
| wine | ไวน์ wie |

| I'd like… | ผม ♂/ฉัน ♀ ขอ… pŏm ♂/cháhn ♀ kŏr… |
| Another…, please. | ขอ…อีกขวดหนึ่ง kŏr…èek kòart nùeng |
| A local…, please. | ขอ…ไทย kŏr…ti |

## Menu Reader

| American fried rice | ข้าวผัดอเมริกัน kôw•pàht ah•me•rih•gahn |
| aniseed | โป๊ยกั๊ก bpóey•gáhk |
| apple | แอ็ปเปิ้ล áp•bpêrn |
| apple juice | น้ำแอ็ปเปิ้ล nárm áp•bpêrn |
| aromatic ginger | กระชาย grah•chie |
| asparagus (tip) | (ยอด) หน่อไม้ฝรั่ง (yôrt) nòr•míe fah•ràhng |
| baby clam | หอยลาย hŏry•lie |
| baby corn | ข้าวโพดอ่อน kôw•poet•òrn |
| bacon | เบคอน be•kôhn |
| banana | กล้วย glôary |
| bananas stewed in coconut milk | กล้วยบวชชี glôary bòart•chee |
| bay leaf | ใบกระวาน bi grah•warn |
| bean | ถั่ว tòar |
| bean sprout | ถั่วงอก tòar•ngôrk |
| beef | เนื้อวัว núea woar |
| beef satay | สะเต๊ะเนื้อ sah•dtéh núea |
| beer | เบียร์ bea |
| bitter gourd | มะระ mah•ráh |

| black-banded kingfish | ปลาสำลี bplar săhm·lee |
| blueberry | บลูเบอรี่ bloo·ber·rêe |
| boiled sticky rice in coconut milk | ข้าวเหนียวเปียก kôw·nĕaw bpèak |
| brandy | บรั่นดี bah·ràhn·dee |
| bread | ขนมปัง kah·nŏm·bpahng |
| broccoli | บร็อคโคลี่ bróhk·koe lêe |
| butter | เนย nery |
| cabbage | กะหล่ำปลี grah·làhm·bplee |
| capon | ไก่ตอน gì dtorn |
| caramelized bananas | กล้วยเชื่อม glôary·chûeem |
| caraway | ยี่หร่า yêe·ràr |
| carrot | แคร์รอท kae·ròht |

| | |
|---|---|
| cashew nut | เม็ดมะม่วงหิมพานต์ méht mah·môarng·hǐhm·mah·parn |
| catfish | ปลาดุก bplar·dùhk |
| cauliflower | กะหล่ำดอก grah·làhm dòrk |
| celery | คื่นช่ายฝรั่ง kûen·chîe fah·ràhng |
| (cold/hot) cereal | ซีเรียล (เย็น/ร้อน) see·rêan (yehn/rórn) |
| champagne | แชมเปญ chaem·bpen |
| cherry | เชอรี่ cher·rêe |
| chicken | ไก่ gì |
| chicken and coconut milk soup flavored with galanga | ต้มข่าไก่ dtôm·kàr gì |
| chicken cooked in pandanus leaves | ไก่ห่อใบเตย gì hòr bi·dtery |
| chicken satay | สะเต๊ะไก่ sah·dtéh gì |
| chicken soup | ซุปไก่ súhp gì |
| chicken stew with soy sauce | ไก่ต้มเค็ม gì dtôm·kehm |
| chilli | พริก príhk |
| Chinese glass noodle | วุ้นเส้น wúhn·sêhn |
| Chinese tea | ชาจีน char·jeen |
| (hot/iced) chocolate | ช็อกโกแล็ต (ร้อน/เย็น) chóhk·goe·lát (rórn/yehn) |
| chrysanthemum tea | น้ำเก๊กฮวย nárm géhk·hoary |
| cilantro [coriander] | ผักชี pàhk·chee |
| clam | หอยกาบ hǒry·gàrp |
| clear soup | แกงจืด gaeng·jùeet |
| clear soup with fish balls | แกงจืดลูกชิ้นปลา gaeng·jùeet lôok·chíhn bplar |

| | |
|---|---|
| clear soup with mixed vegetables, pumpkin and shrimp [prawn] | แกงเลียง gaeng·leang |
| clear soup with noodles, pork and vegetables | แกงจืดวุ้นเส้น gaeng·jùeet wúhn·sêhn |
| clear soup with pickled vegetables | แกงจืดเกี้ยมฉ่าย gaeng·jùeet géam·chìe |
| clear soup with pork ribs and vegetables | ต้มจับฉ่าย dtôm jàhp·chìe |
| clear soup with seaweed | แกงจืดสาหร่ายทะเล gaeng·jùeet sǎr·rìe tah·le |
| clear soup with tofu and ground pork | แกงจืดเต้าหู้หมูสับ gaeng·jùeet dtôu·hôo mǒo·sàhp |
| clear soup with tofu and napa cabbage | แกงจืดเต้าหู้กับผักกาดขาว gaeng·jùeet dtôu·hôo gàhp pàhk·gart·kǒw |
| coconut | มะพร้าว mah·prów |
| coconut milk | กะทิ gah·tíh |
| (hot/iced) coffee | กาแฟ (ร้อน/เย็น) gar·fae (rórn/yehn) |
| cognac | คอนยัค kohn·yàhk |
| corn | ข้าวโพด kôw·pôet |
| crab | ปู bpoo |
| crab fried with curry powder | ปูผัดผงกะหรี่ bpoo pàht pǒng·gah·rèe |
| crab roasted in a clay pot | ปูอบหม้อดิน bpoo òp môr·dihn |
| crispy roast pork | หมูกรอบ mǒo·gròrp |
| crispy, deep-fried gourami fish | ปลาสลิดทอดกรอบ bplar sah·lìht tôrt gròrp |
| cucumber | แตงกวา dtaeng·gwar |

| | |
|---|---|
| custard apple | น้อยหน่า nóry•nàr |
| date | อินทผาลัม ihn•tah•pǎr•lahm |
| deep-fried, battered vegetables | ผักชุบแป้งทอด pàhk chúhp bpâeng tôrt |
| deep-fried bean curd | เต้าหู้ทอด dtôu•hôo tôrt |
| deep-fried beef | เนื้อทอด núea tôrt |
| deep-fried chicken | ไก่ทอด gì tôrt |
| deep-fried, crispy wanton | เกี๊ยวทอด géaw tôrt |
| deep-fried pastry cups with ground [minced] pork | กระทงทอง grah•tong torng |
| deep-fried, spicy fishcakes | ทอดมันปลา tôrt•mahn bplar |
| deep-fried spring roll | เปาะเปี๊ยะ bpor•bpéa tôrt |
| draft [draught] beer | เบียร์สด bea sòt |
| dragon fruit | แก้วมังกร gâew•mahng•gorn |
| dried fruit | ผลไม้แห้ง pǒn•lah•míe hâeng |
| duck | เป็ด bpèht |
| durian | ทุเรียน túh•rean |
| egg custard | สังขยา sǎhng•kah•yǎr |
| egg noodle | บะหมี่ bah•mèe |
| egg noodle in spicy curry with *chicken/ beef* | ข้าวซอย *ไก่/เนื้อ* kôw•sory *gì/núea* |
| egg noodle soup | บะหมี่น้ำ bah•mèe nárm |
| egg yolk mixed with flour and dropped in syrup | ทองหยิบ torng•yìhp |
| eggplant [aubergine] | มะเขือยาว mah•kǔea yow |

| | |
|---|---|
| featherback (fish) | ปลากราย bplar grie |
| fermented rice noodle | เส้นขนมจีน sêhn kah·nŏm·jeen |
| fermented rice noodle with *red curry/sweet sauce* | ขนมจีน น้ำยา/น้ำพริก kah·nŏm·jeen *náhm·yar/ náhm·príhk* |
| fish stew with soy sauce | ปลาต้มเค็ม bplar dtôm·kehm |
| fresh salad with peanut sauce | สลัดแขก sah·làht kàek |
| fresh spring roll | เปาะเปี๊ยะสด bpor·bpéa sòt |
| fried bread with ground [minced] *pork/shrimp [prawn]* | ขนมปังหน้า *หมู/กุ้ง* kah·nŏm·bpahng nâr *mŏo/ gûhng* |
| fried egg | ไข่ดาว kì dow |
| fried egg noodle with chicken | โกยซีหมี่ goey·see·mèe |
| fried fish with sweet, sour and spicy sauce | ปลาสามรส bplar sărm·rót |
| fried noodles with sauce and vegetables | ก๋วยเตี๋ยวราดหน้า gŏary·tĕaw rârt nâr |
| fried rice mixed with fermented shrimp paste | ข้าวคลุกกะปิ kôw klúhk gah·bpìh |
| fried rice with *pork/ shrimp [prawn]* | ข้าวผัด *หมู/กุ้ง* kôw pàht *mŏo/gûhng* |
| fruit | ผลไม้ pŏn·lah·mí |
| galanga (spice) | ข่า kàr |
| garlic | กระเทียม grah·team |
| gin | ยิน yihn |
| ginger | ขิง kĭhng |

| | |
|---|---|
| ginger tea | น้ำขิง nárm·kǐhng |
| gourami (freshwater fish) | ปลาสลิด bplar sah·lìht |
| grape | องุ่น ah·ngùhn |
| green bean | ถั่วแขก tòar kàek |
| green curry | แกงเขียวหวาน gaeng kěaw·wǎrn |
| green onion | ต้นหอม dtôn·hǒrm |
| grilled black-banded kingfish, wrapped in banana leaves | ปลาสำลีเผา bplar sǎhm·lee pǒu |
| grilled catfish | ปลาดุกย่าง bplar·dùhk yârng |
| grilled chicken | ไก่ย่าง gì yârng |
| grilled duck | เป็ดย่าง bpèht yârng |
| grilled pork | หมูย่าง mǒo yârng |
| grilled squid | ปลาหมึกย่าง bplar·mùek yârng |
| grouper | ปลาเก๋า bplar gǒu |
| guava | ฝรั่ง fah·ràhng |
| (smoked) ham | หมูแฮม (รมควัน) mǒo·haem (rom·kwahn) |
| hard-boiled egg | ไข่ต้ม kì dtôm |
| herbal tea | ชาสมุนไพร char sah·mǔhn·pri |
| holy basil | กะเพรา ga·prou |
| hot and sour curry with dried fish and spices | ต้มโคล้งปลาย่าง dtôm·klóeng bplar·yârng |
| hot and sour curry with fish and water mimosa | แกงส้มผักกระเฉด gaeng·sôm pàhk·grah·chèt |
| hot and sour curry with snakehead (fish) and mixed vegetables | แกงส้มปลาช่อน gaeng·sôm bplar·chôrn |

| | |
|---|---|
| hot and sour soup | ต้มยำ dtôm·yahm |
| hot red vegetable curry | แกงเผ็ดเจ gaeng·pèht je |
| house wine | เฮาส์ไวน์ hóus wie |
| imported beer | เบียร์นำเข้า bea nahm kôu |
| Indian-style curry with *beef/chicken* | แกงมัสมั่น *เนื้อ/ไก่* gaeng máht·sah·màhn *núea/gì* |
| jackfruit | ขนุน kah·nǔhn |
| jam | แยม yaem |
| jellied water chestnuts in coconut milk | ทับทิมกรอบ táhp·tihm·gròrp |
| jelly | เยลลี่ yen·lêe |
| juice | น้ำผลไม้ nárm pǒn·lah·míe |
| langsat (fruit) | ลางสาด larng·sàrt |
| large thread rice noodle | ก๋วยเตี๋ยวเส้นใหญ่ gǒary·těaw sêhn·yì |
| layered sweet coconut cream pancakes | ขนมชั้น kah·nǒm cháhn |
| lemon | มะนาว mah·now |
| lemonade | น้ำมะนาว nárm mah·now |
| lemongrass | ตะไคร้ dtah·krí |
| lemongrass tea | น้ำตะไคร้ nárm dtah·krí |
| lentils | ถั่วแขก tòar·kàek |
| lettuce | ผักกาดหอม pàhk·gàrt hörm |
| light beer | ไลท์เบียร์ lí·bea |
| lime | มะนาว mah·now |
| lime juice | น้ำมะนาว nárm mah·now |

| | |
|---|---|
| liqueur | เหล้า lôu |
| liver | ตับ dtàhp |
| lobster | กุ้งมังกร gûhng·mahng·gorn |
| long bean | ถั่วฝักยาว tòar·fàhk·yow |
| longan (fruit) | ลำไย lahm·yi |
| longan tea | น้ำลำไย nárm lahm·yi |
| lychee (fruit) | ลิ้นจี่ líhn·jèe |
| mackerel | ปลาทู bplar too |
| mango | มะม่วง mah·môarng |
| mangosteen | มังคุด mahng·kúht |
| mashed mung beans with coconut milk and egg yolk | เม็ดขนุน méht·kah·nǔhn |
| meatballs | ลูกชิ้นเนื้อ lôok·chíhn núea |
| medium thread rice noodle | ก๋วยเตี๋ยวเส้นเล็ก gǒary·těaw sêhn·léhk |
| melon | แตงไทย dtaeng·ti |
| mild red curry | พะแนง pah·naeng |
| milk | นม nom |
| milkshake | มิลค์เชค míw·chék |
| mineral water | น้ำแร่ nárm râe |
| mint | สะระแหน่ sah·rah·nàe |
| mung bean coconut custard | ขนมหม้อแกง kah·nǒm môr·gaeng |
| mung bean rice crepe | ถั่วแปบ tòar·bpàep |
| mushroom | เห็ด hèht |
| mushroom soup | ซุปเห็ด súhp hèht |

| | |
|---|---|
| mushroom soup cooked in coconut milk and galanga | ต้มข่าเห็ด dtôm·kàr hèht |
| mussels | หอยแมลงภู่ hŏry mah·laeng·pôo |
| napa cabbage | ผักกาดขาว pàhk·gàrt kŏw |
| non-alcoholic beer | เบียร์ไม่มีแอลกอฮอล์ bea mî mee aen·gor·hor |
| noodle soup | ก๋วยเตี๋ยวน้ำ gŏary·tĕaw nárm |
| nutmeg | ลูกจันทน์ lôok·jahn |
| oatmeal | ข้าวโอ๊ต kôw·óet |
| octopus | ปลาหมึกยักษ์ bplar·mùek yáhk |
| okra [ladies' fingers] | กระเจี๊ยบ grah·jéap |
| olive | มะกอก mah·gòrk |
| omelet | ไข่เจียว kì jeaw |
| onion | หอมหัวใหญ่ hŏrm hŏar yì |
| orange | ส้ม sôm |
| orange juice | น้ำส้ม nárm sôm |
| oxtail | หางวัว hărng woar |
| oyster | หอยนางรม hŏry narng·rom |
| pandanus-scented rice noodles in coconut milk | ลอดช่องน้ำกะทิ lôrt·chôhng nárm·gah·tí |
| papaya | มะละกอ mah·lah·gor |
| parsley | ผักชีฝรั่ง pàhk·chee fah·ràhng |
| pasta | เส้นพาสต้า sêhn párs·dtâr |
| peach | ลูกท้อ lôok tór |
| peanut | ถั่วลิสง tòar líh·sŏng |
| pear | สาลี่ săr·lêe |
| pepper (seasoning) | พริกไทย príhk·ti |

| | |
|---|---|
| (green/red) pepper | พริกหยวก (เขียว/แดง) príhk·yòark (kĕaw/daeng) |
| pineapple | สับปะรด sàhp·bpah·rót |
| plums | ลูกไหน lôok năi |
| pomelo (fruit) | ส้มโอ sôm·oe |
| pomfret (fish) | ปลาจาระเม็ด bplar jar·rah·méht |
| pork | เนื้อหมู núea·mŏo |
| pork fried with garlic | หมูทอดกระเทียม mŏo tôrt grah·team |
| pork fried with ginger | หมูผัดขิง mŏo pàht·kĭhng |
| pork satay | สะเต๊ะหมู sah·dtéh mŏo |
| pork stew in Chinese five spice sauce | หมูพะโล้ mŏo pah·lóe |
| pork stew with soy sauce | หมูต้มเค็ม mŏo dtôm·kehm |
| potato | มันฝรั่ง mahn·fah·ràhng |
| prunes | ลูกพรุน lôok pruhn |
| pumpkin | ฟักทอง fáhk·torng |
| pumpkin stewed in coconut milk | ฟักทองบวด fáhk·torng bòart |
| raisins | ลูกเกด lôok·gèt |
| rambutan (fruit) | เงาะ ngóh |
| red roast pork | หมูแดง mŏo·daeng |
| red snapper | ปลากะพงแดง bplar grah·pong daeng |
| red wine | ไวน์แดง wie daeng |
| rice | ข้าว kôw |
| rice porridge with *chicken/pork* | โจ๊ก *ไก่/หมู* jóek *gì/mŏo* |
| rice soup | ข้าวต้ม kôw·dtôm |
| rice vermicelli | เส้นหมี่ sêhn·mèe |

| | |
|---|---|
| rice with curry | ข้าวราดแกง kôw rârt gaeng |
| rice with roast duck | ข้าวหน้าเป็ด kôw nâr bpèht |
| rice with roast pork | ข้าวหมูแดง kôw mŏo•daeng |
| rice with steamed chicken | ข้าวมันไก่ kôw mahn gì |
| rice with stewed leg of pork | ข้าวขาหมู kôw kăr•mŏo |
| rice with stir-fried beef and chili | ข้าวราดผัดพริกเนื้อ kôw rârt pàht•príhk núea |
| rice with stir-fried chicken and chili | ข้าวราดผัดพริกไก่ kôw rârt pàht•príhk gì |
| rice with stir-fried pork and chili | ข้าวราดผัดพริกหมู kôw rârt pàht•príhk mŏo |
| roast beef | เนื้ออบ núea òp |
| roasted shrimp [prawn] | กุ้งเผา gûhng pŏu |
| roasted shrimp [prawn] in a clay pot | กุ้งอบหม้อดิน gûhng òp môr•dihn |
| rock lobster | กั้ง gâhng |
| rose apple | ชมพู่ chom•pôo |
| roselle tea | น้ำกระเจี๊ยบ nárm grah•jéap |
| rum | เหล้ารัม lôu rahm |
| salmon | ปลาแซลมอน bplar san•môrn |
| sapodilla (fruit) | ละมุด lah•múht |
| satay | สะเต๊ะ sah•dtéh |
| sausage | ไส้กรอก sî•gròrk |
| scotch | เหล้าสก็อตช์ lôu sah•góht |
| scrambled egg | ไข่คน kì kon |
| sea bass | ปลากะพงขาว bplar grah•pong kŏw |

| | |
|---|---|
| seafood | อาหารทะเล ar·hărn tah·le |
| sesame | งา ngar |
| shallot | หอมแดง hŏrm·daeng |
| short, clear noodle | เส้นเซี่ยงไฮ้ sêhn sêang·hí |
| short, rolled rice noodle | เส้นก๋วยจั๊บ sêhn gŏary·jáhp |
| shrimp [prawn] | กุ้ง gûhng |
| shrimp [prawn] rice cracker | ข้าวเกรียบกุ้ง kôw·grèap gûhng |
| sirloin | เนื้อสันนอก núea săhn nôrk |
| snakehead (fish) | ปลาช่อน bplar·chôrn |
| snakehead (fish) with spicy herbs | ปลาช่อนแป๊ะซะ bplar·chôrn bpá·sáh |
| snow pea | ถั่วลันเตา tòar lahn·dtou |
| soda | น้ำอัดลม nárm àht·lom |
| soft-boiled egg | ไข่ลวก kì·lôark |
| sparkling wine | สปาร์กลิ่งไวน์ sah·bpárk·lîhng wie |
| spicy catfish salad | ยำปลาดุกฟู yahm bplar·dùk foo |
| spicy deep-fried gourami salad | ยำปลาสลิด yahm bplar·sah·lìht |
| spicy grilled beef salad | ยำเนื้อย่าง yahm núea yârng |
| spicy ground [minced] *chicken/duck* salad | ลาบไก่/เป็ด lârp *gì/bpèht* |
| spicy northeastern sausage | ไส้กรอกอีสาน sî·gròrk ee·sărn |
| spicy papaya salad | ส้มตำ sôm·dtahm |
| spicy pork sausage salad | ยำหมูยอ yahm mŏo·yor |

| | |
|---|---|
| spicy red curry with *beef/chicken* | แกงเผ็ด *เนื้อ/ไก่* gaeng·pèht *núea/gì* |
| spicy red curry with grilled duck | แกงเผ็ดเป็ดย่าง gaeng·pèht bpèht·yârng |
| spicy salad of ground [minced] mushrooms | ลาบเห็ด lârp hèht |
| spicy seafood salad | ยำทะเล yahm tah·le |
| spicy stir-fried catfish | ผัดเผ็ดปลาดุก pàht·pèht bplar·dùhk |
| spinach | ผักโขม pàhk·kŏem |
| squid | ปลาหมึก bplar·mùek |
| steak | สเต็ก sah·dték |
| steamed fish curry | ห่อหมกปลา hòr·mòk bplar |
| steamed pomfret (fish) with sour plums | ปลาจาระเม็ดนึ่งบ๊วย bplar jar·rah·méht nûeng bóary |
| steamed seafood curry | ห่อหมกทะเล hòr·mòk tah·le |
| steamed sticky rice with banana or taro in banana leaves | ข้าวต้มมัด kôw·dtôm·máht |
| stewed beef | เนื้อตุ๋น núea dtŭhn |
| stewed duck | เป็ดตุ๋น bpèht dtŭhn |
| sticky rice, coconut and egg custard | ข้าวเหนียวสังขยา kôw·nĕaw sahng·kah·yăr |
| sticky rice, coconut and mango | ข้าวเหนียวมะม่วง kôw·nĕaw mah·môarng |
| stir-fried baby clams with curry powder | หอยลายผัดผงกะหรี่ hŏry·lie pàht pŏng gah·rèe |
| stir-fried baby clams with chili paste | หอยลายผัดน้ำพริกเผา hŏry·lie pàht náhm·príhk·pŏu |
| stir-fried beef with basil leaves | เนื้อผัดกะเพรา núea pàht gah·prou |

| | |
|---|---|
| stir-fried beef with chili | เนื้อผัดพริก núea pàht príhk |
| stir-fried beef with oyster sauce | เนื้อผัดน้ำมันหอย núea pàht náhm·mahn·hŏry |
| stir-fried chicken with basil leaves | ไก่ผัดกะเพรา gì pàht gah·prou |
| stir-fried chicken with cashew nuts | ไก่ผัดเม็ดมะม่วงหิมพานต์ gì pàht méht·mah·môarng·hĭhm·mah·parn |
| stir-fried chicken with chili | ไก่ผัดพริก gì pàht príhk |
| stir-fried *chicken/pork* with ginger | ไก่/หมู ผัดขิง *gì/mŏo* pàht·kĭhng |
| stir-fried crispy pork with Chinese kale | ผัดคะน้าหมูกรอบ pàht kah·nár mŏo·gròrp |
| stir-fried eggplant | ผัดมะเขือยาว pàht mah·kŭea·yow |
| stir-fried mixed vegetables | ผัดผักรวมมิตรเจ pàht pàk roarm·míht je |
| stir-fried mushrooms, basil and baby corn | ผัดกะเพราเห็ดกับข้าวโพดอ่อน pàht gah·prou hèht gàhp kôw·pôet·òrn |
| stir-fried pork with basil | หมูผัดกะเพรา mŏo pàht gah·prou |
| stir-fried pork with chili | หมูผัดพริก mŏo pàht príhk |
| stir-fried rice noodles in soy sauce with Chinese kale | ผัดซีอิ๊วเจ pàht see·íhw je |
| stir-fried rice noodles in soy sauce with Chinese kale and *chicken/pork* | ผัดซีอิ๊ว *ไก่/หมู* pàht see·íhw *gì/mŏo* |

| | |
|---|---|
| stir-fried rice noodles with shrimp, tofu and peanuts (pad thai) | ผัดไทย pàht·ti |
| stir-fried snow peas with baby corn | ผัดถั่วลันเตากับข้าวโพดอ่อน pàht tòar·lahn·dtou gàhp kôw·pôet·òrn |
| stir-fried water spinach leaves | ผัดผักบุ้ง pàht pàhk·bûhng |
| strawberry | สตรอเบอร์รี่ sah·dtror·ber·rêe |
| stuffed chicken wings | ปีกไก่ยัดไส้ bpèek gì yáht sî |
| suckling pig | หมูหัน mǒo·hǎhn |
| sweet and sour fish | ปลาเปรี้ยวหวาน bplar bprêaw·wǎrn |
| sweet and sour fried vegetables | ผัดเปรี้ยวหวานเจ pàht bprêaw·wǎrn je |
| sweet basil | โหระพา hǒe·rah·par |
| sweet bean thread in coconut milk | ซ่าหริ่ม sâr·rìhm |
| sweet coconut milk jelly | วุ้นกะทิ wúhn gah·tí |
| sweet corn | ข้าวโพดหวาน kôw·pôet·wǎrn |
| sweet potato | มันเทศ mahn·têt |
| tamarind | มะขาม mah·kǎrm |
| tangerine | ส้มจีน sôm·jeen |
| tapioca and beans in coconut milk | สาคูถั่วดำ sǎr·koo tòar·dahm |
| taro balls and sweet eggs in coconut milk | บัวลอยไข่หวาน boar·lory kì wǎrn |
| taro stewed in coconut milk | เผือกบวด pèuak bòart |
| (hot/iced) tea | ชา (ร้อน/เย็น) char (rórn/yehn) |

| | |
|---|---|
| tequila | เตกีล่า dte·gee·lâr |
| thread of egg yolk dropped in syrup | ฝอยทอง fŏry·torng |
| toast | ขนมปังปิ้ง kah·nŏm·bpahng bpîhng |
| tofu | เต้าหู้ dtôu·hôo |
| tomato | มะเขือเทศ mah·kŭea·têt |
| tomato juice | น้ำมะเขือเทศ nárm mah·kŭea·têt |
| tonic water | น้ำโทนิค nárm toe·nìhk |
| tuna | ปลาทูน่า bplar too·nâr |
| turkey | ไก่งวง gì ngoarng |
| vegetable | ผัก pàhk |
| vegetarian spring rolls | เปาะเปี๊ยะเจ bpor·bpéa je |
| vegetarian stir-fried rice noodle with peanut, bean curd and radish | ผัดไทยเจ pàht·ti je |
| vermouth | เวอมัธ wer·máht |
| vodka | ว็อดก้า wóht·gâr |
| water | น้ำ nárm |
| water mimosa | ผักกระเฉด pàhk grah·chèt |
| water spinach | ผักบุ้ง pàhk·bûng |
| watermelon | แตงโม dtaeng·moe |
| whisky | วิสกี้ wíht·sah·gêe |
| white wine | ไวน์ขาว wie kŏw |
| wine | ไวน์ wie |
| yogurt | โยเกิร์ต yoe·gèrt |
| young coconut juice | น้ำมะพร้าวอ่อน nárm mah·prów·òrn |

# ▼ People

| | |
|---|---|
| Hello! | สวัสดี! sah·wàht·dee |
| How are you? | เป็นยังไง bpehn yahng·ngi |
| Fine, thanks. | สบายดี ขอบคุณ sah·bie dee kòrp·kuhn |
| Excuse me! | ขอโทษ! kŏr·tôet |
| Do you speak English? | คุณพูดภาษาอังกฤษได้ไหม? kuhn pôot par·săr ahng·grìht dîe mí |
| What's your name? | คุณชื่ออะไร? kuhn chûee ah·ri |
| My name is… | ผม♂/ฉัน♀ ชื่อ… pŏm♂/cháhn♀ chûee… |
| Nice to meet you. | ยินดีที่ได้รู้จัก yihn dee têe dîe róo·jàhk |
| Where are you from? | คุณมาจากไหน? kuhn mar jàrk nĭ |
| I'm from the *U.S./U.K.* | ผม♂/ฉัน♀ มาจาก *อเมริกา/อังกฤษ* pŏm♂/cháhn♀ mar jàrk *ah·me·rih·gar/ahng·grìht* |
| What do you do? | คุณทำงานอะไร? kuhn tahm·ngarn ah·ri |
| I work for… | ผม♂/ฉัน♀ ทำงานที่… pŏm♂/cháhn♀ tahm·ngarn têe… |
| I'm a student. | ผม♂/ฉัน♀ เป็นนักศึกษา pŏm♂/cháhn♀ bpehn náhk·sùek·săr |
| I'm retired. | ผม♂/ฉัน♀ เกษียณแล้ว pŏm♂/cháhn♀ gah·sĕan láew |
| Do you like…? | คุณชอบ…ไหม? kuhn chôrp…mí |
| Goodbye. | สวัสดี sah·wàht·dee |
| See you later. | แล้วเจอกัน láew jer gahn |

In Thai, an all-purpose form for greeting at any time of the day and for saying goodbye is สวัสดี **sah·wàht·dee.**

## Communication Difficulties

| | |
|---|---|
| Do you speak English? | คุณพูดภาษาอังกฤษได้ไหม? kuhn pôot par·săr ahng·grìht dîe mí |
| Does anyone here speak English? | ที่นี่มีใครพูดภาษาอังกฤษได้บ้าง? têe·nêe mee krai pôot par·săr ahng·grìht dîe bârng |
| I *don't speak/speak a little* Thai. | ผม♂/ฉัน♀ พูดภาษาไทย *ไม่ได้/ได้นิดหน่อย* pŏm♂/cháhn♀ pôot par·săr ti *mî dîe/dîe nít·nòhy* |
| Can you speak more slowly? | พูดช้าลงหน่อยได้ไหม? pôot chár long nòhy dî mí |
| Can you repeat that? | พูดอีกทีได้ไหม? pôot èek tee dî mí |
| Excuse me? | อะไรนะ? ah·ri náh |
| What was that? | นั่นอะไร? nâhn ah·ri |
| Can you spell it? | คุณช่วยสะกดให้ดูหน่อยได้ไหม? kuhn chôary sah·gòt hî doo nòhy dî mí |
| Please write it down. | ช่วยเขียนให้ดูหน่อย chôary kěan hî doo nòhy |
| Can you translate this into English for me? | คุณช่วยแปลอันนี้ให้ ผม♂/ฉัน♀ หน่อยได้ไหม? kuhn chôary bplae ahn née hî pŏm♂/cháhn♀ nòhy dî mí |
| What does *this/that* mean? | นี่/นั่น หมายความว่าอะไร? *nêe/nân* mǐe·kwarm wâr ah·ri |
| I understand. | ผม♂/ฉัน♀ เข้าใจ pŏm♂/cháhn♀ kôu·ji |
| I don't understand. | ผม♂/ฉัน♀ ไม่เข้าใจ pŏm♂/cháhn♀ mî kôu·ji |
| Do you understand? | คุณเข้าใจไหม? kuhn kôu·ji mí |

| | |
|---|---|
| ผม♂/ฉัน♀ พูดภาษาอังกฤษได้ นิดหน่อย pŏm♂/ cháhn♀ pôot par·săr ahng·grìht dîe níht·nòhy | I only speak a little English. |
| ผม♂/ฉัน♀ พูดภาษาอังกฤษไม่ได้ pŏm♂/cháhn♀ pôot par·săr ahng·grìht mî dîe | I don't speak English. |

Thai has various registers appropriate for certain social contexts. For example, different ways of speaking are appropriate for official use, on the street, in religious settings, when addressing the monarchy, etc. Thais who address you are more likely to use your first name rather than your last name. If you hear the word คุณ **kuhn** (Mr., Mrs., Miss) before your name, know that it is a polite form of address.

## Making Friends

| | |
|---|---|
| Hello! | สวัสดี! sah·wàht·dee |
| My name is… | ผม♂/ฉัน♀ ชื่อ… pŏm♂/cháhn♀ chûee… |
| What's your name? | คุณชื่ออะไร? kuhn chûee ah·ri |
| I'd like to introduce you to… | ผม♂/ฉัน♀ อยากแนะนำให้คุณรู้จักกับ… pŏm♂/ cháhn♀ yàrk ná·nahm hî kuhn róo·jàhk gàhp… |
| Nice to meet you. | ยินดีที่ได้รู้จัก yihn dee têe dîe róo·jàhk |
| How are you? | เป็นยังไง bpehn yahng·ngi |
| Fine, thanks. And you? | สบายดี ขอบคุณ แล้วคุณล่ะ? sah·bie dee kòrp·kuhn láew kuhn làh |

In Thailand it is polite to greet people with ไหว้ **wîe** (wai, Thai gesture of greeting). To perform a wai, put your palms together, in a prayer-like gesture, and bow slightly. The higher the hands are held and the deeper the bow, the more reverent the greeting.

## Travel Talk

| | |
|---|---|
| I'm here… | ผม♂/ฉัน♀ มาที่นี่เพื่อ... pŏm♂/cháhn♀ mar têe·nêe pûea… |
| – on business | – ทำธุรกิจ tahm túh·ráh·gìht |
| – on vacation [holiday] | – พักผ่อน páhk·pòhn |
| – studying | – เรียนหนังสือ rean năhng·sŭee |
| I'm staying for… | ผม♂/ฉัน♀ จะอยู่ที่นี่... pŏm♂/cháhn♀ jah yòo têe·nêe… |
| I've been here… | ผม♂/ฉัน♀ มาที่นี่ได้...แล้ว pŏm♂/cháhn♀ mar têe·nêe dîe…láew |
| – a day | – หนึ่งวัน nùeng wahn |
| – a week | – หนึ่งสัปดาห์ nùeng sàhp·dar |
| – a month | – หนึ่งเดือน nùeng duean |

▶ For numbers, see page 165.

| Where are you from? | คุณมาจากไหน? kuhn mar jàrk nǐ |
| I'm from... | ผม♂/ฉัน♀ มาจาก... pǒm♂/cháhn♀ mar jàrk... |

## Relationships

| Who are you with? | คุณมากับใคร? kuhn mar gàhp kri |
| I'm here alone. | ผม♂/ฉัน♀ มาคนเดียว pǒm♂/cháhn♀ mar kon deaw |
| I'm with my... | ผม♂/ฉัน♀ มากับ...ของผม♂/ฉัน♀ pǒm♂/cháhn♀ mar gàhp...kǒhng pǒm♂/cháhn♀ |
| – husband/wife | – สามี/ภรรยา sǎr·mee/pahn·rah·yar |
| – boyfriend/girlfriend | – แฟน faen |
| – father/mother | – พ่อ/แม่ pôr/mâe |
| – friend/colleague | – เพื่อน/เพื่อนร่วมงาน pûean/pûean·rôarm·ngarn |
| – *older/younger* brother | – พี่ชาย/น้องชาย pêe chie/nórng chie |
| – *older/younger* sister | – พี่สาว/น้องสาว pêe sǒw/nórng sǒw |
| When's your birthday? | วันเกิดของคุณเมื่อไหร่? wahn gèrt kǒhng kuhn mûea·rì |
| How old are you? | คุณอายุเท่าไหร่? kuhn ar·yúh tôu·rì |
| I'm... | ผม♂/ฉัน♀ อายุ... pǒm♂/cháhn♀ ar·yúh... |

▶ For numbers, see page 165.

| Are you married? | คุณแต่งงานแล้วหรือยัง? kuhn dtàng·ngarn láew rúe yahng |
| I'm... | ผม♂/ฉัน♀ ... pǒm♂/cháhn♀ ... |
| – single/in a relationship | – ยังโสด/มีแฟนแล้ว yahng sòet/mee faen láew |
| – engaged/married | – มีคู่หมั้นแล้ว/แต่งงานแล้ว mee kôo·mâhn láew/dtàng·ngarn láew |
| – divorced/separated | – หย่าแล้ว/แยกกันอยู่ yàr láew/yâek gahn yòo |

– widowed — เป็นหม้าย bpehn mîe

Do you have *children/* คุณมี ลูก/หลาน ไหม? kuhn mee lôok/lărn mí
*grandchildren*?

## Work and School

| | |
|---|---|
| What do you do? | คุณทำงานอะไร? kuhn tahm·ngarn ah·ri |
| What are you studying? | คุณกำลังเรียนอะไรอยู่? kuhn gahm·lahng rean ah·ri yòo |
| I'm studying Thai. | ผม♂/ฉัน♀ กำลังเรียนภาษาไทย pŏm♂/cháhn♀ gahm·lahng rean par·săr ti |
| Who do you work for? | คุณทำงานที่ไหน? kuhn tahm·ngarn têe·nĭ |
| I work for… | ผม♂/ฉัน♀ ทำงานที่... pŏm♂/cháhn♀ tahm·ngarn têe… |
| Here's my business card. | นี่นามบัตรของผม♂/ฉัน♀ nêe narm·bàht kŏhng pŏm♂/cháhn♀ |

▶ For business travel, see page 140.

## Weather

| | |
|---|---|
| What's the forecast? | พยากรณ์อากาศ เป็นยังไง? pah·yar·gorn ar·gàrt bpehn yahng·ngi |
| What *beautiful/ terrible* weather! | อากาศ ดี/แย่ จัง! ar·gàrt dee/yâe jahng |
| Will it be…tomorrow? | พรุ่งนี้... ไหม? prûhng·née…mí |
| – cool/warm | – เย็น/อุ่น yehn/ùhn |
| – cold/hot | – หนาว/ร้อน nŏw/rórn |
| – rainy/sunny | – ฝนตก/แดดออก fŏn dtòk/dàet òrk |
| Do I need *a jacket/ an umbrella*? | ผม♂/ฉัน♀ ต้องใช้ เสื้อแจ็กเก็ต/ร่ม ไหม? pŏm♂/cháhn♀ dtôhng chí sûea·ják·géht/rôm mí |

▶ For temperature, see page 171.

# *Romance*

## Essential

| | |
|---|---|
| Would you like to go out for *a drink/ dinner*? | คุณอยากไป ดื่ม/ทานอาหารเย็น ข้างนอกไหม? kuhn yàrk bpi *dùeem/tarn ar·hărn yehn* kâhng·nôrk mí |
| What are your plans for *tonight/tomorrow*? | คืนนี้/พรุ่งนี้ คุณมีแผนอะไรไหม? *kueen née/ prûhng·née* kuhn mee păen ah·ri mí |
| Can I have your number? | ผม♂/ฉัน♀ ขอเบอร์โทรศัพท์ของคุณหน่อยได้ไหม? pŏm♂/cháhn♀ kŏr ber toe·rah·sàhp kŏhng kuhn nòhy dî mí |
| Can I join you? | ผม♂/ฉัน♀ ขอนั่งด้วยได้ไหม? pŏm♂/cháhn♀ kŏr nâhng dôary dî mí |
| Can I get you a drink? | คุณจะดื่มอะไรไหม? kuhn jah dùeem ah·ri mí |
| I *like/love* you. | ผม♂/ฉัน♀ ชอบ/รัก คุณ pŏm♂/cháhn♀ *chôrp/ráhk* kuhn |

## Making Plans ━━━━━━━━━━━━━━━━━━━━━

| | |
|---|---|
| Would you like to go out for…? | คุณอยากออกไปหา...ทานไหม? kuhn yàrk òrk bpi hăr…tarn mí |
| – coffee | – กาแฟ gar·fae |
| – a drink | – เครื่องดื่ม krûeang·dùeem |
| – dinner | – อาหารเย็น ar·hărn yehn |
| What are your plans for…? | คุณมีแผนอะไรสำหรับ...ไหม? kuhn mee păen ah·ri săhm·ràhp…mí |
| – today | – วันนี้ wahn·née |
| – tonight | – คืนนี้ kueen née |
| – tomorrow | – พรุ่งนี้ prûhng·née |
| – this weekend | – สุดสัปดาห์นี้ sùht sàhp·dar née |

| Where would you like to go? | คุณอยากจะไปไหน? kuhn yàrk·jah bpi nǐ |
| Can I have your *number/e-mail*? | ผม♂/ฉัน♀ ขอ *เบอร์โทรศัพท์/อีเมล์* ของคุณหน่อยได้ไหม? pǒm♂/cháhn♀ kǒr *ber toe·rah·sàhp/ee·mew* kǒhng kuhn nòhy dî mí |

▶ For e-mail and phone, see page 48.

## Pick-up [Chat-up] Lines

| Can I join you? | ผม♂/ฉัน♀ ขอนั่งด้วยได้ไหม? pǒm♂/cháhn♀ kǒr nâhng dôary dî mí |
| You're very attractive. | คุณมีเสน่ห์มาก kuhn mee sah·nè mârk |
| Let's go somewhere quieter. | ไปหาที่ที่เงียบกว่านี้ดีกว่า bpi hǎr têe têe ngêap gwàr née dee gwàr |

## Accepting and Rejecting

| I'd love to. | ผม♂/ฉัน♀ สนใจมาก pǒm♂/cháhn♀ sǒn·ji mârk |
| Where should we meet? | เราจะเจอกันที่ไหนดีล่ะ? rou jah jer gahn têe·nǐ dee làh |
| I'll meet you at *the bar/your hotel*. | ผม♂/ฉัน♀ จะไปเจอคุณที่ *บาร์/โรงแรมของคุณ* pǒm♂/cháhn♀ jah bpi jer kuhn têe *bar/ roeng·raem kǒhng kuhn* |
| I'll come by at… | ผม♂/ฉัน♀ จะไปถึงตอน… pǒm♂/cháhn♀ jah bpi tǔeng dtorn… |

▶ For time, see page 167.

| I'm busy. | ขอบคุณ แต่ว่าผม♂/ฉัน♀ ยุ่งมาก kòrp·kuhn dtàe·wâr pǒm♂/cháhn♀ yûhng mârk |
| I'm not interested. | ผม♂/ฉัน♀ ไม่สนใจ pǒm♂/cháhn♀ mî sǒn·ji |
| Leave me alone. | ขอร้อง อย่ายุ่งกับผม♂/ฉัน♀ ได้ไหม kǒr·rórng yàr yûhng gàhp pǒm♂/cháhn♀ dî mí |
| Stop bothering me! | เลิกมากวนใจผม♂/ฉัน♀ ซะที! lêrk mar goarn·ji pǒm♂/cháhn♀ sáh tee |

## Getting Physical

| | |
|---|---|
| Can I *hug/kiss* you? | ผม♂/ฉัน♀ ขอ *กอด/จูบ* คุณได้ไหม? pǒm♂/cháhn♀ kǒr *gòrt/jòop* kuhn dîe mí |
| Yes. | ครับ♂/ค่ะ♀ kráhp♂/kâh♀ |
| No. | ไม่ได้ mî đîe |
| Stop! | หยุดนะ! yùht náh |
| I *like/love* you. | ผม♂/ฉัน♀ *ชอบ/รัก* คุณ pǒm♂/cháhn♀ *chôrp/ráhk* kuhn |

## Sexual Preferences

| | |
|---|---|
| Are you gay? | คุณเป็นเกย์หรือเปล่า? kuhn bpehn ge rúe·bplòw |
| I'm… | ผม♂/ฉัน♀ … pǒm♂/cháhn♀ … |
| – heterosexual | – ไม่ได้เป็นเกย์ mî đîe bpehn ge |
| – homosexual | – เป็นเกย์ bpehn ge |
| – bisexual | – เป็นไบเซ็กช่วล bpehn bi séhk·chôarn |

▼ **Fun**

# *Sightseeing*

| | |
|---|---|
| Where's the tourist information office? | สำนักงานท่องเที่ยวอยู่ที่ไหน? săhm·náhk·ngarn tôhng·têaw yòo têe·nî |
| What are the main attractions? | มีอะไรที่น่าสนใจบ้าง? mee ah·ri têe nâr·sŏn·ji bârng |
| Do you have tours in English? | คุณมีทัวร์ที่เป็นภาษาอังกฤษไหม? kuhn mee toar têe bpehn par·săr ahng·grìht mí |
| Can I have a *map/ guide*? | ผม♂/ฉัน♀ ขอ *แผนที่/หนังสือแนะนำการท่อง เที่ยว* ได้ไหม? pŏm♂/chán♀ kŏr *păen·têe/ năhng·sŭee ná·nahm garn tôhng·têaw* dî mí |

## Tourist Information Office

| | |
|---|---|
| Do you have information on…? | คุณมีข้อมูลเกี่ยวกับ…ไหม? kuhn mee kôr·moon gèaw gàhp…mí |
| How do we get there? | ผม♂/ฉัน♀ จะไปที่นั่นได้ยังไง? pŏm♂/chán♀ jah bpi têe nâhn dî yahng·ngi |
| Can you recommend…? | ช่วยแนะนำ…ให้หน่อยได้ไหม? chôary ná·nahm…hî nòhy dî mí |
| – a boat trip | – ทัวร์ทางเรือ toar tarng ruea |
| – a bus tour | – ทัวร์ทางรถ toar tarng rót |
| – an excursion to… | – ทัวร์ระยะสั้น… toar rah·yáh sâhn… |
| – a sightseeing tour | – ทัวร์ชมเมือง toar chom mueang |

---

*i* The Tourism Authority of Thailand (TAT) has offices throughout Thailand. The main office is located in Bangkok. TAT information counters are open daily, 8:30 a.m. to 4:30 p.m.

## Tours

| | |
|---|---|
| I'd like to go on the tour to… | ผม♂/ฉัน♀ ต้องการทัวร์ไป… pŏm♂/cháhn♀ dtôhng·garn toar bpi… |
| When's the next tour? | ทัวร์กรุ๊ปต่อไปออกเมื่อไหร่? toar grúhp dtòr·bpi òrk mûea·rì |
| Are there tours in English? | มีทัวร์ที่เป็นภาษาอังกฤษไหม? mee toar têe bpehn par·săr ahng·grìht mí |
| Is there an English *guide book*/*audio guide*? | มี *หนังสือนำเที่ยว*/*เทปนำเที่ยว* เป็นภาษาอังกฤษไหม? mee *năhng·sŭee nahm·têaw*/*tép nahm·têaw* bpehn par·săr ahng·grìht mí |
| I'd like to see… | ผม♂/ฉัน♀ อยากไปดู… pŏm♂/cháhn♀ yàrk bpi doo… |
| Can we stop here…? | เราขอหยุดตรงนี้เพื่อ…ได้ไหม? rou kŏr yùht dtrong·née pûea…dî mí |
| – to take photos | – ถ่ายรูป tìe rôop |
| – for souvenirs | – ซื้อของที่ระลึก sûee kŏrng têe·rah·lúek |
| – for the restrooms [toilets] | – เข้าห้องน้ำ kôu hôhng·nárm |
| Can we look around? | เราขอดูรอบ ๆ หน่อยได้ไหม? rou kŏr doo rôrp·rôrp nòry dî mí |
| Is it handicapped [disabled]-accessible? | มีทางเข้าออกสำหรับคนพิการไหม? mee tarng kôu òrk săhm·ràhp kon píh·garn mí |

▶ For ticketing, see page 20.

## Sights

| | |
|---|---|
| Where's…? | …อยู่ที่ไหน? …yòo têe·nĭ |
| – the battleground | – สมรภูมิ sah·mŏr·rah·poom |
| – the botanical garden | – สวนพฤกษศาสตร์ sŏarn prúek·sah·sârt |

| Where's...? | ...อยู่ที่ไหน? ...yòo têe·nǐ |
|---|---|
| – the downtown area | – ย่านใจกลางเมือง yârn ji·glarng mueang |
| – the fountain | – น้ำพุ náhm·púh |
| – the library | – ห้องสมุด hôhng sah·mùht |
| – the market | – ตลาด dtah·làrt |
| – the (war) memorial | – อนุสาวรีย์ (สงคราม) ah·nûh·sǎr·wah·ree (sǒng·krarm) |
| – the museum | – พิพิธภัณฑ์ píh·píht·tah·pahn |
| – the old town | – เมืองเก่า mueang gòu |
| – the palace | – วัง wahng |
| – the park | – สวนสาธารณะ sǒarn sǎr·tar·rah·náh |
| – the shopping area | – ย่านช็อปปิ้ง yârn chóhp·bpîhng |
| Can you show me on the map? | คุณช่วยชี้ในแผนที่ให้หน่อยได้ไหม? kuhn chôary chée ni pǎen·têe hî nòhy dî mí |

▶ For directions, see page 35.

## Impressions

| It's... | มัน... mahn... |
|---|---|
| – beautiful | – สวย sŏary |
| – interesting | – น่าสนใจ nâr·sŏn·ji |
| – romantic | – โรแมนติก roe·maen·dtìhk |
| – strange | – แปลก plàek |
| – stunning | – น่าตกตะลึง nâr·dtòk·dtàh·lueng |
| – terrible | – แย่สุดๆ yâe sùht·sùht |
| I (don't) like it. | ผม♂/ฉัน♀ (ไม่) ชอบ pŏm♂/cháhn♀ (mî) chôrp |

## Religion

| Where's...? | ...อยู่ที่ไหน? ...yòo têe·nĭ |
|---|---|
| – the *Catholic/ Protestant* church | – โบสถ์ *คาทอลิก/โปรเตสแตนต์* bòet *kar·tor·lìhk/proe·dtés·dtáen* |
| – the mosque | – มัสยิด/สุเหร่า máht·sah·yíht/suh·ròu |
| – the shrine | – ศาลเจ้า sărn·jârw |
| – the synagogue | – โบสถ์ยิว bòet yihw |
| – the temple | – วัด wáht |
| What time is *mass/ the service*? | เวลาทำมิสซา/สวดมนต์ กี่โมง? we·lar *tahm míht·sar/sòart·mon* gèe moeng |

# *Shopping*

| | |
|---|---|
| Where's the *market/* *mall [shopping* *centre]?* | ตลาด/ศูนย์การค้า อยู่ที่ไหน? *dtah·làrt/ sŏon·garn·kár* yòo têe·nĭ |
| I'm just looking. | ผม♂/ฉัน♀ แค่ดูเฉยๆ pŏm♂/cháhn♀ kâe doo chŏey·chŏey |
| Can you help me? | ช่วยผม♂/ฉัน♀ หน่อยได้ไหม? chôary pŏm♂/ cháhn♀ nòhy dî mí |
| I'm being helped. | ผม♂/ฉัน♀ มีคนช่วยแล้ว pŏm♂/cháhn♀ mee kon chôary láew |
| How much? | เท่าไหร่? tôu·rì |
| That one, please. | ขออันนั้นหน่อย kŏr ahn náhn nòhy |
| That's all. | แค่นี้แหละ kâe née là |
| Where can I pay? | ผม♂/ฉัน♀ จะจ่ายเงินดีไหน? pŏm♂/cháhn♀ jah jìe ngern dîe têe·nĭ |
| I'll pay *in cash/by* *credit card.* | ผม♂/ฉัน♀ จะจ่ายด้วย เงินสด/บัตรเครดิต pŏm♂/ cháhn♀ jah jìe dôary *ngern·sòt/bàht·kre·diht* |
| A receipt, please. | ขอใบเสร็จด้วย kŏr bi·sèht dôary |

## Stores ————

| | |
|---|---|
| Where's…? | …อยู่ที่ไหน? …yòo têe·nĭ |
| – the antiques store | – ร้านขายของเก่า rárn kĭe kŏrng·gòu |
| – the bakery | – ร้านเบเกอรี่ rárn be·ger·rêe |
| – the bank | – ธนาคาร tah·nar·karn |
| – the bookstore | – ร้านหนังสือ rárn năhng·sŭee |

| – the camera store | – ร้านขายกล้องถ่ายรูป rárn kǐe glôhng·tìe·rôop |
|---|---|
| – the clothing store | – ร้านขายเสื้อผ้า rárn kǐe sûea·pâr |
| – the department store | – ห้างสรรพสินค้า hârng sàhp·pah·sǐhn·kár |
| – the gift shop | – ร้านกิฟต์ช็อป rárn gíhp·chòhp |
| – the health food store | – ร้านขายอาหารสุขภาพ rárn kǐe ar·hǎrn sùhk·kah·pârp |
| – the jeweler | – ร้านขายเครื่องประดับ rárn kǐe krûeang·bprah·dàhp |
| – the liquor store [off–licence] | – ร้านขายเหล้า rárn kǐe lôu |
| – the market | – ตลาด dtah·làrt |
| – the music store | – ร้านขายซีดีเพลง rárn kǐe see·dee pleng |
| – the pharmacy [chemist] | – ร้านขายยา rárn kǐe yar |
| – the produce [grocery] store | – ร้านขายของชำ rárn kǐe kǒrng·chahm |
| – the shoe store | – ร้านขายรองเท้า rárn kǐe rorng·tów |
| – the shopping mall [shopping centre] | – ศูนย์การค้า sǒon·garn·kár |
| – the souvenir store | – ร้านขายของที่ระลึก rárn kǐe kǒrng·têe·rah·lúehk |
| – the supermarket | – ซุปเปอร์มาร์เก็ต súhp·bpêr mar·gêht |
| – the toy store | – ร้านขายของเล่น rárn kǐe kǒrng·lên |

*i* There are countless malls and markets in Thailand. During your stay, be sure to visit one of the many night markets. The largest are located in Bangkok and Chiang Mai. Night markets offer the opportunity to buy many designer and unique goods that are not available in regular shopping malls or day markets.

## Services

| Can you recommend...? | คุณช่วยแนะนำ...ให้หน่อยได้ไหม? kuhn chôary ná·nahm...hî nòhy dî mí |
|---|---|
| – a barber | – ร้านตัดผมผู้ชาย rárn dtàht·pŏm pôo·chie |
| – a dry cleaner | – ร้านซักแห้ง rárn sáhk·hâeng |
| – a hairstylist | – ร้านทำผม rárn tahm·pŏm |
| – a laundromat [launderette] | – ร้านซักผ้า rárn sáhk·pâr |
| – a nail salon | – ร้านทำเล็บ rárn tahm·léhp |
| – a spa | – สปา sah·bpar |
| – a travel agency | – บริษัททัวร์ bor·rih·sàht toar |
| Can you...this? | คุณช่วย...นี่ให้หน่อยได้ไหม? kuhn chôary...née hî nòhy dîe mí |
| – alter | – แก้ gǎe |
| – clean | – ทำความสะอาด tahm kwarm sah·àrt |
| – fix [mend] | – ซ่อม sôhm |
| – press | – รีด rêet |
| When will it be ready? | จะเสร็จเมื่อไหร่? jah sèht mûea·rì |

## Spa

| | |
|---|---|
| I'd like… | ผม♂/ฉัน♀ อยากจะ… pŏm♂/cháhn♀ yàrk jah… |
| – an *eyebrow/bikini* wax | – แว็กซ์ ขนคิ้ว/แนวบิกินี่ wák kŏn kíhw/naew bih·gih·nêe |
| – a facial | – นวดหน้า nôart·nâr |
| – a *manicure/ pedicure* | – ทำ เล็บมือ/เล็บเท้า tahm léhp·muee/léhp·tów |
| – a massage | – นวดตัว nôart·dtoar |
| Do you *have/do*…? | คุณมีบริการ… ไหม? kuhn mee bor·rih·garn…mí |
| – acupuncture | – ฝังเข็ม fähng·kĕhm |
| – aromatherapy | – อโรมาเทราปี ah·roe·mâr te·rar·pêe |
| – oxygen treatment | – ทำทรีตเมนต์ด้วยอ๊อกซิเจน tahm tréet·méhn dôary óhk·sih·jên |
| – a sauna | – อบซาวน่า òp sou·nâr |

## Hair Salon

| | |
|---|---|
| I'd like… | ผม♂/ฉัน♀ อยากจะ… pŏm♂/cháhn♀ yàrk jah… |
| – an appointment for *today/tomorrow* | – ขอนัดเวลาสำหรับ วันนี้/พรุ่งนี้ kŏr náht we·lar sähm·ràhp *wahn·née/prûhng·née* |
| – some *color/ highlights* | – ทำสี/ทำไฮไลท์ ผม tahm·sĕe/tahm hie·lí pŏm |
| – my hair *styled/ blow-dried* | – เซ็ต/เป่า ผม *séht/bpòu* pŏm |
| – a haircut | – ตัดผม dtàht·pŏm |
| Not too short. | ไม่ต้องสั้นมาก mî dtôhng sâhn mârk |
| Shorter here. | ตรงนี้สั้นอีกนิด dtrong·née sâhn èek níht |

## Sales Help

| When do you *open/close*? | คุณ เปิด/ปิด เมื่อไหร่? kuhn bpèrt/bpìht mûea·rì |
| Where's...? | ...อยู่ที่ไหน? ...yòo têe·nǐ |
| – the cashier | – แคชเชียร์ káet·chea |
| – the escalator | – บันไดเลื่อน bahn·di lûean |
| – the elevator [lift] | – ลิฟต์ líhp |
| – the fitting room | – ห้องลองเสื้อผ้า hôhng lorng sûea·pâr |
| – the store directory | – รายการร้านค้า rie·garn rárn·kár |
| Can you help me? | ช่วยผม♂/ฉัน♀ หน่อยได้ไหม? chôary pǒm♂/cháhn♀ nòhy dî mí |
| I'm just looking. | ผม♂/ฉัน♀ แค่ดูเฉยๆ pǒm♂/cháhn♀ kâe doo chǒey·chǒey |
| I'm being helped. | ผม♂/ฉัน♀ มีคนช่วยแล้ว pǒm♂/cháhn♀ mee kon chôary láew |
| Do you have...? | คุณมี...ไหม? kuhn mee...mí |
| Can you show me...? | ขอดู...หน่อยได้ไหม? kǒr doo...nòhy dî mí |
| Can you *ship/wrap* it? | ช่วย ส่ง/ห่อ ให้หน่อยได้ไหม? chôary sòng/hòr hî nòhy dî mí |
| How much? | เท่าไหร่? tôu·rì |
| That's all. | แค่นี้แหละ kâe née là |

## You May See...

| | |
|---|---|
| เปิด/ปิด bpèrt/bpìht | open/closed |
| ห้องลองเสื้อผ้า hôhng lorng sûea•pâr | fitting room |
| แคชเชียร์ káet•chea | cashier |
| รับเฉพาะเงินสด ráhp chah•póh ngern•sòt | cash only |
| ยินดีรับบัตรเครดิต yihn•dee ráhp bàht•kre•dîht | credit cards accepted |
| ทางเข้า/ทางออก tarng kôu/tarng òrk | entrance/exit |

## Preferences

| | |
|---|---|
| I'd like something... | ผม♂/ฉัน♀ อยากได้อะไรที่... pŏm♂/cháhn♀ yàrk•dîe ah•ri têe... |
| – cheap/expensive | – ถูก/แพง tòok/paeng |
| – nicer | – สวยกว่านี้ sŏary gwàr née |
| – from this region | – เป็นของในท้องถิ่น bpehn kŏrng ni tórng•tìn |
| Around...baht. | ประมาณ...บาท bprah•marn...bàrt |
| Is it real? | ของแท้หรือเปล่า? kŏrng táe rúe•bplòw |
| Can you show me *this/that*? | ขอดู *อันนี้/อันนั้น* หน่อยได้ไหม? kŏr doo *ahn née/ahn náhn* nòhy dî mí |

## Decisions

| | |
|---|---|
| That's not quite what I want. | มันไม่ใช่สิ่งที่ผม♂/ฉัน♀ ต้องการชะทีเดียว mahn mî chî sìhng têe pŏm♂/cháhn♀ dtôhng•garn sáh tee deaw |
| No, I don't like it. | ไม่ ผม♂/ฉัน♀ ไม่ชอบอันนี้ mî pŏm♂/cháhn♀ mî chôrp ahn née |
| I have to think about it. | ผม♂/ฉัน♀ ขอคิดดูก่อน pŏm♂/cháhn♀ kŏr kíht doo gòrn |

| I'll take it. | ผม♂/ฉัน♀ เอาอันนี้แหละ pŏm♂/cháhn♀ ou ahn née là |
|---|---|

## Bargaining

| That's too much. | แพงไป paeng bpi |
|---|---|
| I'll give you...baht. | ตกลง...บาทก็แล้วกัน dtòk·long...bàrt gôr·láew·gahn |
| Is that your best price? | ราคาต่ำสุดแล้วหรือ? rar·kar dtàhm sùht láew rěr |
| Can you give me a discount? | ลดให้ผม♂/ฉัน♀ หน่อยได้ไหม? lót hî pŏm♂/cháhn♀ nòhy dîe mí |

▶ For numbers, see page 165.

## Paying

| How much? | เท่าไหร่? tôu·rì |
|---|---|
| I'll pay... | ผม♂/ฉัน♀ จะจ่าย... pŏm♂/cháhn♀ jah jàry... |
| – in cash | – เป็นเงินสด bpehn ngern·sòt |
| – by credit card | – ด้วยบัตรเครดิต dôary bàht·kre·dìht |
| – by traveler's check [cheque] | – ด้วยเช็คเดินทาง dôary chéhk dern·tarng |
| A receipt, please. | ขอใบเสร็จด้วย kŏr bi·sèht dôary |

## Complaints

| | |
|---|---|
| I'd like… | ผม♂/ฉัน♀ อยากจะ... pŏm♂/cháhn♀ yàrk jah… |
| – to exchange this | – เปลี่ยนของชิ้นนี้ bplèan kŏrng chíhn née |
| – a refund | – ขอเงินคืน kŏr ngern kueen |
| – to see the manager | – พบผู้จัดการ póp pôo·jàht·garn |

## Souvenirs

| | |
|---|---|
| Buddha image | พระพุทธรูป práh·púht·tah·rôop |
| ceramics | เซรามิค se·rar·mìhk |
| doll | ตุ๊กตา dtúhk·gah·dtar |
| handmade flowers | ดอกไม้ประดิษฐ์ dòrk·mí bprah·dìht |
| hill tribe clothes | ชุดชาวเขา chúht chow kŏu |
| jewelry | เครื่องประดับ krûeang·bprah·dàhp |
| key ring | พวงกุญแจ poarng guhn·jae |
| kite | ว่าว wôw |
| lacquerware | เครื่องเขิน krûeang kĕrn |
| nielloware | เครื่องถม krûeang tŏm |
| postcard | โปสการ์ด bpóet·sah·gárt |
| pottery | เครื่องปั้นดินเผา krûeang bpâhn dihn·pŏu |
| silk | ผ้าไหม pâr mĭ |
| silverware | เครื่องเงิน krûeang ngern |
| T-shirt | เสื้อยืด sûea·yûeet |
| wooden elephant | ช้างไม้ chárng·mié |
| Can I see *this/that*? | ผม♂/ฉัน♀ ขอดู *อันนี้/อันนั้น* หน่อยได้ไหม? pŏm♂/cháhn♀ kŏr doo *ahn née/ahn náhn* nòhy dî mí |

| | |
|---|---|
| It's in the *window/display case*. | มันอยู่ใน *ที่จัดโชว์/ตู้โชว์* mahn yòo ni *têe jàht choe/dtôo·choe* |
| I'd like… | ผม♂/ฉัน♀ อยากได้… pŏm♂/cháhn♀ yàrk·dîe… |
| – a battery | – แบ็ตเตอรี่ bàt·dter·rêe |
| – a bracelet | – สร้อยข้อมือ sôry kôr·muee |
| – a brooch | – เข็มกลัด kěhm·glàht |
| – a clock | – นาฬิกา nar·líh·gar |
| – earrings | – ตุ้มหู dtûm·hŏo |
| – a necklace | – สร้อยคอ sôry·kor |
| – a ring | – แหวน wăen |
| – a watch | – นาฬิกาข้อมือ nar·líh·gar kôr·muee |
| I'd like… | ผม♂/ฉัน♀ อยากได้ที่เป็น… pŏm♂/cháhn♀ yàrk·dîe têe bpehn… |
| – copper | – ทองแดง torng·daeng |
| – crystal | – คริสตัล kríhs·dtâhn |
| – cut glass | – แก้วเจียระไน gâew jea·rah·ni |

| | |
|---|---|
| – diamonds | – เพชร péht |
| – enamel | – ลงยา/เคลือบ long·yar/klûeap |
| – gold | – ทองคำ torng·kahm |
| – pearls | – ไข่มุก ki·múhk |
| – pewter | – พิวเตอร์ pihw·dtêr |
| – platinum | – ทองขาว torng·kǎrw |
| – sterling silver | – เงินสเตอร์ลิง ngern sah·dter·lihng |
| Is this real? | นี่ของแท้หรือเปล่า? nêe kǒrng táe rúe·bplòw |
| Is there a certificate for it? | มีใบรับรองหรือเปล่า? mee bi·ráhp·rorng rúe·bplòw |
| Can you engrave it? | ช่วยสลักตัวอักษรให้ด้วยได้ไหม? chôary sàh·làhk dtoar·àhk·sǒrn hî dôary dî mí |

## Antiques

| | |
|---|---|
| How old is it? | มันเก่าขนาดไหน? mahn gòu kah·nàrt nǐ |
| Do you have anything from the…period? | คุณมีของที่อยู่ในสมัย…ไหม? kuhn mee kǒrng têe·yòo ni sah·mǐ…mí |
| Do I have to fill out any forms? | ผม♂/ฉัน♀ ต้องกรอกแบบฟอร์มอะไรหรือเปล่า? pǒm♂/cháhn♀ dtôhng gròrk baep·form ah·ri rúe·bplòw |
| Is there a certificate of authenticity? | มีใบรับรองว่าเป็นของแท้หรือเปล่า? mee bi·ráhp·rorng wâr bpehn kǒrng·táe rúe·bplòw |

## Clothing

| | |
|---|---|
| I'd like… | ผม♂/ฉัน♀ อยากจะ… pǒm♂/cháhn♀ yàrk jah… |
| Can I try this on? | ขอลองหน่อยได้ไหม? kǒr lorng nòhy dî mí |
| It doesn't fit. | มันไม่พอดี mahn mî por·dee |

| It's too… | มัน…เกินไป mahn…gern bpi |
| – big /small | – ใหญ่/เล็ก yì/léhk |
| – short /long | – สั้น/ยาว sâhn/yow |
| – tight /loose | – คับ/หลวม káhp/lŏarm |
| Do you have this in size…? | คุณมีขนาด…ไหม? kuhn mee kah·nàrt…mí |
| Do you have this in a *bigger/smaller* size? | คุณมีขนาด*ใหญ่กว่า/เล็กกว่า* นี้ไหม? kuhn mee kàh·nàrt *yâi gwàr/léhk gwar* née mí |

▶For numbers, see page 165.

## You May See…

| สำหรับผู้ชาย săhm·ràhp pôo·chie | men's |
| สำหรับผู้หญิง săhm·ràhp pôo·yĭhng | women's |
| สำหรับเด็ก săhm·ràhp dèhk | children's |

### Color

| I'd like something in… | ผม♂/ฉัน♀ อยากได้ที่เป็น… pŏm♂/cháhn♀ yàrk·dîe têe bpehn… |
| – beige | – สีน้ำตาลอ่อน sĕe náhm·dtarn òrn |
| – black | – สีดำ sĕe dahm |
| – blue | – สีน้ำเงิน sĕe náhm·ngern |
| – brown | – สีน้ำตาล sĕe náhm·dtarn |
| – green | – สีเขียว sĕe kĕaw |
| – gray | – สีเทา sĕe tou |
| – orange | – สีส้ม sĕe sôm |
| – pink | – สีชมพู sĕe chom·poo |
| – purple | – สีม่วง sĕe môarng |

| – red | – สีแดง sĕe daeng |
| – white | – สีขาว sĕe kŏw |
| – yellow | – สีเหลือง sĕe lŭeang |

## Clothes and Accessories

| backpack | เป้สะพายหลัง bpê sah·pie lăhng |
| belt | เข็มขัด kĕhm·kàht |
| bikini | บิกินี่ bih·gih·nêe |
| blouse | เสื้อผู้หญิง sûea pôo·yĭhng |
| bra | ยกทรง yók·song |
| briefs [underpants] | กางเกงใน garng·geng ni |
| coat | เสื้อโค้ท sûea kóet |
| dress | ชุดกระโปรง chúht gràh·bproeng |
| hat | หมวก mòark |
| jacket | เสื้อแจ็กเก็ต sûea jáek·gèht |
| jeans | กางเกงยีนส์ garng·geng yeen |
| pajamas | ชุดนอน chúht norn |
| pants [trousers] | กางเกงขายาว garng·geng kăr yow |
| pantyhose [tights] | ถุงน่อง tŭhng·nôhng |
| purse [handbag] | กระเป๋าถือ grah·bpŏu tŭee |
| raincoat | เสื้อกันฝน sûea gahn fŏn |
| scarf | ผ้าพันคอ pâr·pahn·kor |
| shirt | เสื้อเชิร์ต sûea·chért |
| shorts | กางเกงขาสั้น garng·geng kăr sâhn |
| skirt | กระโปรง grah·bproeng |
| socks | ถุงเท้า tŭhng·tóu |
| suit | ชุดสูท chúht·sòot |

| | |
|---|---|
| sunglasses | แว่นกันแดด wân gahn dàet |
| sweater | เสื้อสเว็ตเตอร์ sûea sah·wéht·dtêr |
| sweatshirt | เสื้อสเว็ตเชิร์ต sûea sah·wéht·chért |
| swimsuit | ชุดว่ายน้ำ chúht wîe·nárm |
| T-shirt | เสื้อยืด sûea·yûeet |
| tie | เนคไท néhk·ti |
| underwear | ชุดชั้นใน chúht cháhn ni |

## Fabric

| | |
|---|---|
| I'd like… | ผม♂/ฉัน♀ อยากได้… pǒm♂/cháhn♀ yàrk·dîe… |
| – cotton | – ผ้าฝ้าย pâr fîe |
| – denim | – ผ้ายีนส์ pâr yeen |
| – lace | – ผ้าลูกไม้ pâr lôok·mí |
| – leather | – หนัง nǎhng |
| – linen | – ผ้าลินิน pâr lih·nihn |
| – silk | – ผ้าไหม pâr mǐ |
| – wool | – ผ้าวูล pâr woon |
| Is it machine washable? | อันนี้ซักด้วยเครื่องซักผ้าได้ไหม? ahn née sáhk dôary krûeang·sáhk·pâr dîe mí |

## Shoes

| | |
|---|---|
| I'd like… | ผม♂/ฉัน♀ อยากได้… pǒm♂/cháhn♀ yàrk·dîe… |
| – high-heels/flats | – รองเท้าส้นสูง/รองเท้าส้นแบน rorng·tów sôn sǒong/rorng·tów sôn baen |
| – boots | – รองเท้าบู๊ท rorng·tów bóot |
| – flip-flops | – รองเท้าแตะ rorng·tów dtà |
| – hiking boots | – รองเท้าเดินเขา rorng·tów dern·kǒu |

| – loafers | – รองเท้าสวม rorng·tów sŏarm |
| – sandals | – รองเท้าแตะ rorng·tów dtà |
| – shoes | – รองเท้า rorng·tów |
| – slippers | – รองเท้าแตะ rorng·tów dtà |
| – sneakers | – รองเท้าผ้าใบ rorng·tów pâr·bi |
| Size… | ไซส์… sí… |

▶ For numbers, see page 165.

## Sizes

| small | เล็ก léhk |
| medium | กลาง glarng |
| large | ใหญ่ yì |
| extra large | ใหญ่พิเศษ yì píh·sèt |
| petite | สำหรับคนตัวเล็ก sǎhm·ràhp kon dtoar léhk |

## Newsstand and Tobacconist

| Do you sell English-language newspapers? | คุณมีหนังสือพิมพ์ภาษาอังกฤษขายไหม? kuhn mee nǎhng·sǔee·pihm par·sǎr ahng·grìht kǐe mí |
| I'd like… | ผม♂/ฉัน♀ อยากได้… pǒm♂/cháhn♀ yàrk·dîe… |
| – chewing gum | – หมากฝรั่ง mark·fah·ràhng |
| – a cigar | – ซิการ์ síh·gâr |
| – a *pack/carton* of cigarettes | – บุหรี่หนึ่ง ซอง/ห่อ buh·rèe nùeng *sorng/hòr* |
| – a lighter | – ไฟแช็ก fi·chák |
| – a magazine | – นิตยสาร níht·tah·yah·sǎrn |
| – matches | – ไม้ขีด mí·kèet |

| I'd like… | ผม♂/ฉัน♀ อยากได้... pŏm♂/cháhn♀ yàrk·dîe… |
|---|---|
| – a newspaper | – หนังสือพิมพ์ năhng·sŭee·pihm |
| – a postcard | – โปสการ์ด bpóet·sah·gárt |
| – a *road/town* map of… | – แผนที่ *ถนน/เมือง* ของ... păen·têe *tah·nŏn/ mueang* kŏrng… |
| – stamps | – แสตมป์ sah·dtaem |

## Photography

| I'd like…camera. | ผม♂/ฉัน♀ อยากได้กล้อง... pŏm♂/cháhn♀ yàrk·dîe glôhng… |
|---|---|
| – an automatic | – อัตโนมัติ àht·tah·noe·máht |
| – a digital | – ดิจิตอล dih·jih·dtôhn |
| – a disposable | – ใช้แล้วทิ้ง chí láew tíhng |
| I'd like… | ผม♂/ฉัน♀ อยากได้... pŏm♂/cháhn♀ yàrk·dîe… |
| – a battery | – แบ็ตเตอรี่ bàt·dter·rêe |
| – digital prints | – ภาพดิจิตอล pârp dih·jih·dtôhn |
| – a memory card | – เมมโมรี่การ์ด mem·moe·rêe gárt |
| Can I print digital photos here? | ที่นี่มีบริการอัดภาพดิจิตอลไหม? têe·nêe mee bor·rih·garn àht pârp dih·jih·dtôhn mí |

# *Sports and Leisure*

## Essential

| When's the game? | เริ่มแข่งกี่โมง? rêrm kàng gèe moeng |
|---|---|
| Where's…? | ...อยู่ที่ไหน? …yòo têe·nĭ |
| – the beach | – ชายหาด chie·hàrt |

| | |
|---|---|
| – the park | – สวนสาธารณะ sŏarn săr·tar·rah·náh |
| – the pool | – สระว่ายน้ำ sàh wîe·nárm |
| Is it safe to swim here? | ที่นี่ปลอดภัยพอที่จะ ว่ายน้ำไหม? têe·nêe bplòrt·pi por têe jah wîe·nárm mí |
| Can I rent [hire] golf clubs? | ผม♂/ฉัน♀ ขอเช่าไม้กอล์ฟได้ไหม? pŏm♂/ cháhn♀ kŏr chôu mí·górf dîe mí |
| How much per hour? | ชั่วโมงละเท่าไหร่? chôar·moeng lah tôu·rì |
| How far is it to…? | ไป…ไกลไหม? bpi…gli mí |
| Show me on the map, please. | ช่วยชี้ในแผนที่ให้หน่อย chôary chée ni păen·têe hî nòhy |

## Spectator Sports

| | |
|---|---|
| When's…*game/match*? | …นัด นี้เริ่มแข่งกี่โมง? …nát née rêrm kàng gèe moeng |
| – the badminton | – แบดมินตัน bàt·mihn·tâhn |
| – the basketball | – บาสเก็ตบอล bárt·sah·gêht bohn |
| – the boxing | – มวย moary |
| – the golf | – กอล์ฟ górf |
| – the soccer [football] | – ฟุตบอล fúht·bohn |
| – the table tennis | – ปิงปอง bpihng·bpohng |
| – the takraw | – ตะกร้อ dtah·grôr |
| – the tennis | – เทนนิส ten·níht |
| – the volleyball | – วอลเลย์บอล wohn·lê·bohn |
| Who's playing? | ใครแข่งกับใคร? kri kàng gàhp kri |
| Where's the *racetrack*/*stadium*? | สนามแข่ง/สนามกีฬา อยู่ที่ไหน? *sah·nărm kàng/ sah·nărm gee·lar* yòo têe·nĭ |

▶ For ticketing, see page 20.

The national sport in Thailand is Muay Thai or Thai boxing. It differs from other martial arts in that it allows eight points of contact: the two hands, shins, elbows and knees compared to just the fists and feet. Another popular game is takraw; it's similar to volleyball but one's head and feet are used to play.

## Participating

| | |
|---|---|
| Where *is/are*…? | …อยู่ที่ไหน? …yòo têe·nǐ |
| – the golf course | – สนามกอล์ฟ sah·nǎrm górf |
| – the gym | – โรงยิม roeng yihm |
| – the park | – สวนสาธารณะ sŏarn sǎr·tar·rah·náh |
| – the tennis courts | – สนามเทนนิส sah·nǎrm ten·níht |
| How much per…? | …ละเท่าไหร่? …lah tôu·rì |
| – day | – วัน wahn |
| – hour | – ชั่วโมง chôar·moeng |
| – game | – เกม gem |
| – round | – รอบ rôrp |

## At the Beach/Pool

| | |
|---|---|
| Where's the *beach/pool*? | ชายหาด/สระว่ายน้ำอยู่ที่ไหน? chie·hàrt/sàh wîe·nárm yòo têe·nǐ |
| Is there…? | มี…ไหม? mee…mí |
| – a kiddie [paddling] pool | – สระเด็ก sàh dèhk |
| – an *indoor/outdoor* pool | – สระในร่ม/กลางแจ้ง sàh ni·rôm/glarng·jâeng |
| – a lifeguard | – ยามไลฟ์การ์ด yarm lí·gàrt |

| Is it safe…? | ปลอดภัย…ไหม? bplòrt·pi…mí |
| – to swim | – ที่จะว่ายน้ำ têe jah wâie·nárm |
| – to dive | – ที่จะดำน้ำ têe jah dahm·nárm |
| – for children | – สำหรับเด็ก săhm·ràhp dèhk |
| I'd like to rent [hire]… | ผม♂/ฉัน♀ อยากเช่า… pŏm♂/cháhn♀ yàrk chôu… |
| – diving equipment | – อุปกรณ์ดำน้ำ ùhp·bpah·gorn dahm·nárm |
| – a jet ski | – เจ็ทสกี jéht sah·gee |
| – a motorboat | – เรือยนต์ ruea yon |
| – a rowboat | – เรือพาย ruea pie |
| – snorkeling equipment | – อุปกรณ์สนอร์กเกิ๊ล ùhp·bpah·gorn sah·nórk·gêrn |
| – a surfboard | – กระดานโต้คลื่น grah·darn dtôe·klûeen |
| – an umbrella | – ร่ม rôm |
| – water skis | – สกีน้ำ sah·gee nárm |
| – a windsurfer | – วินด์เซิร์ฟ wihn·sérp |
| For…hours. | สำหรับ…ชั่วโมง săhm·ràhp…chôar·moeng |

## In the Countryside

| A map of…, please. | ขอแผนที่ของ…หน่อย kŏr păen·têe kŏhng…nòhy |
| – this region | – แถวนี้ tăew·née |
| – the walking routes | – เส้นทางเดินเท้า sên·tarng dern·tóu |
| – the bike routes | – เส้นทางจักรยาน sên·tarng jàhk·grah·yarn |
| – the trails | – เส้นทางเดินป่า sên·tarng dern·bpàr |

| Is it…? | อันนี้…หรือเปล่า? ahn née…rúe•bplòw |
| – easy | – ง่าย ngîe |
| – difficult | – ยาก yârk |
| – far | – ไกล gli |
| – steep | – ชัน chahn |
| How far is it to…? | ไป…ไกลไหม? bpi…gli mí |
| Show me on the map, please. | ช่วยชี้ในแผนที่ให้หน่อย chôary chée ni păen•têe hî nòhy |
| I'm lost. | ผม♂/ฉัน♀ หลงทาง pŏm♂/cháhn♀ lŏng•tarng |
| Where's…? | …อยู่ที่ไหน? …yòo têe•nî |
| – the cave | – ถ้ำ tâhm |
| – the forest | – ป่า bpàr |
| – the lake | – ทะเลสาบ tah•le•sàrp |
| – the mountain | – ภูเขา poo•kŏu |
| – the nature preserve | – เขตอนุรักษ์ธรรมชาติ kèt àh•núh•ráhk tahm•mah•chárt |
| – the overlook [viewpoint] | – จุดชมวิว jùht chom wihw |
| – the park | – สวนสาธารณะ sŏarn săr•tar•rah•náh |
| – the picnic area | – ที่ปิกนิก têe bpíhk•níhk |
| – the rainforest | – ป่าดิบชื้น bpàr•dìhp chúeen |
| – the river | – แม่น้ำ mâe•nárm |
| – the sea | – ทะเล tah•le |
| – the hot spring | – บ่อน้ำร้อน bòr•nárm•rórn |
| – the waterfall | – น้ำตก náhm•dtòk |

# *Culture and Nightlife*

## Essential

| | |
|---|---|
| What's there to do at night? | ที่นี่มีอะไรให้ทำตอนกลางคืนบ้าง? têe nêe mee ah·ri hî tahm dtorn glarng·kueen bârng |
| Do you have a program of events? | คุณมีโปรแกรมกิจกรรมไหม? kuhn mee bproe·graem giht·jah·gahm mí |
| Where's…? | …อยู่ที่ไหน? …yòo têe·nî |
| – the downtown area | – ย่านใจกลางเมือง yârn ji·glarng mueang |
| – the bar | – บาร์ bar |
| – the dance club | – คลับเต้นรำ klàhp dtên·rahm |
| Is there a cover charge? | มีค่าเข้าไหม? mee kâr·kôu mí |

## Entertainment

| | |
|---|---|
| Can you recommend…? | คุณช่วยแนะนำ…ให้หน่อยได้ไหม? kuhn chôary ná·nahm…hî nòhy dî mí |
| – a ballet | – บัลเล่ต์ bahn·lê |
| – a concert | – คอนเสิร์ต kohn·sèrt |
| – a movie | – ภาพยนตร์ pârp·pah·yon |
| – a play | – ละครเวที lah·korn we·tee |
| When does it *start/ end*? | มันเริ่ม/เลิกเมื่อไหร่? mahn *rêrm/lêrk* mûee·rì |
| Where's…? | …อยู่ที่ไหน? …yòo têe·nî |
| – the concert hall | – โรงคอนเสิร์ต roeng kohn·sèrt |
| – the movie theater [cinema] | – โรงหนัง roeng năng |
| – the theater | – โรงละคร roeng lah·korn |

| What's the dress code? | ต้องใส่เสื้อผ้าแบบไหน? dtôrng sì sêua•pâr bàep nĭ |
|---|---|

▶ For ticketing, see page 20.

## You May Hear...

| กรุณาปิดมือถือของท่านด้วย gah•rúh•nar bpìht muee•tŭee kŏhng tâhn dôary | Turn off your cell [mobile] phones, please. |
|---|---|

## Nightlife

| What's there to do at night? | ที่นี่มีอะไรให้ทำตอนกลางคืนบ้าง? têe nêe mee ah•ri hî tahm dtorn glarng•kuen bârng |
|---|---|
| Can you recommend...? | คุณช่วยแนะนำ...ให้หน่อยได้ไหม? kuhn chôary ná•nahm...hî nòhy dî mí |
| – a bar | – บาร์ bar |
| – a dance club | – คลับเต้นรำ klàhp dtên•rahm |
| – a jazz club | – คลับที่เล่นเพลงแจ๊ซ klàhp têe lên pleng jáet |
| – a club with Thai music | – คลับที่เล่นเพลงไทย klàhp têe lên pleng ti |
| Is there live music? | มีดนตรีเล่นสดไหม? mee don•dtree lên sòt mí |
| How do I get there? | ผม♂/ฉัน♀ จะไปที่นั่นได้ยังไง? pŏm♂/cháhn♀ jah bpi têe nân dîe yahng•ngi |
| Is there a cover charge? | มีค่าเข้าไหม? mee kâr•kôu mí |
| Let's go dancing. | ไปเต้นรำกันเถอะ bpi dtên•rahm gahn tèr |

# Special Needs

# *Business Travel*

## Essential

| | |
|---|---|
| I'm here on business. | ผม♂/ฉัน♀ มาธุระ pǒm♂/cháhn♀ mar túh•ráh |
| Here's my business card. | นี่นามบัตรของผม♂/ฉัน♀ nêe narm•bàht kǒhng pǒm♂/cháhn♀ |
| Can I have your card? | ผม♂/ฉัน♀ ขอนามบัตรของคุณได้ไหม? pǒm♂/cháhn♀ kǒr narm•bàht kǒhng kuhn dî mí |
| I have a meeting with… | ผม♂/ฉัน♀ มีประชุมกับ… pǒm♂/cháhn♀ mee bprah•chuhm gàhp… |
| Where's…? | …อยู่ที่ไหน …yòo têe•nǐ |
| – the business center | – ศูนย์บริการทางธุรกิจ sǒon bor•rih•garn tarng túh•ráh•giht |
| – the convention hall | – ห้องคอนเวนชั่น hôhng kohn•wen•châhn |
| – the meeting room | – ห้องประชุม hôhng bprah•chuhm |

In Thailand it is polite to refer to someone by the title คุณ **kuhn** (Mr., Mrs., Miss), then the first name. The traditional greeting is the wai, made by pressing the palms together under the chin and making a slight bow; hand-shaking is also common in business settings. In Thai culture, age deserves respect; however, you should always be courteous: impatience and displays of anger are frowned upon. Thais are reluctant to say "no" directly, so be alert to non-verbal communication.

## Business Communication

| | |
|---|---|
| I'm here… | ผม♂/ฉัน♀ มาที่นี่เพื่อ… pǒm♂/cháhn♀ mar têe•nêe pûea… |
| – on business | – ทำธุระ tahm túh•ráh |
| – for a seminar | – สัมมนา sǎhm•mah•nar |

| | |
|---|---|
| – for a conference | – ประชุมสัมมนา bprah·chuhm săhm·mah·nar |
| – for a meeting | – ประชุม bprah·chuhm |
| My name is… | ผม♂/ฉัน♀ ชื่อ… pŏm♂/cháhn♀ chûee… |
| May I introduce my colleague… | ผม♂/ฉัน♀ ขอแนะนำเพื่อนร่วมงานของผม ♂/ฉัน♀… pŏm♂/cháhn♀ kŏr ná·nahm pûean·rôarm·ngarn kŏhng pŏm♂/cháhn♀… |
| I have *a meeting/an appointment* with… | ผม♂/ฉัน♀ มีประชุม/นัดกับ… mee *bprah·chuhm/náht* gàhp… |
| I'm sorry I'm late. | ขอโทษ ที่มาสาย kŏr·tôet têe mar sĭe |
| I need an interpreter. | ผม♂/ฉัน♀ ต้องการล่าม pŏm♂/cháhn♀ dtôhng·garn lârm |
| You can reach me at the…Hotel. | คุณติดต่อผม♂/ฉัน♀ ได้ที่โรงแรม… kuhn dtiht·dtòr pŏm♂/cháhn♀ dîe têe roeng·raem… |
| I'm here until… | ผม♂/ฉัน♀ จะอยู่ที่นี่จนถึง… pŏm♂/cháhn♀ jah yòo têe·nêe jon·tŭeng… |
| I need to… | ผม♂/ฉัน♀ ต้องการ… pŏm♂/cháhn♀ dtôhng·gam… |
| – make a call | – โทรศัพท์ toe·rah·sàhp |
| – make a photocopy | – ถ่ายเอกสาร tìe èk·gah·sărn |
| – send an e-mail | – ส่งอีเมล์ sòng ee·mew |
| – send a fax | – ส่งแฟกซ์ sòng fàk |
| – send a package | – ส่งพัสดุ sòng páht·sah·dùh |
| It was a pleasure to meet you. | ยินดีที่ได้พบคุณ yihn·dee têe dîe póp kuhn |

▶ For internet and communications, see page 48.

## You May Hear…

| | | |
|---|---|---|
| คุณนัดไว้หรือเปล่า? kuhn náht wí rúe·bplòw | | Do you have an appointment? |

| กับใคร? gàhp kri | With whom? |
| กรุณารอสักครู่ gah·rúh·nar ror sáhk krôo | One moment, please. |

## *Travel with Children*

### Essential

| Is there a discount for kids? | มีส่วนลดสำหรับเด็กไหม? mee sòarn·lót sǎhm·ràhp dèhk mí |
| Can you recommend a babysitter? | คุณช่วยแนะนำพี่เลี้ยงเด็กให้หน่อยได้ไหม? kuhn chôary ná·nahm pêe·léang dèhk hî nòhy dî mí |
| Do you have a *child's seat/highchair*? | คุณมีที่นั่งเด็ก/เก้าอี้เด็กไหม? kuhn mee *têe·nâhng dèhk/gôu·êe dèhk* mí |
| Where can I change the baby? | ผม♂/ฉัน♀ จะเปลี่ยนผ้าอ้อมให้เด็กได้ที่ไหน? pǒm♂/cháhn♀ jah bplèan pâr·ôrm hî dèhk dîe têe·nǐ |

## Fun with Kids

| | |
|---|---|
| Can you recommend something for kids? | คุณมีอะไรที่จะแนะนำสำหรับเด็กไหม? kuhn mee ah·ri têe jah ná·nahm sǎhm·ràhp dèhk mí |
| Where's...? | ...อยู่ที่ไหน? ...yòo têe·nǐ |
| – the amusement park | – สวนสนุก sǒarn·sah·nùhk |
| – the arcade | – ตู้เล่นเกมอาเขต dtôo·lêhn·gem ar·kèt |
| – the kiddie [paddling] pool | – สระเด็ก sàh dèhk |
| – the park | – สวนสาธารณะ sǒarn sǎr·tar·rah·náh |
| – the playground | – สนามเด็กเล่น sah·nǎrm dèhk·lên |
| – the zoo | – สวนสัตว์ sǒarn·sàht |
| Are kids allowed? | เด็กเข้าได้ไหม? dèhk kôu dîe mí |
| Is it safe for kids? | ปลอดภัยสำหรับเด็กหรือเปล่า? bplòrt·pi sǎhm·ràhp dèhk rúe·bplòw |
| Is it suitable for...year olds? | อันนี้เหมาะสำหรับเด็กอายุ...ปีไหม? ahn née mòh sǎhm·ràhp dèhk ar·yúh...bpee mí |

▶ For numbers, see page 165.

## Basic Needs for Kids

| | |
|---|---|
| Do you have...? | คุณมี...ไหม? kuhn mee...mí |
| – a baby bottle | – ขวดนมเด็ก kòart·nom dèhk |
| – baby food | – อาหารเด็ก ar·hǎrn dèhk |
| – baby wipes | – กระดาษเช็ดก้นเด็ก grah·dàrt chéht gôn dèhk |
| – a car seat | – ที่นั่งในรถสำหรับเด็ก têe·nâhng ni rót sǎhm·ràhp dèhk |
| – a children's *menu/ portion* | – เมนู/ขนาด สำหรับเด็ก *me·noo/kah·nàrt* sǎhm·ràhp dèhk |

▶ For dining with kids, see page 60.

| Do you have…? | คุณมี…ไหม? kuhn mee…mí |
|---|---|
| – a *child's seat/ highchair* | – ที่นั่งเด็ก/เก้าอี้เด็ก têe·nâhng dèhk/gôu·êe dèhk |
| – a *crib/cot* | – เปล/อู่นอน bple/òo·norn |
| – diapers [nappies] | – ผ้าอ้อม pâr·ôrm |
| – formula [baby food] | – นมผงเด็ก/อาหารเด็ก nom·pǒng·dèhk/ar·hǎrn dèhk |
| – a pacifier [soother] | – จุกนม jùhk nom |
| – a playpen | – คอกเด็กเล่น kôrk dèhk lêhn |
| – a stroller [pushchair] | – รถเข็นเด็ก rót kěhn dèhk |
| Can I breastfeed the baby here? | ฉันให้นมลูกตรงนี้ได้ไหม? cháhn hî nom lôok dtrong·née dîe mí |
| Where can I *breastfeed/change* the baby? | ฉันจะ ให้นม/เปลี่ยนผ้าอ้อม เด็กได้ที่ไหน? cháhn jah *hî nom/bplèan pâr·ôrm* dèhk dîe têe·nî |

## Babysitting

| Can you recommend a babysitter? | คุณช่วยแนะนำพี่เลี้ยงเด็กให้หน่อยได้ไหม? kuhn chôary ná·nahm pêe léang dèhk hî nòhy dî mí |
|---|---|
| What's the charge? | คิดเท่าไหร่? kíht tôu·rì |
| Is there constant supervision? | มีการดูแลตลอดหรือเปล่า? mee garn doo·lae dtah·lòrt rúe·bplòw |
| I'll be back by… | ผม♂/ฉัน♀ จะกลับมาเวลา… pǒm♂/cháhn♀ jah glàhp mar we·lar… |
| I can be reached at… | คุณติดต่อผม♂/ฉัน♀ ได้ที่… kuhn dtìht·dtòr pǒm♂/cháhn♀ dîe têe… |

▶ For time, see page 167.

## Health and Emergency

| | |
|---|---|
| Can you recommend a pediatrician? | คุณช่วยแนะนำหมอเด็กให้หน่อยได้ไหม? kuhn chôary ná·nahm mŏr·dèhk hî nòhy đie mí |
| My child is allergic to… | ลูกของผม♂/ฉัน♀ แพ้… lôok kŏhng pŏm♂/ cháhn♀ páe… |
| My child is missing. | ลูกของผม♂/ฉัน♀ หาย lôok kŏhng pŏm♂/ cháhn♀ hǐe |
| Have you seen a *boy/girl*? | คุณเห็นเด็กผู้ชาย/เด็กผู้หญิงไหม? kuhn hěhn *dèhk pôo·chie/dèhk pôo·yǐhng* mí |

▶ For food items, see page 86.

▶ For health, see page 151.

▶ For police, see page 149.

# For the Disabled

## Essential

| | |
|---|---|
| Is there…? | มี…ไหม? mee…mí |
| – access for the disabled | – ทางเข้าออกสำหรับคนพิการ tarng kôu òrk săhm·ràhp kon píh·garn |
| – a wheelchair ramp | – ทางขึ้นสำหรับรถเข็นคนพิการ tarng kûen săhm·ràhp rót·kĕhn kon píh·garn |
| – a handicapped-[disabled-] accessible toilet | – ห้องน้ำสำหรับคนพิการ hôhng·nárm săhm·ràhp kon píh·garn |
| I need… | ผม♂/ฉัน♀ ต้องการ… pŏm♂/cháhn♀ dtôhng·garn… |
| – assistance | – ความช่วยเหลือ kwarm chôary·lŭea |
| – an elevator [a lift] | – ลิฟต์ líhp |
| – a ground-floor room | – ห้องชั้นล่าง hôhng cháhn lârng |

## Getting Help

| | |
|---|---|
| I'm… | ผม♂/ฉัน♀… pŏm♂/cháhn♀… |
| – disabled | – พิการ píh·garn |
| – visually impaired | – พิการทางสายตา píh·garn tarng săry·dtar |
| – hearing impaired/ deaf | – พิการทางหู/หูหนวก píh·garn tarng hŏo/ hŏo·nòark |
| – unable to *walk far/ use the stairs* | – เดินไกล/ใช้บันไดไม่ได้ *dern gli/chí bahn·di* mî die |
| Please speak louder. | กรุณาพูดดังขึ้นหน่อย gah·rúh·nar pôot dahng kûeen nòhy |

| Can I bring my wheelchair? | ผม♂/ฉัน♀ เอารถเข็นไปด้วยได้ไหม? pŏm♂/cháhn♀ ou rót·kĕhn bpi dôary dîe mí |
|---|---|
| Are guide dogs permitted? | อนุญาตให้นำสุนัขนำทางไปด้วยไหม? àh·núh·yârt hî nahm sùh·náhk nahm·tarng bpi dôary mí |
| Can you help me? | คุณช่วยผม♂/ฉัน♀ หน่อยได้ไหม? kuhn chôary pŏm♂/cháhn♀ nòhy dî mí |
| Please *open/hold* the door. | ช่วย *เปิด/ดึง* ประตูให้หน่อย chôary *bpèrt/dueng* bprah·dtoo hî nòhy |

# ▼ Resources

# Emergencies

## Essential

| | |
|---|---|
| Help! | ช่วยด้วย! chôary dôary |
| Go away! | ไปให้พ้น! bpi hî pón |
| Stop, thief! | หยุดนะ ขโมย! yùht náh kah•moey |
| Get a doctor! | เรียกหมอให้หน่อย! rêak mŏr hî nòhy |
| Fire! | ไฟไหม้! fi mî |
| I'm lost. | ผม♂/ฉัน♀ หลงทาง pŏm♂/cháhn♀ lŏng tarng |
| Can you help me? | คุณช่วยผม♂/ฉัน♀ หน่อยได้ไหม? kuhn chôary pŏm♂/cháhn♀ nòhy dî mí |

# Police

## Essential

| | |
|---|---|
| Call the police! | ช่วยเรียกตำรวจให้หน่อย! chôary rêak dtahm•ròart hî nòhy |
| Where's the police station? | สถานีตำรวจอยู่ที่ไหน? sah•tăr•nee dtahm•ròart yòo têe•nǐ |
| There was an *accident/attack*. | มี อุบัติเหตุ/คนถูกทำร้าย mee *uh•bàht•dtih•hèt/ kon tòok tahm•ríe* |
| My child is missing. | ลูกของผม♂/ฉัน♀ หาย lôok kŏhng pŏm♂/ cháhn♀ hǐe |
| I need… | ผม♂/ฉัน♀ ต้องการ… pŏm♂/cháhn♀ dtôhng•garn… |
| – an interpreter | – ล่าม lârm |

| I need... | ผม♂/ฉัน♀ ต้องการ... pŏm♂/chăhn♀ dtôhng•garn... |
| --- | --- |
| – to contact my lawyer | – ติดต่อทนายของผม♂/ฉัน♀ dtìht•dtòr tah•nie kŏhng pŏm♂/chăhn♀ |
| – to make a phone call | – โทรศัพท์ toe•rah•sàhp |
| – to contact the consulate | – ติดต่อสถานกงสุล dtìht•dtòr sah•tărn gong•sŭhn |
| I'm innocent. | ผม♂/ฉัน♀ บริสุทธิ์ pŏm♂/chăhn♀ bor•rih•sùht |

## You May Hear...

| กรอกแบบฟอร์มนี้ gròrk bàep•form née | Fill out this form. |
| --- | --- |
| ขอบัตรประจำตัวของคุณหน่อย kŏr bàht•bprah•jahm•dtoar kŏhng kuhn nòhy | Your identification, please. |

Contact your consulate, ask the concierge at your hotel, or ask the tourist information office for telephone numbers of the local ambulance, emergency services and police.

## Lost Property and Theft

| I'd like to report... | ผม♂/ฉัน♀ มาแจ้งความเรื่อง... pŏm♂/chăhn♀ mar jâeng•kwarm rûeang... |
| --- | --- |
| – a mugging | – การจี้ garn jêe |
| – a rape | – การข่มขืน garn kòm•kŭeen |
| – a theft | – ขโมยของ kah•moey kŏrng |
| I was *mugged/ robbed*. | ผม♂/ฉัน♀ ถูก จี้/ปล้น pŏm♂/chăhn♀ tòok jêe/bplôn |

| I lost my… | …ของผม♂/ฉัน♀ หาย …kŏhng pom♂/cháhn♀ hĭe |
|---|---|
| My…was/were stolen. | …ของผม♂/ฉัน♀ ถูกขโมย …kŏhng pŏm♂/cháhn♀ tòok kah·moey |
| – backpack | – เป้สะพายหลัง bpê sah·pie·lăhng |
| – bicycle | – จักรยาน jàhk·grah·yarn |
| – camera | – กล้องถ่ายรูป glôhng tie·rôop |
| – (rental [hire]) car | – รถ (เช่า) rót (chôu) |
| – computer | – คอมพิวเตอร์ kohm·pihw·dtêr |
| – credit card | – บัตรเครดิต bàht·kre·dìht |
| – jewelry | – เครื่องประดับ krûeang bprah·dàhp |
| – money | – เงิน ngern |
| – passport | – หนังสือเดินทาง năhng·sŭee dern·tarng |
| – purse [handbag] | – กระเป๋าถือ grah·bpŏu tŭee |
| – traveler's checks [cheques] | – เช็คเดินทาง chéhk dern·tarng |
| – wallet | – กระเป๋าสตางค์ grah·bpŏu sah·dtarng |
| I need a police report. | ผม♂/ฉัน♀ ต้องการใบแจ้งความ pŏm♂/cháhn♀ dtôhng·garn bi·jâeng·kwarm |

# Health

| I'm sick [ill]. | ผม♂/ฉัน♀ ไม่สบาย pŏm♂/cháhn♀ mî sah·bie |
| I need an English-speaking doctor. | ผม♂/ฉัน♀ ต้องการหมอที่พูดภาษาอังกฤษได้ pŏm♂/cháhn♀ dtôhng·garn mŏr têe pôot par·săr ahng·grìht dîe |

| It hurts here. | มันเจ็บตรงนี้ mahn jèhp dtrong·née |
| I have a stomachache. | ผม♂/ฉัน♀ ปวดท้อง pŏm♂/cháhn♀ bpòart tórng |

## Finding a Doctor

| Can you recommend a *doctor/dentist*? | คุณช่วยแนะนำ *หมอ/หมอฟัน* ให้หน่อยได้ไหม? kuhn chôary ná·nahm *mŏr/mŏr fahn* hî nòhy dî mí |
| Can the doctor come here? | ให้หมอมาที่นี่ได้ไหม? hî mŏr mar têe·nêe dî mí |
| I need an English-speaking doctor. | ผม♂/ฉัน♀ ต้องการหมอที่พูดภาษาอังกฤษได้ pŏm♂/cháhn♀ dtôhng·garn mŏr têe pôot par·săr ahng·grìht dîe |
| What are the office hours? | เวลาทำการกี่โมง? we·lar tahm·garn gèe moeng |
| I'd like an appointment for… | ผม♂/ฉัน♀ จะขอนัด… pŏm♂/cháhn♀ jah kŏr náht… |
| – today | – วันนี้ wahn·née |

| – tomorrow | – พรุ่งนี้ prûhng·née |
|---|---|
| – as soon as possible | – เร็วที่สุดเท่าที่จะเร็วได้ rehw têe·sùht tôu têe jah rehw dîe |
| It's urgent. | มันด่วนมาก mahn dòarn mârk |
| I have an appointment with Doctor… | ผม♂/ฉัน♀ นัดหมอ…ไว้ pŏm♂/cháhn♀ náht mŏr…wí |

## Symptoms

| I'm… | ผม♂/ฉัน♀… pŏm♂/cháhn♀… |
|---|---|
| – bleeding | – เลือดออก lûeat òrk |
| – constipated | – ท้องผูก tórng·pòok |
| – dizzy | – เวียนหัว wean·hŏar |
| – nauseous | – คลื่นไส้ klueen·si |
| – vomiting | – อาเจียน ar·jean |
| It hurts here. | มันเจ็บตรงนี้ mahn jèhp dtrong·née |
| I have… | ผม♂/ฉัน♀ มีอาการ… pŏm♂/cháhn♀ mee ar·garn… |
| – an allergic reaction | – ภูมิแพ้ poom·páe |
| – chest pain | – เจ็บหน้าอก jèhp nâr·òk |
| – cramps | – เป็นตะคริว bpehn dtah·krihw |
| – diarrhea | – ท้องร่วง tórng rôarng |
| – an earache | – ปวดหู bpòart hŏo |
| – a fever | – ไข้ kî |
| – pain | – เจ็บ jèhp |
| – a rash | – ผื่นคัน bpehn pùeen·kahn |
| – a sprain | – แพลง plaeng |

| I have… | ผม♂/ฉัน♀ มีอาการ... pǒm♂/cháhn♀ mee ar·garn… |
| – some swelling | – บวม boarm |
| – a sore throat | – เจ็บคอ jèhp kor |
| – a stomachache | – ปวดท้อง bpòart tórng |
| – sunstroke | – เป็นลมแดด bpehn lom·dàet |
| I've been sick [ill] for…days. | ผม♂/ฉัน♀ ไม่สบายมา...วันแล้ว pǒm♂/cháhn♀ mî sah·bie mar…wahn láew |

▶For numbers, see page 165.

## Health Conditions

| I'm… | ผม♂/ฉัน♀ เป็น... pǒm♂/cháhn♀ bpehn… |
| – anemic | – โรคโลหิตจาง rôek loe·hìht jarng |
| – asthmatic | – โรคหอบหืด rôek hòrp·hùeet |
| – diabetic | – โรคเบาหวาน rôek bou·wǎrn |
| I'm allergic to *antibiotics/penicillin*. | ผม♂/ฉัน♀ แพ้ ยาปฏิชีวนะ/เพนิซิลลิน pǒm♂/cháhn♀ páe yar *bpah·dtìh·chee·wah·náh/pe·níh·sihn·lihn* |

▶For food items, see page 86.

| I have… | ผม♂/ฉัน♀ เป็น... pǒm♂/cháhn♀ bpehn… |
| – arthritis | – โรคไขข้อเสื่อม rôek kǐ·kôr sùeam |
| – a heart condition | – โรคหัวใจ rôek hǒar·ji |
| – *high/low* blood pressure | – โรคความดัน *สูง/ต่ำ* rôek kwarm·dahn *sǒong/dtàhm* |
| I'm on medication. | ผม♂/ฉัน♀ กินยาอยู่ pǒm♂/cháhn♀ gihn yar yòo |

## You May Hear...

| | |
|---|---|
| ตรงนี้เจ็บไหม? dtrong·née jèhp mí | Does it hurt here? |
| คุณใช้ยาอะไรอยู่หรือเปล่า? kuhn chí yar ah·ri yòo rúe·bplòw | Are you on medication? |
| คุณแพ้อะไรไหม? kuhn páe ah·ri mí | Are you allergic to anything? |
| อ้าปากหน่อย âr bpàrk nòhy | Open your mouth. |
| หายใจลึกๆ hǎry·ji lúek·lúek | Breathe deeply. |
| ไอให้ฟังหน่อย ai hî fahng nòhy | Cough please. |
| คุณต้องไปหาหมอเฉพาะทาง kuhn dtôhng bpi hǎr mǒr chah·póh·tarng | See a specialist. |
| คุณต้องไปโรงพยาบาล kuhn dtôhng bpi roeng·pah·yar·barn | Go to the hospital. |

## Treatment

| | |
|---|---|
| Do I need a *prescription/medicine*? | ผม♂/ฉัน♀ ต้องใช้ *ใบสั่งยา/ยา* ไหม? pǒm♂/ cháhn♀ dtôhng chí *bi·sàhng·yar/yar* mí |
| Can you prescribe a generic drug [unbranded medication]? | คุณช่วยสั่งยาสามัญทั่วไปให้ได้ไหม? kuhn chôary sàhng yar sǎr·mahn dtôar·bpi hî dî mí |
| Where can I get it? | ผม♂/ฉัน♀ จะหาซื้อได้ที่ไหน? pǒm♂/cháhn♀ jah hǎr súee dîe têe·nî |

▶ For dosage instructions, see page 158.

## Hospital

| | |
|---|---|
| Notify my family, please. | ช่วยแจ้งให้ครอบครัว ของผม♂/ฉัน♀ ทราบด้วย chôary jâeng hî krôrp·kroar kǒhng pǒm♂/cháhn♀ sârp dôary |

| I'm in pain. | ผม♂/ฉัน♀ ปวดมาก pŏm♂/cháhn♀ bpòart mârk |
|---|---|
| I need a *doctor/ nurse*. | ผม♂/ฉัน♀ ต้องการ หมอ/พยาบาล pŏm♂/ cháhn♀ dtôhng·garn *mŏr/pah·yar·barn* |
| When are visiting hours? | เวลาเยี่ยมกี่โมงถึงกี่โมง? we·lar yêam gèe moeng tŭeng gèe moeng |
| I'm visiting… | ผม♂/ฉัน♀ มาเยี่ยม… pŏm♂/cháhn♀ mar yêam… |

## Dentist

| I have… | ผม♂/ฉัน♀ มาเพราะ… pŏm♂/cháhn♀ mar próh… |
|---|---|
| – a broken tooth | – ฟันบิ่น fahn bìhn |
| – a lost filling | – ที่อุดฟันหลุด têe·ùht·fahn lùht |
| – a toothache | – ปวดฟัน bpòart fahn |
| Can you fix this denture? | ช่วยซ่อมฟันปลอมให้หน่อยได้ไหม? chôary sôrm fahn·bplorm hî nòhy dî mí |

## Gynecologist

| I have *cramps/a vaginal infection*. | ฉันมีอาการ *ปวดประจำเดือน/ ติดเชื้อในช่องคลอด* cháhn mee ar·garn *bpòart bprah·jahm·duean/dtìht chúea ni chôhng·klôrt* |
|---|---|
| I missed my period. | ประจำเดือนของฉันไม่มา bprah·jahm·duean kŏhng cháhn mî mar |
| I'm on the Pill. | ฉันกินยาคุมอยู่ cháhn gihn yar·kuhm yòo |
| I'm (…months) pregnant. | ฉันท้อง (…เดือน แล้ว) cháhn tórng (… duean láew) |
| I'm not pregnant. | ฉันไม่ได้ท้อง cháhn mî·dî tórng |
| My last period was… | ประจำเดือนของฉันมาครั้งสุดท้ายเมื่อ… bprah·jahm·duean kŏhng cháhn mar kráhng sùht·tíe mûee… |

## Optician

| I lost… | ผม♂/ฉัน♀ ทำ…หาย pŏm♂/chán♀ tahm…hĭe |
| – a contact lens | – คอนแท็คเลนส์ kohn·tàk·len |
| – my glasses | – แว่นตาของผม♂/ฉัน♀ wăen·dtar kŏhng pŏm♂/chán♀ |
| – a lens | – เลนส์ len |

## Payment and Insurance

| How much? | เท่าไหร่? tôu·rì |
| Can I pay by credit card? | ผม♂/ฉัน♀ จ่ายด้วยบัตรเครดิตได้ไหม? pŏm♂/chán♀ jìe dôary bàht·kre·dìht dîe mí |
| I have insurance. | ผม♂/ฉัน♀ มีประกัน pŏm♂/chán♀ mee bprah·gahn |
| I need a receipt for my insurance. | ผม♂/ฉัน♀ ต้องการใบเสร็จสำหรับเบิกประกัน pŏm♂/chán♀ dtôhng·garn bi·sèht săhm·ràhp bèrk bprah·gahn |

## Pharmacy [Chemist]

| Where's the pharmacy [chemist]? | ร้านขายยาอยู่ที่ไหน? rárn·kĭe·yar yòo têe·nĭ |
| What time does it *open/close*? | ร้านขายยา *เปิด/ปิด* กี่โมง? rárn·kĭe·yar *bpèrt/ bpìht* gèe moeng |
| What would you recommend for…? | คุณมียาที่แนะนำสำหรับอาการ…ไหม? kuhn mee yar têe ná·nahm săhm·ràhp ar·garn…mí |
| How much do I take? | ผม♂/ฉัน♀ ต้องทานยานี้ยังไง? pŏm♂/chán♀ dtôhng tarn yar née yahng·ngi |

| Can you fill [make up] this prescription? | ช่วยจัดยาตามใบสั่งยาให้หน่อยได้ไหม? chôary jàht yar dtarm bi·sàhng·yar hî nòhy dî mí |
| I'm allergic to… | ผม♂/ฉัน♀ แพ้… pŏm♂/cháhn♀ páe… |

You'll find that pharmacies in Thailand are abundant and that many of the drugs that are sold only with a prescription in other countries are sold freely as over-the-counter drugs. If you rely on regular prescription medicine, take a supply with you.

**Dosage Instructions**

| How much do I take? | ผม♂/ฉัน♀ ต้องทานยังไง? pŏm♂/cháhn♀ dtôhng tarn yahng·ngi |
| How often? | บ่อยแค่ไหน? bòhy kâe nǐ |
| Is it safe for children? | ปลอดภัยสำหรับเด็กหรือเปล่า? bplòrt·pi sǎhm·rahp dèhk rúe·bplòw |
| I'm taking… | ผม♂/ฉัน♀ ทานยา…อยู่ pŏm♂/cháhn♀ tarn yar…yòo |
| Are there side effects? | มีผลข้างเคียงไหม? mee pǒn·kârng·keang mí |

## You May See…

| วันละ หนึ่ง/สาม ครั้ง wahn lah *nùeng/sǎrm* krǎhng | *once/three* times a day |
| หลัง/ก่อน/พร้อม อาหาร *lǎhng/gòrn/prórm* ar·hǎrn | *after/before/with* meals |
| ตอนท้องว่าง dtorn tórng·wârng | on an empty stomach |
| อาจจะทำให้ง่วง àrt·jah tahm·hî ngôarng | may cause drowsiness |
| สำหรับใช้ภายนอกเท่านั้น sǎhm·ràhp chí pie·nôrk tôu·náhn | for external use only |

## Health Problems

| I need something for… | ผม♂/ฉัน♀ อยากได้ยาแก้... pǒm♂/cháhn♀ yàrk·dîe yar gâe… |
|---|---|
| – a cold | – หวัด wàht |
| – a cough | – ไอ i |
| – diarrhea | – ท้องร่วง tórng rôarng |
| – insect bites | – แมลงกัดต่อย mah·laeng gàht·dtòry |
| – motion sickness | – เมารถ mou rót |
| – seasickness | – เมาเรือ mou ruea |
| – a sore throat | – เจ็บคอ jèhp kor |
| – sunburn | – แดดเผา dàet pǒu |
| – an upset stomach | – ท้องเสีย tórng sěa |

## Basic Needs

| I'd like… | ผม♂/ฉัน♀ อยากได้... pǒm♂/cháhn♀ yàrk·dîe… |
|---|---|
| – acetaminophen [paracetamol] | – พาราเซตตามอล par·rar·séht·dtar·môhn |
| – aftershave | – โลชั่นทาหลังโกนหนวด loe·châhn tar lǎhng goen·nòart |
| – antiseptic cream | – ครีมแก้อักเสบ kreem gâe àhk·sèp |
| – aspirin | – แอสไพริน àet·sah·pi·rihn |
| – bandages [plasters] | – ผ้าพันแผล pâr pahn plǎe |
| – a comb | – หวี wěe |
| – condoms | – ถุงยางอนามัย tǔhng·yarng ah·nar·mi |
| – contact lens solution | – น้ำยาแช่คอนแท็คเลนส์ náhm·yar châe kohn·tàk·len |
| – deodorant | – ยาระงับกลิ่นตัว yar rah·ngáhp glìhn·dtoar |
| – a hairbrush | – แปรงแปรงผม bpraeng·pǒm |

| I'd like... | ผม♂/ฉัน♀ อยากได้... pǒm♂/cháhn♀ yàrk•dîe... |
|---|---|
| – ibuprofen | – อีบูโปรเฟน ee•boo•bproc•fen |
| – insect repellent | – ยาทากันแมลง yar tar gahn mah•laeng |
| – lotion | – โลชั่น loe•châhn |
| – a nail file | – ตะไบเล็บ dtah•bi léhp |
| – a pain killer | – ยาแก้ปวด yar•gâe•bpòart |
| – a (disposable) razor | – มีดโกน (ใช้แล้วทิ้ง) mêet•goen (chí láew tíhng) |
| – razor blades | – ใบมีดโกน bi mêet•goen |
| – sanitary napkins [pads] | – ผ้าอนามัย pâr ah•nar•mi |
| – shampoo/ conditioner | – แชมพู/ครีมนวดผม chaem•poo/kreem nôart pǒm |
| – soap | – สบู่ sah•bòo |
| – sunscreen | – ครีมกันแดด kreem gahn dàet |
| – tampons | – ผ้าอนามัยแบบสอด pâr ah•nar•mi bàep•sòrt |
| – tissues | – กระดาษทิชชู่ grah•dàrt tíht•chôo |
| – toilet paper | – กระดาษชำระ grah•dàrt chahm•ráh |
| – a toothbrush | – แปรงสีฟัน bpraeng sěe fahn |
| – toothpaste | – ยาสีฟัน yar sěe fahn |

▶ For baby products, see page 143.

# *Reference*

## Grammar

### Gender

In Thai, the first person pronoun "I" varies by gender: A man would refer to himself as ผม pǒm, a female speaker would say ฉัน

cháhn (or in very formal situation ดิฉัน dih•cháhn). A similar gender distinction applies when ending a statement politely or to say "yes": A man uses ครับ kráhp, while a woman uses ค่ะ kâh.

Most of the time, the subject pronoun—I, pŏm ♂/cháhn ♀; you, kuhn; we, rou, etc.—can be omitted from the sentence.

## Verbs

Verbs are not conjugated in Thai, nor is there a change in tense (present, past, future, etc.). Instead, distinctions between tenses are marked by adverbs and expressions of time, or by the context of the sentence.

A past event can be indicated by the addition of either แล้ว láew (already) after the verb, or of ได้ dî (to get or receive) immediately in front of the verb, to emphasize that the event is completed. However, these are used only sparingly and are not necessary if the past tense is implicit in the context. Sentences beginning with the time expression เมื่อ mûea (when), for example, are automatically considered a past event.

A future or hypothetical event is indicated by the addition of จะ jah (immediately) in front of the verb.

## Nouns

Instead of articles, Thai nouns have classifiers. Common classifiers include:

| | | |
|---|---|---|
| คน | kon | for people |
| ตัว | dtoar | for animals, tables, chairs and items of clothing |
| ลูก | lôok | for fruit, eggs and other round objects |
| ชิ้น | chíhn | meaning a "piece", can be used for items served or sold in pieces |
| ใบ | bi | for fruit, bags and banknotes |
| ฉบับ | chah•bàhp | for letters and newspapers |
| เล่ม | lêhm | for books, candles and knives |

Portions of food and drink are classified according to the dishes and containers in which they are served. Therefore, fried rice would be classified by the word plate, coffee by cup, soup by bowl and so forth:

| | | |
|---|---|---|
| ข้าวผัดจานหนึ่ง | kôw·pàht jarn nueng | one plate of fried rice |
| ก๋วยเตี๋ยวชามหนึ่ง | gŏary·tĕaw charm nueng | one bowl of noodles |

When the number of a certain noun is to be specified, the word order is as follows: noun + number + classifier:

| | | |
|---|---|---|
| รถ+สอง+คัน | rót+sŏrng+kahn | two cars |
| ขวด+สาม+ขวด | kòart+sărm+kòart | three bottles |

## Word Order

Like English, Thai is a subject-verb-object language. For example:

| | | |
|---|---|---|
| เธอซื้อหนังสือ | ter súee năhng·sŭee | She buys books. |

Questions can be formed by putting question words at the end of the affirmative sentences. For example:

1. หรือ rŭee
   เธอซื้อหนังสือหรือ
   ter súee năhng·sŭee rŭee
   Did she buy books?

2. ใช่ไหม chî·mí
   เธอซื้อหนังสือใช่ไหม
   ter súee năhng·sŭee chî·mí
   She buys books, doesn't she?

To negate, place ไม่ได้ mî·dîe before the verb.

เธอไม่ได้ซื้อหนังสือ
ter mî·dîe súee năhng·sŭee
She doesn't buy books.

## Pronouns

Pronouns in Thai can be complicated, as that they can indicate hierarchy, relationship, gender, etc. The pronouns shown in the following table are the most frequently used in normal situations.

| I | ผม♂/ฉัน♀ pŏm♂/cháhn♀ |
|---|---|
| you | คุณ kuhn |
| he | เขา kóu |
| she | เธอ ter |
| it | มัน manh |
| we | เรา rou |
| they | เขา kóu |

## Possessive Pronouns

Place ของ kŏhng before a noun or pronoun to indicate possession, for example:

ของผม♂/ฉัน♀ kŏhng pŏm♂/cháhn♀ (mine)

## Adjectives

An adjective in Thai is placed after the noun to which it refers, for example:

| หมอฉลาด | mŏr chah·làrt | the clever doctor |
|---|---|---|

To add emphasis, some adjectives in Thai can be repeated; note that the tone of the first word may change, for example:

| ช้วยสวย | sóary sŏary | extremely beautiful |
|---|---|---|
| ว้านหวาน | wárn wărn | incredibly sweet |

## Comparative and Superlative

Use กว่า gwàr for the comparative:

| ใหญ่กว่า | yì gwàr | bigger |
| เล็กกว่า | léhk gwàr | smaller |

Use ที่สุด têe·sùht for the superlative:

| ใหญ่ที่สุด | yì têe·sùht | biggest |
| เล็กที่สุด | léhk têe·sùht | smallest |

## Adverbs and Adverbial Expressions

Where an adverb in Thai is placed depends on its function. Adverbs that describe a manner or degree are placed after the verb, for example:

| เขาขับช้า | kóu kàhp chár | He drives <u>slowly</u>. |

Adverbs of time and frequency can be placed before or after the verb, for example:

| เขาจะทำงาน<u>คืนนี้</u> | kóu jah tahm·ngarn <u>kueen née</u> | He will work <u>tonight</u>. |
| <u>คืนนี้</u>เขาจะทำงาน | <u>kueen née</u> kóu jah tahm·ngarn | |

Adverbs of negation precede the verb:

| ผม ♂/ฉัน ♀ <u>ไม่เคย</u>ดื่มเหล้า | pŏm ♂/cháhn ♀ <u>mî·kery</u> dùeem lôu | I <u>never</u> drink alcohol. |

## Numbers

 Thai numbers are mostly used in formal writing. Otherwise, Arabic numbers are commonly used.

# Essential

| 0 | ๐ sǒon |
|---|---|
| 1 | ๑ nùeng |
| 2 | ๒ sǒrng |
| 3 | ๓ sǎrm |
| 4 | ๔ sèe |
| 5 | ๕ hâr |
| 6 | ๖ hòk |
| 7 | ๗ jèht |
| 8 | ๘ bpàet |
| 9 | ๙ gôw |
| 10 | ๑๐ sìhp |
| 11 | ๑๑ sìhp·èht |
| 12 | ๑๒ sìhp sǒrng |
| 13 | ๑๓ sìhp sǎrm |
| 14 | ๑๔ sìhp sèe |
| 15 | ๑๕ sìhp hâr |
| 16 | ๑๖ sìhp hòk |
| 17 | ๑๗ sìhp jèht |
| 18 | ๑๘ sìhp bpàet |
| 19 | ๑๙ sìhp gôw |
| 20 | ๒๐ yêe·sìhp |
| 21 | ๒๑ yêe·sìhp·èht |
| 22 | ๒๒ yêe·sìhp sǒrng |
| 30 | ๓๐ sǎrm sìhp |

| 31 | ๓๑ sǎrm sìhp èht |
| 40 | ๔๐ sèe sìhp |
| 50 | ๕๐ hâr sìhp |
| 60 | ๖๐ hòk sìhp |
| 70 | ๗๐ jèht sìhp |
| 80 | ๘๐ bpàet sìhp |
| 90 | ๙๐ gôw sìhp |
| 100 | ๑๐๐ nùehng róry |
| 101 | ๑๐๑ nùehng róry nùehng |
| 200 | ๒๐๐ sǒrng róry |
| 500 | ๕๐๐ hâr róry |
| 1,000 | ๑๐๐๐ nùeng pahn |
| 10,000 | ๑๐,๐๐๐ nùeng mùeen |
| 1,000,000 | ๑๐๐,๐๐๐ nùeng sǎen |

## Ordinal Numbers

| first | ที่หนึ่ง têe nùeng |
| second | ที่สอง têe sǒrng |
| third | ที่สาม têe sǎrm |
| fourth | ที่สี่ têe sèe |
| fifth | ที่ห้า têe hâr |
| once | ครั้งหนึ่ง/หนึ่งครั้ง kráhng nùeng/nùeng kráhng |
| twice | สองครั้ง sǒrng kráhng |
| three times | สามครั้ง sǎrm kráhng |

## Time

| | |
|---|---|
| What time is it? | ตอนนี้เวลา เท่าไหร่? dtorn·née we·lar tôu·rì |
| It's noon [midday]. | ตอนนี้ เที่ยงวัน dtorn·née têang·wahn |
| At midnight. | เที่ยงคืน têang·kueen |
| From one to two a.m. | ตั้งแต่ตีหนึ่งถึงตีสอง dtâhng·dtàe dtee nùeng tŭeng dtee sŏrng |
| From one to two p.m. | ตั้งแต่บ่ายโมงถึงบ่ายสองโมง dtâhng·dtàe bìe moeng tŭeng bìe sŏrng moeng |
| 3:45 a.m. | ตีสามสี่สิบห้านาที dtee sărm sèe·sìhp·hâr nar·tee |
| 3:45 p.m. | บ่ายสามโมงสี่สิบห้านาที bìe sărm moeng sèe·sìhp·hâr nar·tee |
| 5:30 a.m. | ตีห้าครึ่ง dtee hâr krûeng |
| 5:30 p.m. | บ่ายห้าโมงครึ่ง bìe hâr moeng krûeng |

# Days

## Essential

| Monday | วันจันทร์ wahn jahn |
| Tuesday | วันอังคาร wahn ahng·karn |
| Wednesday | วันพุธ wahn púht |
| Thursday | วันพฤหัสบดี wahn páh·rúe·hàht·sàh·bor·dee |
| Friday | วันศุกร์ wahn sùhk |
| Saturday | วันเสาร์ wahn sŏu |
| Sunday | วันอาทิตย์ wahn ar·tíht |

## Dates

| yesterday | เมื่อวาน mûea·warn |
| today | วันนี้ wahn·née |
| tomorrow | พรุ่งนี้ prûhng·née |
| day | วัน wahn |
| week | สัปดาห์ sàhp·dar |
| month | เดือน duean |
| year | ปี bpee |

## Months

| January | มกราคม mók·gah·rar·kom |
| February | กุมภาพันธ์ guhm·par·pahn |
| March | มีนาคม mee·nar·kom |
| April | เมษายน me·săr·yon |
| May | พฤษภาคม prúet·sah·par·kom |

| June | มิถุนายน míh·tuh·nar·yon |
|------|--------------------------|
| July | กรกฎาคม gàh·ráhk·gah·dar·kom |
| August | สิงหาคม sǐhng·hǎr·kom |
| September | กันยายน kahn·yar·yon |
| October | ตุลาคม dtùh·lar·kom |
| November | พฤศจิกายน prúet·sah·jih·gar·yon |
| December | ธันวาคม tahn·war·kom |

## Seasons

| spring | ฤดูใบไม้ผลิ rúe·doo bi·mí plì |
|--------|------------------------------|
| summer | ฤดูร้อน rúe·doo rórn |
| fall [autumn] | ฤดูใบไม้ร่วง rúe·doo bi·mí rûang |
| winter | ฤดูหนาว rúe·doo nǒw |
| rainy season | ฤดูฝน rúe·doo fǒn |

## Holidays

| January 1, New Year's Day | วันขึ้นปีใหม่ wahn kûehn bpee mì |
|---------------------------|----------------------------------|
| April 6, Chakri Day | วันจักรี wahn jàhk·gree |
| April 13-15, Songkran (Thai New Year) | วันสงกรานต์ wahn sǒng·grarn |
| May 1, Labor Day | วันแรงงาน wahn raeng·ngarn |
| May 5, Coronation Day | วันฉัตรมงคล wahn chàht·trah·mong·kon |
| August 12, H.M. Queen's Birthday (Mother's Day) | วันเฉลิมพระชนมพรรษา สมเด็จพระบรมราชินีนาถ wahn chah·lěrm práh chon·mah·pahn·sǎr sǒm·dèht práh bor·rom·mah·rar·chíh·nee·nârt |
| October 23, Chulalongkorn Day | วันปิยมหาราช wahn bpih·yáh mah·hǎr·rârt |

| December 5, H.M. King's Birthday (National Day) | วันเฉลิมพระชนมพรรษา พระบาทสมเด็จพระเจ้าอยู่หัว wahn chah·lěrm práh·chon·mah·pahn·sǎr pǐah·bàrt sǒm·dèht práh·jôw·yòo·hǒar |
|---|---|
| December 10, Constitution Day | วันรัฐธรรมนูญ wahn ráht·tah·tahm·mah·noon |

## Moveable Holidays

| Buddha Commemoration Day | มาฆบูชา mar·káh boo·char |
|---|---|
| Buddha's Birthday | วิสาขบูชา wíh·sǎr·kàh boo·char |
| Buddha's First Sermon | อาสาฬหบูชา ar·sǎrn·hàh boo·char |
| First Day of Buddhist Lent | เข้าพรรษา kôu pahn·sǎr |
| The Festival of Lights | ลอยกระทง lory grah·tong |

## Conversion Tables ———————————————

| When you know | Multiply by | To find |
|---|---|---|
| ounces | 28.3 | grams |
| pounds | 0.45 | kilograms |
| inches | 2.54 | centimeters |
| feet | 0.3 | meters |
| miles | 1.61 | kilometers |
| square inches | 6.45 | sq. centimeters |
| square feet | 0.09 | sq. meters |
| square miles | 2.59 | sq. kilometers |
| pints (US/Brit) | 0.47/0.56 | liters |
| gallons (US/Brit) | 3.8/4.5 | liters |
| Fahrenheit | 5/9, after -32 | Centigrade |
| Centigrade | 9/5, then +32 | Fahrenheit |

**Mileage**

| | |
|---|---|
| 1 km – 0.62 miles | 50 km – 31 miles |
| 5 km – 3.1 miles | 100 km – 62 miles |
| 10 km – 6.2 miles | |

**Measurement**

| 1 gram | กรัม grahm | 0.035 oz. |
|---|---|---|
| 1 kilogram (kg) | กิโลกรัม (ก.ก.) gih·loe·grahm | 2.2 lb |
| 1 liter (l) | ลิตร (ล.) líht | 1.06 U.S/0.88 Brit. quarts |
| 1 centimeter (cm) | เซ็นติเมตร (ซ.ม.) sehn·dti·mét | 0.4 inch |
| 1 meter (m) | เมตร (ม.) mét | 3.28 feet |
| 1 kilometer (km) | กิโลเมตร (ก.ม.) gih·loe·mét | 0.62 mile |

**Temperature**

| | | |
|---|---|---|
| -40° C – -40° F | -1° C – 30° F | 20° C – 68° F |
| -30° C – -22° F | 0° C – 32° F | 25° C – 77° F |
| -20° C – -4° F | 5° C – 41° F | 30° C – 86° F |
| -10° C – 14° F | 10° C – 50° F | 35° C – 95° F |
| -5° C – 23° F | 15° C – 59° F | |

**Oven Temperature**

| | |
|---|---|
| 100° C – 212° F | 177° C – 350° F |
| 121° C – 250° F | 204° C – 400° F |
| 149° C – 300° F | 260° C – 500° F |

## Useful Websites

www.tourismthailand.org
*Tourism Authority of Thailand*

www2.airportthai.co.th/airportnew/sun/index.asp
*Thai airport information*

www.railway.co.th/English/index.asp
*State Railway of Thailand*

www.bmta.co.th/en/index.php
*Bangkok Mass Transit Authority*

www.bangkokmetro.co.th
*MRT (Mass Rapid Transit) information*

www.bts.co.th/en/index.asp
*BTS (Bangkok Transit System) information*

www.chaophrayaboat.co.th/index.htm
*Chao Praya Express Boat information*

www.bangkoktourist.com
*Bangkok Tourism Division*

www.berlitzpublishing.com
*Berlitz language and travel guides*

# English–Thai Dictionary

## A

**abroad** ต่างประเทศ dtàrng•bprah•têt

**accept** ยอมรับ yorm•ráhp

**access** เข้าถึง kôu•tŭeng

**accident** อุบัติเหตุ uh•bàht•dtih•hèt

**accommodation** ที่พัก têe•pâhk

**accompany** มาด้วย mar dôary

**acetaminophen** พาราเซตตามอล par•rar•séht•dtar•môhn

**across** ตรงข้าม dtrong•kârm

**acupuncture** ฝังเข็ม fǎhng•kěhm

**adapter** ปลั๊กแปลงไฟฟ้า bpláhk bplaeng fi•fár

**additional** เพิ่มเติม pêrm•dterm

**address** ที่อยู่ têe•yòo

**admission charge** ค่าเข้า kâr•kôu

**adult** ผู้ใหญ่ pôo•yì

**after** หลังจาก lǎhng•jàrk

**afternoon** ตอนบ่าย dtorn bìe

**agree** เห็นด้วย hěhn•dôary

**air** (tire) ลม lom; อากาศ ar•gàrt

**air conditioning** แอร์ ae

**air mattress** ที่นอนอัดลม têe•norn àht lom

**airline** สายการบิน sǐe•garn•bihn

**airmail** ไปรษณีย์อากาศ bpri•sah•nee ar•gàrt

**airport** สนามบิน sah•nǎrm•bihn

**airsickness** เมาเครื่องบิน mou krûeang•bihn

**alarm clock** นาฬิกาปลุก nar•li•gar bplùhk

**allergy** ภูมิแพ้ poom•páe

**allow** อนุญาต ah•núh•yârt

**allowance** ค่าใช้จ่าย kâr chí•jie

**almost** เกือบจะ gùeap•jah

**alone** คนเดียว kon•deaw

**already** แล้ว láew

**alter (a garment)** แก้ gâe

**alternate** สลับ sah•làhp

**aluminum foil** กระดาษฟอยล์ grah•dàrt fory

**ambassador** เอกอัครราชทูต èk•àhk•kah•rârt•chah•tôot

**ambulance** รถพยาบาล rót pah•yar•barn

**American** อเมริกัน ah•me•rih•gahn

**amount** จำนวน jahm•noarn

**amusement park** สวนสนุก sǒarn sah•nùhk

**and** และ lá

**anemia** โรคโลหิตจาง rôek loe•hìht jarng

**anesthetic** ยาชา yar•char

**animal** สัตว์ sàht

**antacid** ยาลดกรด yar lót gròt

**antibiotics** ยาปฏิชีวนะ yar bpah•dtih•chee•wah•náh

**antique** ของเก่า kǒrng gòu

**antiseptic cream** ครีมแก้อักเสบ kreem gǎe àhk•sèp

**any** ใด di

**anyone** ใคร kri

**anything** อะไร ah•ri

**apartment** อพาร์ตเมนต์ ah•párt•méhn

**apologize** ขอโทษ kǒr•tôet

**appointment** นัด náht

**approve** ยอมรับ yorm•ráhp

**approximately** ประมาณ bprah•marn

---

| **adj** | adjective | **BE** | British English | **n** | noun |
|---|---|---|---|---|---|
| **v** | verb | | | | |

**area code** รหัสพื้นที่ rah·hàht púeen·têe
**arm** แขน kǎen
**aromatherapy** อโรมาเทราปี ah·roe·mâr te·rar·pêe
**around** รอบ ๆ rôrp·rôrp
**arrivals** ขาเข้า kǎr·kôu
**arrive** มาถึง mar·tǔeng
**art gallery** หอศิลป์ hǒr·sǐhn
**arthritis** โรคไขข้อเสื่อม rôek kǐ·kôr sùeam
**ashtray** ที่เขี่ยบุหรี่ têe kèar buh·rèe
**ask** ถาม tǎrm
**aspirin** แอสไพริน áet·sah·pi·rihn
**assistance** ความช่วยเหลือ kwarm chôary·lǔea
**asthma** โรคหอบหืด rôek hòrp·hùeet
**ATM** เอทีเอ็ม e·tee·ehm
**attack** ∨ ทำร้าย tahm·ríe; n การทำร้าย garn tahm·rie
**attractive** มีเสน่ห์ mee sah·nè
**audio guide** เทปนำเที่ยว tép nahm·têaw
**authentic** แท้ táe
**available** ว่าง wârng
**away** ห่าง hàrng

# B

**baby** เด็กอ่อน dèhk òrn
**baby bottle** ขวดนมเด็ก kòart·nom dèhk
**baby food** อาหารเด็ก ar·hǎrn dèhk
**babysitter** พี่เลี้ยงเด็ก pêe·léang dèhk
**back** หลัง lǎhng
**backache** ปวดหลัง bpòart lǎhng
**backpack** เป้สะพายหลัง bpê sah·pie lǎhng
**bad** เลว lew
**bag** กระเป๋า grah·bpǒu
**baggage [BE]** กระเป๋า grah·bpǒu
**baggage claim** ที่รับกระเป๋า têe ráhp grah·bpǒu
**bakery** ร้านเบเกอรี่ rárn be·ger·rêe
**balcony** ระเบียง rah·beang

**ball** ลูกบอล lôok·bohn
**ballet** บัลเลต์ bahn·lê
**bandage** ผ้าพันแผล pâr pahn plǎe
**bank** ธนาคาร tah·nar·karn
**bar** บาร์ bar
**barber** ร้านตัดผมผู้ชาย rárn dtàht·pǒm pôo·chie
**bargain** ต่อราคา tòr rar·kar
**basement** ชั้นใต้ดิน cháhn tí·dihn
**basket** ตะกร้า dtah·grâr
**basketball** บาสเก็ตบอล bárt·sah·gêht bohn
**bath** อาบน้ำ àrp·nárm
**bathroom** ห้องน้ำ hôhng·nárm
**battery** แบตเตอรี่ bàt·dter·rèe
**be** เป็น bpehn
**beach** ชายหาด chie·hàrt
**beautiful** สวย sǒary
**because** เพราะว่า próh·wâr
**bed** เตียง dteang
**bedding** เครื่องนอน krûeang·norn
**bedroom** ห้องนอน hôhng·norn
**before** ก่อน gòrn
**begin** เริ่ม rêrm
**behind** หลัง lǎhng
**belong** เป็นของ bpehn kǒhng
**belt** เข็มขัด kěhm·kàht
**bet** พนัน pah·nahn
**between** ระหว่าง rah·wàrng
**beware** ระวัง rah·wahng
**bicycle** จักรยาน jàhk·grah·yarn
**big** ใหญ่ yì
**bike path** ทางจักรยาน tarng jàhk·grah·yarn
**bikini** บิกินี่ bih·gih·nêe
**bill** บิล bihn
**binoculars** กล้องส่องทางไกล glôhng sòng tarng gli
**bird** นก nók

**birthday** วันเกิด wahn•gèrt
**bite** กัด gàht
**blanket** ผ้าห่ม pâr•hòm
**bleed** เลือดออก lûeat•òrk
**blister** แผลพุพอง plăe púh•porng
**blood** เลือด lûeat
**blood pressure** ความดันเลือด kwarm•dahn lûeat
**blouse** เสื้อผู้หญิง sûea pôo•yĭhng
**board** กระดาน grah•darn
**boarding card** ตั๋วขึ้นเครื่อง dtŏar kûen krûeang
**boat trip** ทัวร์ทางเรือ toar tarng ruea
**bone** กระดูก grah•dòok
**book** หนังสือ năhng•sŭee
**bookstore** ร้านหนังสือ rárn năhng•sŭee
**boots** รองเท้าบูท rorng•tów bóot
**born** เกิด gèrt
**borrow** ยืม yueem
**botanical garden** สวนพฤกษศาสตร์ sŏarn prúek•sah•sàrt
**bother** รบกวน róp•goarn
**bottle** ขวด kòart
**bottle opener** ที่เปิดขวด têe bpèrt kòart
**bowl** ชาม charm
**box** กล่อง glòhng
**boxing** ชกมวย chók•moary
**boy** เด็กผู้ชาย dèhk•pôo•chie
**bra** ยกทรง yók•song
**bracelet** สร้อยข้อมือ sôry kôr•muee
**brake** v หยุด yùht; n เบรก brèk
**break** แตก dtàek
**breakfast** อาหารเช้า ar•hăhn chów
**breast** หน้าอก nâr•òk
**breastfeed** ให้นม hî•nom
**breathe** หายใจ hĭe•ji
**bridge** สะพาน sah•parn
**bring** เอามา ou•mar
**British (person)** คนอังกฤษ kon ahng•grìht

**brochure** แผ่นพับ pàen•páhp
**broken** เสีย sĕa
**broom** ไม้กวาด mie•gwàrt
**browse** เปิดดู bpèrt•doo
**bruise** รอยฟกช้ำ rory fók•cháhm
**bucket** ถัง tăhng
**Buddha image** พระพุทธรูป práh•púht•tah•rôop
**bug** แมลง mah•laeng
**build** สร้าง sârng
**building** ตึก dtùek; อาคาร ar•karn
**burn** ไหม้ mî
**bus** รถเมล์ rót•me
**bus station** สถานีขนส่ง sah•tăr•nee kŏn•sòng
**bus stop** ป้ายรถเมล์ bpîe rót•me
**bus ticket** ตั๋วรถเมล์ dtŏar rót•me
**business** ธุรกิจ túh•ráh•gìht
**business card** นามบัตร narm•bàht
**business center** ศูนย์บริการทางธุรกิจ sŏon bor•rih•garn tarng túh•ráh•gìht
**business class** ชั้นธุรกิจ cháhn túh•ráh•gìht
**business district** ย่านธุรกิจ yârn túh•ráh•gìht
**busy** ยุ่ง yûhng
**but** แต่ dtàe
**button (clothing)** กระดุม grah•duhm; **(device)** ปุ่ม bpùhm
**buy** ซื้อ súee
**by** โดย doey
**bye** สวัสดี sah•wàht•dee

## C

**cafe** ร้านกาแฟ rárn gar•fae
**calendar** ปฏิทิน bpah•dtìh•tihn
**call (phone)** โทรศัพท์ toe•rah•sàhp; **(summon)** เรียก rêak
**camera** กล้องถ่ายรูป glôhng tìe•rôop

camp ตั้งแคมป์ dtâhng·káem

campsite ที่ตั้งแคมป์ têe dtâhng·káem

can กระป๋อง grah·bpŏhng

can opener ที่เปิดกระป๋อง têe bpèrt grah·bpŏhng

canal คลอง klorng

cancel ยกเลิก yók·lêrk

cancer มะเร็ง mah·rehng

candle เทียน tean

candy store ร้านขายขนม rárn kĭe kah·nŏm

canoe เรือแคนู rua kae·noo

car รถยนต์ rót·yon

car hire [BE] รถเช่า rót·chôu

car park [BE] ที่จอดรถ têe jòrt rót

car rental รถเช่า rót·chôu

car seat ที่นั่งในรถสำหรับเด็ก têe·nâhng ni rót sǎhm·ràhp dèhk

carafe เหยือก yùeak

card บัตร bàht

careful ระวัง rah·wahng

carpet พรม prom

carry-on luggage กระเป๋าถือขึ้นเครื่อง grah·bpŏu tǔee kûen krûeang

cart รถเข็น rót·kěhn

carton (of cigarettes) กล่อง glòhng

cash v ขึ้นเงิน kûen·ngern; n เงินสด ngern·sòt

cash register เครื่องคิดเงิน krûeang kít·ngern

cashier แคชเชียร์ káet·chea

casino คาสิโน kar·sĭh·noe

catch จับ jàhp

cathedral โบสถ์ฝรั่ง bòet fah·ràhng

caution ระมัดระวัง rah·máht rah·wahng

cave ถ้ำ tǎhm

CD ซีดี see·dee

CD player เครื่องเล่นซีดี krûeang lêhn see·dee

cell phone โทรศัพท์มือถือ toe·rah·sàhp muee·tǔee

cemetery สุสาน sùh·sǎrn

ceramics เซรามิก se·rar·mihk

certificate ใบรับรอง bi ráhp·rorng

change v เปลี่ยน bplèan; (money) v แลกเงิน lâek ngern; n เงินทอน ngern·torn

charcoal ถ่าน tàrn

charge v คิดเงิน kíht·ngern; n ค่า kâr

cheap ถูก tòok

check n (bank) เช็ค chéhk; v ตรวจ dtròart; v (luggage) ฝากกระเป๋า fàrk grah·bpŏu

check in เช็คอิน chéhk·ihn

check out เช็คเอาท์ chéhk·óu

check-in desk โต๊ะเช็คอิน dtó chéhk·ihn

checking account บัญชีกระแสรายวัน bahn·chee grah·sǎe rie·wahn

chemical toilet ส้วมเคมี sôarm ke·mee

chemist [BE] ร้านขายยา rárn kĭe yar

cheque [BE] เช็ค chéhk

chest หน้าอก nâr·òk

child เด็ก dèhk

child seat ที่นั่งเด็ก têe·nâhng dèhk

children's menu เมนูสำหรับเด็ก me·noo sǎhm·ràhp dèhk

children's portion ขนาดสำหรับเด็ก kah·nàrt sǎhm·ràhp dèhk

choose เลือก lûeak

church โบสถ์ bòet

cigar ซิการ์ sĭh·gâr

cigarette บุหรี่ bùh·rèe

cinema [BE] โรงหนัง roeng·nǎng

clean adj สะอาด sah·àrt; v ทำความสะอาด tahm kwarm sah·àrt

clearance (sale) ลดราคา lót rar·kar

cliff หน้าผา nâr·pǎr

cling film [BE] ฟิล์มถนอมอาหาร feem tah·nŏrm ar·hǎrn

**clinic** คลินิก klee•nihk

**clock** นาฬิกา nar•lih•gar

**close (shut)** ปิด bpiht; **(near)** ใกล้ glî

**clothes shop [BE]** ร้านขายเสื้อผ้า rárn kǐe sûea•pâr

**clothing store** ร้านขายเสื้อผ้า rárn kǐe sûea•pâr

**club** คลับ klàhp

**coast** ชายฝั่ง chie•fàhng

**coat** เสื้อโค้ท sûea•kóet

**coat check** ที่รับฝากเสื้อโค้ท têe ráhp fàrk sûea•kóet

**code** รหัส rah•hàht

**coin** เหรียญ rěan

**cold (weather)** adj หนาว nǒw; n หวัด wàht

**collapse** ล้ม lóm

**colleague** เพื่อนร่วมงาน pûean•rôarm•ngarn

**collect (call)** โทรเก็บเงินปลายทาง toe gèhp ngern bplie tarng

**color** สี sěe

**comb** หวี wěe

**come** มา mar

**commission** ค่าบริการ kâr bor•rih•garn

**company** บริษัท bor•rih•sàht

**compartment** ที่ใส่ของ têe sì kǒrng

**computer** คอมพิวเตอร์ kohm•pihw•dtêr

**concert** คอนเสิร์ต kohn•sèrt

**conditioner (hair)** ครีมนวดผม kreem nôart pǒm

**condom** ถุงยางอนามัย tǔhng•yarng ah•nar•mi

**conductor (bus)** กระเป๋ารถ grah•bpǒu rót

**conference** การประชุมสัมมนา garn bprah•chuhm sǎhm•mah•nar

**confirm** ยืนยัน yueen•yahn

**congratulations** ขอแสดงความยินดี kǒr sah•daeng kwarm yihn•dee

**connect** เชื่อมต่อ chûeam•dtòr

**connection** การเชื่อมต่อ garn chûeam•dtòr

**conscious** รู้สึกตัว róo•sùek dtoar

**conservation area** เขตอนุรักษ์ kèt àh•nú•ráhk

**constant** คงที่ kong•têe

**constipation** อาการท้องผูก ar•garn tórng•pòok

**consulate** กงสุล gong•sǔhn

**consult** ปรึกษา bprùek•sǎr

**contact** v ติดต่อ dtiht•dtòr; n การติดต่อ garn dtiht•dtòr

**contact lens** คอนแท็คเลนส์ korn•tàk•lehn

**contact lens solution** น้ำยาคอนแท็คเลนส์ náhm•yar kohn•tàk•lehn

**contraceptive** คุมกำเนิด kuhm•gahm•nèrt

**control** ควบคุม kôarp•kuhm

**convention** การประชุม garn bprah•chuhm

**convention hall** ห้องคอนเวนชั่น hôhng kohn•wen•châhn

**cook** v ทำอาหาร tahm ar•hǎrn; n คนครัว kon•kroar

**cool** เย็น yehn

**copy** ทำสำเนา tahm sǎhm•nou

**corkscrew** ที่เปิดจุกก๊อก têe bpèrt jùhk•góhk

**corner** มุม muhm

**correct** ถูกต้อง took•dtôhng

**cosmetic** เครื่องสำอาง krûeang sǎhm•arng

**cost** n ค่าใช้จ่าย kâr chí•jie; v ราคา rar•kar

**cot** เตียงพับ dteang•páhp

**cottage** กระท่อม grah•tôhm

**cotton** ผ้าฝ้าย pâr fie

**cough** ไอ i

**counter** เคาน์เตอร์ kóu•dtêr

**country** ประเทศ bprah•têt

**country code** รหัสประเทศ rah•hàht bprah•têt

**course** วิชา wih•char

**cover charge** ค่าบริการต่อหัว kâr
bor·rih·garn dtòr hǔa

**craft shop** ร้านขายงานฝีมือ rárn kǐe
ngarn·fěe·muee

**cramp (sports)** ตะคริว dtah·kríhw;
**(period)** ปวดประจำเดือน bpòart
bprah·jahm·duean

**credit card** บัตรเครดิต bàht kre·diht

**crib** เปลเด็ก bple dèhk

**crowd** ฝูงคน fǒong·kon

**cruise** ล่องเรือ lôhng·ruea

**crutch** ไม้เท้า mí·tów

**crystal** คริสตัล kríhs·dtâhn

**cup** ถ้วย tôary

**currency** เงิน ngern

**currency exchange office**
ที่รับแลกเงิน têe ráhp lâek ngern

**curtain** ผ้าม่าน pâr·mârn

**customer service** บริการลูกค้า
bor·rih·garn lôok·kár

**customs** ศุลกากร sǔhn·lah·gar·gorn

**cut** v (knife) บาด bàrt; n บาดแผล
bàrt·plǎe

**cute** น่ารัก nâr·ráhk

# D

**daily** รายวัน rie·wahn

**damage** เสียหาย sěa·hǐe

**damp** ชื้น chúeen

**dance** เต้นรำ dtêhn·rahm

**dance club** คลับเต้นรำ klàhp dtêhn·rahm

**dangerous** อันตราย ahn·dtah·rie

**dark** มืด mûeet

**day** วัน wahn

**day trip** ทัวร์วันเดียว toar wahn deaw

**dead** ตาย dtie

**deaf** หูหนวก hǒo·nòark

**deck chair** เก้าอี้ผ้าใบ gôu·ee pâr·bi

**declare** แสดงรายการสิ่งของ sah·daeng
rie·garn sìhng·kǒrng

**decorative** ตกแต่ง dtok·dtàng

**deep** ลึก lúek

**degree** องศา ong·sǎr

**delay** ช้า chár

**delete** ลบ lóp

**delicious** อร่อย ah·ròhy

**deliver** ส่ง sòng

**delivery** การส่ง garn·sòng

**dental floss** ไหมขัดฟัน mǐ kàht fahn

**dentist** หมอฟัน mǒr fahn

**denture** ฟันปลอม fahn bplorm

**deodorant** ยาระงับกลิ่นตัว yar rah·ngáhp
glìhn·dtoar

**depart** จาก jàrk

**department store** ห้างสรรพสินค้า hârng
sàhp·pah·sǐhn·kár

**departure gate** ประตูทางออกขึ้นเครื่อง
bprah·dtoo tarng·òrk kûen krûeang

**departures** ขาออก kǎr·òrk

**deposit** v ฝากเงิน fàrk ngern; n เงินมัดจำ
ngern máht·jahm

**describe** อธิบาย ah·tíh·bie

**destination** ปลายทาง bplie·tarng

**detail** รายละเอียด rie·lah·èat

**detergent** ผงซักฟอก pǒng·sáhk·fôrk

**detour** ทางเบี่ยง tarng·bèang

**develop** พัฒนา páht·tah·nar

**diabetes** โรคเบาหวาน rôek bou·wǎrn

**diabetic** adj เบาหวาน bou·wǎrn;
n คนเป็นโรคเบาหวาน kon bpehn rôek
bou·wǎrn

**dial (phone)** กด gòt

**diaper** ผ้าอ้อม pâr·ôrm

**diarrhea** ท้องร่วง tórng·rôarng

**dice** v หั่น hàhn; n ลูกเต๋า lôok·dtǒu

**dictionary** พจนานุกรม
pót·jah·nar·núh·grom

**diesel** ดีเซล dee·sen

**diet** v ควบคุมอาหาร kôarp•kuhm ar•hǎrn

**difficult** ยาก yârk

**digital** ดิจิตอล dih•jih•dtôhn

**dine** กินอาหาร gihn ar•hǎrn

**dining car** รถเสบียง rót sah•beang

**dining room** ห้องอาหาร hôhng ar•hǎrn

**dinner** อาหารเย็น ar•hǎrn yehn

**direct** adj ตรง dtrong; v กำกับ gahm•gàhp

**direction** ทิศ tíht

**director (company)** ผู้อำนวยการ pôo•ahm•noary•garn

**directory (phone)** สมุดโทรศัพท์ sàh•mùht toe•rah•sàhp

**dirty** สกปรก sòk•grah•bpròk

**disabled** adj พิการ pih•garn; n คนพิการ kon pih•garn

**disconnect** ตัดการเชื่อมต่อ dtàht garn chûeam•dtòr

**discount** ส่วนลด sòarn•lót

**dish** จาน jarn

**dishwasher** เครื่องล้างจาน krûeang lárng jarn

**dishwashing liquid** น้ำยาล้างจาน náhm•yar lárng jarn

**display case** ตู้โชว์ tôo•choe

**disposable** ใช้แล้วทิ้ง chí láew tíhng

**dissolve** ละลาย lah•lie

**distance** ระยะทาง ráh•yáh•tarng

**disturb** รบกวน róp•goarn

**dive** ดำน้ำ dahm•nárm

**diving equipment** อุปกรณ์ดำน้ำ ùhp•bpah•gorn dahm•nárm

**divorce** หย่า yàr

**dizzy** เวียนศีรษะ wean sěe•sàh

**do** ทำ tahm

**dock** อู่เรือ òo•ruea

**doctor** หมอ mǒr

**dog** สุนัข suh•náhk

**doll** ตุ๊กตา dtúhk•gah•dtar

**dollar** ดอลลาร์ dohn•lâr

**domestic** ในประเทศ ni bprah•têht

**donation** เงินบริจาค ngern bor•rih•jàrk

**door** ประตู bprah•dtoo

**dosage (medicine)** ขนาดรับประทาน kah•nàrt ráhp•bprah•tarn

**double** คู่ kôo

**double room** ห้องคู่ hôhng kôo

**downstairs** ชั้นล่าง cháhn lârng

**downtown** ย่านใจกลางเมือง yârn ji•glarng mueang

**dress** ชุดกระโปรง chúht grah•bproeng

**drink** v ดื่ม dùeem; n เครื่องดื่ม krûeang•dùeem

**drip** หยด yòt

**drive** ขับ kàhp

**driver** คนขับ kon kàhp

**driver's license** ใบขับขี่ bi•kàhp•kèe

**drown** จมน้ำ jom nárm

**drowsy** ง่วง ngôarng

**drugstore** ร้านขายยา rárn kǐe yar

**dry** adj แห้ง hâeng

**dry clean** ซักแห้ง sáhk•hâeng

**dry cleaner** ร้านซักแห้ง rárn sáhk•hâeng

**dummy [BE]** จุกนม jùhk•nom

**during** ระหว่าง rah•wàrng

**duty (tax)** ภาษี par•sěe

**duty-free** ร้านค้าปลอดภาษี rárn•kár bplòrt par•sěe

# E

**ear** หู hǒo

**earache** ปวดหู bpòart hǒo

**earrings** ตุ้มหู dtûhm•hǒo

**east** ทิศตะวันออก tíht dtah•wahn•òrk

**easy** ง่าย ngîe

**eat** กิน gihn

**economy class** ชั้นประหยัด cháhn bprah•yàht

**electrical outlet** ปลั๊กไฟ bpláhk•fi

electronic ไฟฟ้า fi·fár

elevator ลิฟต์ lihp

e-mail อีเมล์ ee·mew

e-mail address อีเมล์แอดเดรส ee·mew áht·drét

embassy สถานทูต sah·tárn·tôot

emergency ฉุกเฉิน chùhk·chěrn

emergency brake เบรคฉุกเฉิน brèk chùhk·chěrn

emergency exit ทางออกฉุกเฉิน tarng·òrk chùhk·chěrn

emergency service บริการฉุกเฉิน bor·rih·garn chùhk·chěrn

empty ว่าง wârng

end v จบ jòp; n ปลาย bplie

engaged หมั้น mâhn

England (ประเทศ)อังกฤษ (bprah·têt) ahng·griht

English (language) ภาษาอังกฤษ par·sǎr ahng·griht; (person) คนอังกฤษ kon ahng·griht

engrave สลัก sah·làhk

enjoy สนุก sah·nùhk

enlarge ขยาย kah·yǐe

enough พอ por

entrance ทางหน้า tarng·kôu

entry visa วีซ่าเข้าประเทศ wee·sâr kôu bprah·têt

envelope ซองจดหมาย sorng·jòt·mǐe

equipment เครื่องมือ krûeang·muee

error ข้อผิดพลาด kôr·piht·plârt

escalator บันไดเลื่อน bahn·di·lûean

essential จำเป็น jahm·bpehn

e-ticket ตั๋วอิเล็กทรอนิกส์ dtǒar ee·léhk·tror·nihk

Eurocheque ยูโรเช็ค yoo·roe chéhk

evening ตอนเย็น dtorn·yehn

event เหตุการณ์ hèt·garn

every ทุก túhk

exact แน่นอน nâe·norn

examination การสอบ garn·sòrp

example ตัวอย่าง dtoar·yàrng

except ยกเว้น yók·wéhn

excess luggage กระเป๋าเกิน grah·bpǒu gern

exchange แลกเปลี่ยน lâek·bplèan

exchange rate อัตราแลกเปลี่ยน àht·dtrar lâek·bplèan

excursion ทัวร์ระยะสั้น toar rah·yáh sâhn

exhausted หมดแรง mòt raeng

exit v ออก òrk; n ทางออก tarng·òrk

expensive แพง paeng

express mail ไปรษณีย์ด่วน bpri·sah·nee dòarn

extension (phone) เบอร์ต่อ ber dtòr

extra เพิ่ม pêrm

eye ตา dtar

eyebrow คิ้ว kíhw

fabric เนื้อผ้า núea·pâr

face หน้า nâr

facility สถานที่ sah·tárn·têe

faint เป็นลม bpehn·lom

family ครอบครัว krôrp·kroar

famous มีชื่อเสียง mee chûee·sěang

fan พัดลม páht·lom

far ไกล gli

farm ฟาร์ม farm

fast เร็ว rehw

fast food อาหารจานด่วน ar·hǎrn jarn dòarn

faucet ก๊อกน้ำ góhk·nárm

faulty บกพร่อง bòk·prôhng

favorite ที่ชอบ têe chôrp

fax แฟ็กซ์ fàk

fax machine เครื่องแฟ็กซ์ krûeang fàk

fax number เบอร์แฟ็กซ์ ber fàk

feature รูปแบบ rôop·baep

feed ป้อน bpôrn

feeding bottle [BE] ขวดนม kòart•nom

feel รู้สึก róo•sùek

female เพศหญิง pêt•yĭhng

ferry เรือข้ามฟาก ruea kârm•fârk

fever ไข้ kî

few น้อย nóry; (a few) ไม่กี่ mî•gèe

field ทุ่ง tûhng

fight ต่อสู้ dtòr•sôo

fill เติม dterm

fill out กรอก gròrk

fill up เติมให้เต็ม dterm hî dtehm

filling (dental) ที่อุดฟัน têe•ùht•fahn

film หนัง năhng

find หา hăr

fine (health) สบายดี sah•bie dee

finger นิ้ว níhw

fire ไฟ fi

fire alarm สัญญาณไฟไหม้ săhn•yarn fi•mî

fire escape ทางหนีไฟ tarng nêe fi

fire exit ทางหนีไฟ tarng nêe fi

fire extinguisher ถังดับเพลิง tăhng dàhp•plerng

first ที่หนึ่ง têe nùeng

first class ชั้นหนึ่ง cháhn nùeng

fishing ตกปลา dtòk•bplar

fit พอดี por•dee

fitting room ห้องลองเสื้อผ้า hôhng lorng sûea•pâr

fix (repair) ซ่อม sôhm

flash (camera) แฟลช flàt

flashlight ไฟฉาย fi•chĭe

flat [BE] (apartment) แฟลต flàt

flavor รสชาติ rót•chârt

flea market ตลาดนัด dtah•làrt náht

flight เที่ยวบิน têaw•bihn

flight attendant พนักงานต้อนรับ pah•náhk•ngarn dtôrn•ráhp

flight number เที่ยวบินที่ têaw•bihn têe

floor (level) ชั้น cháhn

flower ดอกไม้ dòrk•mie

flu ไข้หวัดใหญ่ kî•wàht•yì

flush (toilet) กดชักโครก gòt cháhk•krôek

fly บิน bihn

fog หมอก mòrk

follow ตาม dtarm

food อาหาร ar•hărn

food poisoning อาหารเป็นพิษ ar•hărn bpehn•píht

foot เท้า tów

football [BE] ฟุตบอล fúht•bohn

footpath [BE] ทางเท้า tarng•tów

for เพื่อ pêua

for sale สำหรับขาย săhm•ràhp kĭe

foreign ต่างชาติ dtarng•chârt

forest ป่า bpàr

forget ลืม lueem

fork ส้อม sôhm

form แบบฟอร์ม bàep•form

formal dress ชุดเป็นทางการ chúht bpehn tarng•garn

formula (baby) นมผงเด็ก nom•pŏng•dèhk

fountain น้ำพุ nárm•púh

fracture ร้าว rárw

free ว่าง wârng

freezer ตู้แช่แข็ง dtôo•châe•kăeng

frequent บ่อย bòhy

fresh สด sòt

friend เพื่อน pûean

from จาก jàrk

front ด้านหน้า dârn•nâr

frying pan กระทะ grah•táh

fuel น้ำมัน náhm•mahn

full เต็ม dtehm

fun สนุก sah•nùhk

funny ตลก dtah•lòk

furniture เฟอร์นิเจอร์ fer•nih•jêr

## G

**gallery** หอศิลป์ hŏr•sĭn

**game** เกม gem

**garage** โรงรถ roeng•rót

**garbage bag** ถุงใส่ขยะ tŭhng sì kah•yàh

**garden** สวน sŏarn

**gas** เบนซิน ben•sihn

**gas station** ปั๊มน้ำมัน bpáhm náhm•mahn

**gate** ประตู bprah•dtoo

**gauze** ผ้ากอซ pâr•górt

**gear** เกียร์ gear

**genuine** แท้ táe

**get off (bus, train, etc.)** ลง long

**gift** ของฝาก kŏrng•fàrk

**gift store** ร้านกิฟต์ช็อป rárn gíp•chòhp

**girl** เด็กหญิง dèhk•yĭhng

**give** ให้ hî

**glass** แก้ว gâew

**glasses (optical)** แว่นตา wâen•dtar

**gloves** ถุงมือ tŭhng•muee

**go** ไป bpi

**gold** ทอง torng

**golf** กอล์ฟ górp

**golf club** ไม้กอล์ฟ mí•górp

**golf course** สนามกอล์ฟ sah•nărm górp

**good** ดี dee

**goodbye** สวัสดี sah•wàht•dee

**gram** กรัม grahm

**grass** หญ้า yâr

**Great Britain** สหราชอาณาจักร sah•hàh•rârt•chah•ar•nar•jahk

**grocery store** ร้านขายของชำ rárn kĭe kŏrng•chahm

**group** กลุ่ม glùhm

**guarantee** รับประกัน ráhp bprah•gahn

**guesthouse** เกสต์เฮาส์ gét•hóus

**guide (person)** ไกด์ gí

**guide book** หนังสือนำเที่ยว năhng•sŭee nahm•têaw

**guide dog** สุนัขนำทาง sùh•náhk nahm tarng

**guided tour** ทัวร์นำเที่ยว toar nahm•têaw

**guided walk** ทัวร์เดินนำเที่ยว toar dern nahm•têaw

**guitar** กีตาร์ gee•dtâr

**gym** โรงยิม roeng•yihm

**gynecologist** สูตินรีแพทย์ sŏo•dtih•nah•ree•pâet

## H

**hair** ผม pŏm

**hairbrush** แปรงแปรงผม bpraeng bpraeng•pŏm

**hairdresser** ช่างทำผม chârng tahm•pŏm

**halal** ฮาลาล har•larn

**half** ครึ่ง krûeng

**hammer** ฆ้อน kórn

**hand** มือ muee

**hand luggage** กระเป๋าถือ grah•bpŏu tŭee

**handbag [BE]** กระเป๋าถือ grah•bpŏu tŭee

**handicapped** *adj* พิการ píh•garn; *n* **(person)** คนพิการ kon píh•garn

**handicrafts** หัตถกรรม hàht•tah•gahm

**hanger** ไม้แขวนเสื้อ mí•kwăen•sûea

**happy** มีความสุข mee kwarm•sùhk

**harbor** ท่าเรือ târ•ruea

**hard** แข็ง kăng

**hardware store** ร้านขายเครื่องมืออุปกรณ์ rárn kĭe krûeang•muee ùhp•bpah•gorn

**hat** หมวก mòark

**have** มี mee

**hay fever** โรคแพ้อากาศ rôek páe•ar•gàrt

**head** หัว hŏar

**headache** ปวดหัว bpòart•hŏar

**health** สุขภาพ sùhk•kah•pârp

**health food store** ร้านขายอาหารสุขภาพ rárn kǐe ar·hǎrn sùhk·kah·pârp

**health insurance** ประกันสุขภาพ bprah·gahn sùhk·kah·pârp

**hear** ได้ยิน dî·yin

**hearing aid** เครื่องช่วยฟัง krûeang·chôary·fahng

**hearing impaired** พิการทางหู pih·garn tarng·hǒo

**heart** หัวใจ hǔa·ji

**heart attack** หัวใจวาย hǔa·ji wary

**heart condition** โรคหัวใจ rôek hǔa·ji

**heat** ความร้อน kwarm·rórn

**heavy** หนัก nàhk

**heel** ส้น sôn

**height (person)** ความสูง kwarm·sǒong

**hello** สวัสดี sah·wàht·dee; **(phone)** ฮัลโหล hahn·lǒe

**helmet** หมวกนิรภัย mòark níh·ráh·pi

**help** n ความช่วยเหลือ kwarm chôary·lǔea; v ช่วย chôary; **(request)** ช่วยด้วย chôary·dôary

**here** ที่นี่ têe·nêe

**high** สูง sǒong

**highchair** เก้าอี้เด็ก gôu·êe dèhk

**highway** ทางหลวง tarng·lǒarng

**hike** เดินป่า dern·bpàr

**hill** เนินเขา nern·kǒu

**hire** เช่า chôu

**hold** ถือ tǔee

**hole** รู roo

**holiday [BE]** วันหยุด wan yùht

**home** บ้าน bârn

**homemade** ทำเอง tahm·eng

**honeymoon** ฮันนีมูน hahn·nee·moon

**horn (car)** แตร dtrae

**horse** ม้า már

**horse racing** แข่งม้า kàeng már

**horseback riding** ขี่ม้า kèe·már

**horsetrack** ลู่ม้าวิ่ง lôo már wîhng

**hospital** โรงพยาบาล roeng pah·yar·barn

**hot** adj ร้อน rórn; **(spicy)** เผ็ด pèht

**hotel** โรงแรม roeng·raem

**hour** ชั่วโมง chôar·moeng

**house** บ้าน bârn

**how** ยังไง yahng·ngi

**how many** เท่าไหร่ tôu·rì

**how much** เท่าไหร่ tôu·rì

**hug** กอด gòrt

**hungry** หิว hǐhw

**hunt** ล่า lâr

**hurry** รีบ rêep

**hurt** เจ็บ jèhp

## I

**ibuprofen** อีบูโปรเฟน ee·boo·bproe·fen

**identification** บัตรประจำตัว bàht bprah·jahm·dtoar

**ill [BE]** ไม่สบาย mî sah·bie

**illegal** ผิดกฎหมาย piht gòt·mǐe

**imitation (fake)** ของเลียนแบบ kǒrng lean·bàep

**important** สำคัญ sǎhm·kahn

**improve** ปรับปรุง bpràhp·bpruhng

**in** ใน ni

**include** รวม roarm

**indigestion** อาหารไม่ย่อย ar·hǎrn mî yôhy

**indoor pool** สระว่ายน้ำในร่ม sàh wîe·nárm ni·rôm

**inexpensive** ไม่แพง mî paeng

**infection** การติดเชื้อ garn dtiht·chúea

**inflammation** อาการอักเสบ ar·garn àhk·sèp

**informal** ไม่เป็นทางการ mî bpehn tarng·garn

**information** ข้อมูล kôr·moon

**information desk** ประชาสัมพันธ์ bprah·char·sǎhm·pahn

injection ฉีดยา chèet yar

injure บาดเจ็บ bàrt∙jèhp

innocent บริสุทธิ์ bor∙rih∙sùht

insect แมลง mah∙laeng

insect bite แมลงกัดต่อย mah∙laeng gàht dtòhy

insect repellent ยากันแมลง yar gahn mah∙laeng

insert แทรก sâek

inside ข้างใน kârng∙ni

insist ยืนกราน yueen∙grarn

insomnia นอนไม่หลับ norn∙mî∙làhp

instant messenger
โปรแกรมส่งข้อความ bproe∙graem sòng kôr∙kwarm

instead แทนที่ taen∙têe

instructions คำสั่ง kahm∙sàhng

instructor ผู้สอน pôo∙sŏrn

insulin อินซูลิน ihn∙soo∙lihn

insurance ประกันภัย bprah∙gahn∙pi

interest (hobby) ความสนใจ kwarm sŏn∙ji

international ระหว่างประเทศ rah∙wàrng bprah∙têt

International Student Card
บัตรนักศึกษาสากล bàht náhk∙sùek∙săr săr∙gon

internet อินเตอร์เน็ต ihn∙dter∙nèht

internet cafe อินเตอร์เน็ตคาเฟ่ ihn∙dter∙nèht kar∙fê

internet service บริการอินเตอร์เน็ต bor∙rih∙garn ihn∙dter∙nèht

interpreter ล่าม lârm

intersection สี่แยก sèe∙yâek

introduce แนะนำ ná∙nahm

invite เชิญ chern

iron *n* เตารีด dtou∙rêet; *v* รีด rêet

itch คัน kahn

itemized แยกตามรายการ yâek dtarm rie∙garn

jacket เสื้อแจ็กเก็ต sûea ják∙gèht

jar ขวด kòart

jaw ขากรรไกร kăr gahn∙gri

jazz แจส jáet

jeans ยีนส์ yeen

jet lag เจ็ทแล็ก jéht∙làk

jet-ski เจ็ทสกี jéht sah∙gee

jeweler ร้านขายเครื่องประดับ rárn kĭe krûeang bprah∙dàhp

jewelry เครื่องประดับ krûeang bprah∙dàhp

job งาน ngarn

join ต่อ dtòr

joke เรื่องตลก rûeang dtah∙lôk

journey การเดินทาง garn dern∙tarng

keep เก็บ gèhp

keep out ห้ามเข้า hârm kôu

key กุญแจ guhn∙jae

key card คีย์การ์ด kee∙gárt

key ring พวงกุญแจ poarng guhn∙jae

kiddie pool สระเด็ก sàh dèhk

kidney ไต dti

kilogram กิโลกรัม gih∙loe grahm

kilometer กิโลเมตร gih∙loe mét

kind *adj* ใจดี ji∙dee; (type) ประเภท bprah∙pêt

kiss จูบ jòop

kitchen ห้องครัว hôhng∙kroar

kitchen foil [BE] กระดาษฟอยล์ grah∙dàrt fory

knee เข่า kòu

knife มีด mêet

knock เคาะ kóh

know รู้จัก róo∙jàhk

kosher โคเชอร์ koe∙chêr

# L

**label** ป้าย bpîe

**lace** ผ้าลูกไม้ pâr lôok•míe

**lactose intolerant** กินนมไม่ได้ gihn nohm mî dîe

**ladder** บันได bahn•di

**lake** ทะเลสาบ tah•le•sàrp

**lamp** โคมไฟ koem•fi

**land** ที่ดิน têe•dihn

**lane** เลน len

**large** ใหญ่ yì

**last (previous)** ที่แล้ว têe•láew; **(final)** สุดท้าย sùht•tie

**late** สาย sǐe

**launderette [BE]** ร้านซักรีด rárn sáhk•rêet

**laundromat** ร้านซักรีด rárn sáhk•rêet

**laundry service** บริการซักรีด bor•rih•garn sáhk•rêet

**lawyer** ทนายความ tah•nie•kwarm

**laxative** ยาระบาย yar rah•bie

**lead** นำ nahm

**leader (group)** ผู้นำ pôo•nahm

**learn** เรียน rean

**leather** หนัง nǎhng

**leave** v ออกจาก òrk•jàrk; **(deposit)** ฝากไว้ fàrk•wí

**left** ซ้าย síe

**left-luggage office [BE]** แผนกกรัมภาระ pàh•nàek sǎhm•par•ráh

**leg** ขา kǎr

**legal** ถูกกฎหมาย tòok gòt•mǐe

**lend** ให้ยืม hî•yueem

**length** ความยาว kwarm•yarw

**lens** เลนส์ lehn

**less** น้อยกว่า nóry gwàr

**lesson** บทเรียน bòt•rean

**let** ปล่อย bplòhy

**letter** จดหมาย jòt•mǐe

**level** ระดับ rah•dàhp

**library** ห้องสมุด hôhng sah•mùht

**life** ชีวิต chee•wíht

**life boat** เรือชูชีพ ruea choo•chêep

**lifeguard** ยามไลฟ์การ์ด yarm lí•gàrt

**lifejacket** เสื้อชูชีพ sûea choo•chêep

**lift [BE]** ลิฟต์ líhp

**light** adj **(weight)** เบา bou; **(color)** อ่อน òrn; v จุดไฟ jùht fi; n ไฟ fi

**lightbulb** หลอดไฟ lòrt•fi

**lighter** ไฟแช็ก fi•cháhk

**lighthouse** ประภาคาร bprah•par•karn

**like** v **(same)** เหมือนกับ mǔean•gàhp; **(want)** อยากได้ yàrk•dîe; **(please)** ชอบ chôrp

**line** เส้น sêhn

**linen** ลินิน lih•nihn

**lip** ริมฝีปาก rihm•fěe•bpàrk

**lipstick** ลิปสติก líhp•sah•dtihk

**liquor store** ร้านขายเหล้า rárn kǐe lôu

**liter** ลิตร líht

**little** น้อย nóry

**live** v อยู่ yòo; **(performance)** adj สด sòht

**lobby (theater, hotel)** ล็อบบี้ lóhp•bêe

**local** ท้องถิ่น tórng•tìhn

**lock** ล็อก lóhk

**log off** ออกจากระบบ òrk•jark rah•bòp

**log on** เข้าระบบ kôu rah•bòp

**long** ยาว yow

**long-distance bus** รถบัสทางไกล rót báht tarng gli

**look** ดู doo

**loose** หลวม lǒarm

**lorry [BE]** รถบรรทุก rót bahn•túhk

**lose** หาย hǐe

**lost** หลงทาง lǒng•tarng

**lost and found office** แผนกของหาย pah•nàek kǒrng•hǐe

**lost-property office [BE]** แผนกของหาย pah·nàek kŏrng·hǐe

**lottery** ล็อตเตอรี่ lóht·dter·rêe

**loud** ดัง dahng

**love** รัก ráhk

**low** ต่ำ dtàhm

**luggage** กระเป๋า grah·bpŏu

**luggage cart** รถเข็นกระเป๋า rót kĕhn grah·bpŏu

**luggage trolley [BE]** รถเข็นกระเป๋า rót kĕhn grah·bpŏu

**lunch** อาหารกลางวัน ar·hǎrn glarng·wahn

**lung** ปอด bpòrt

## M

**magazine** นิตยสาร níht·tah·yah·sǎrn

**mail** *n* จดหมาย jòt·mǐe; *v* ส่งจดหมาย sòng jòt·mǐe

**mailbox** ตู้จดหมาย dtôo jòt·mǐe

**main** สำคัญ sǎhm·kahn

**make-up** *v* แต่งหน้า dtàng·nâr

**male** เพศชาย pêt·chie

**mall** ศูนย์การค้า sŏon garn·kár

**man** ผู้ชาย pôo·chie

**manager** ผู้จัดการ pôo·jàht·garn

**mandatory** บังคับ bahng·káhp

**manicure** ทำเล็บมือ tahm léhp·muee

**many** หลาย lǐe

**map** แผนที่ păen·têe

**market** ตลาด dtah·làrt

**marry** แต่งงาน dtàng·ngarn

**mask** หน้ากาก nâr·gàrk

**mass (church)** มิสซา míht·sar

**massage** นวด nôart

**matches** ไม้ขีด mí·kèet

**matinée** รอบกลางวัน rôrp glarng·wahn

**mattress** ที่นอน têe·norn

**maybe** อาจจะ àrt·jah

**meal** อาหาร ar·hǎrn

**measure** วัดขนาด wáht kah·nàrt

**measurement** การวัด garn wáht

**mechanic** ช่าง chârng

**medication** การใช้ยา garn chí yar

**medicine** ยา yar

**medium** ขนาดกลาง kah·nàrt glarng

**meet** พบ póp

**meeting** การประชุม garn bprah·chuhm

**meeting room** ห้องประชุม hôhng bprah·chuhm

**member** สมาชิก sah·mar·chíhk

**memorial** อนุสาวรีย์ ah·núh·sǎr·wah·ree

**memory card** เมมโมรี่การ์ด mem·moe·rêe gárt

**mend (clothes)** ชุน chuhn

**menstrual cramps** ปวดประจำเดือน bpòart bprah·jahm·duean

**menu** เมนู me·noo

**merge** รวม roarm

**message** ข้อความ kôr·kwarm

**metal** โลหะ loe·hàh

**microwave (oven)** (เตาอบ)ไมโครเวฟ (dtou) mi·kroe·wép

**midday [BE]** เที่ยง têang

**midnight** เที่ยงคืน têang·kueen

**migraine** ไมเกรน mi·gren

**mini-bar** มินิบาร์ míh·níh bar

**minute** นาที nar·tee

**mirror** กระจกเงา grah·jòk ngou

**missing** หาย hǐe

**mistake** ผิดพลาด piht·plârt

**mobile phone [BE]** โทรศัพท์มือถือ toe·rah·sàhp muee·tǔee

**money** เงิน ngern

**money order** ธนาณัติ tah·nar·náht

**monsoon** มรสุม mor·rah·sǔhm

**month** เดือน duean

**mop** ไม้ถูพื้น mie tŏo·púeen

**moped** จักรยานมอเตอร์ไซค์ jàhk·grah·yarn mor·dter·si

**more** มากกว่า mârk•gwàr
**morning** ตอนเช้า dtorn•chóu
**mosque** สุเหร่า suh•ròu
**mosquito bite** ยุงกัด yuhng•gàht
**motion sickness** เมารถ mou rót
**motor** เครื่องยนต์ krûeang•yon
**motorboat** เรือยนต์ ruea yon
**motorcycle** มอเตอร์ไซค์ mor•dter•si
**motorway [BE]** ทางด่วน tarng•dòarn
**mountain** ภูเขา poo•kŏu
**mouth** ปาก bpàrk
**move** ขยับ kah•yàhp
**movie** หนัง năhng
**movie theater** โรงหนัง roeng•năhng
**Mr.** นาย nie
**Mrs.** นาง narng
**much** มาก mârk
**mugging** จี้ jêe
**muscle** กล้ามเนื้อ glârm•núea
**museum** พิพิธภัณฑ์ píh•piht•tah•pahn
**music** ดนตรี don•dtree
**must** ต้อง dtôhng

# N

**nail** เล็บ léhp
**nail file** ตะไบขัดเล็บ dtah•bi kàht léhp
**nail salon** ร้านทำเล็บ rárn tahm•léhp
**name** ชื่อ chûee
**napkin** กระดาษเช็ดปาก grah•dàrt chéht bpàrk
**nappy [BE]** ผ้าอ้อม pâr•ôrm
**nationality** สัญชาติ săn•chârt
**native** พื้นเมือง púeen•mueang
**nature** ธรรมชาติ tahm•mah•chârt
**nature trail** ทางเดินชมธรรมชาติ tarng•dern chom tahm•mah•chârt
**nausea** คลื่นไส้ klûeen sî
**near** ใกล้ glî
**nearby** ใกล้ๆ glî•glî

**necessary** จำเป็น jahm•bpehn
**neck** คอ kor
**necklace** สร้อยคอ sôry•kor
**need** ต้องการ dtôhng•garn
**network** เครือข่าย kruea•kie
**never** ไม่เคย mî•kery
**new** ใหม่ mì
**news** ข่าว kòw
**newspaper** หนังสือพิมพ์ năhng•sŭee•pihm
**newsstand** แผงขายหนังสือพิมพ์ păeng kie năhng•sŭee•pihm
**next** ถัดไป tàht•bpi
**next to** ติดกับ dtiht•gàhp
**nice** ดี dee
**night** กลางคืน glarng•kueen
**night club** ไนท์คลับ ni•klàhp
**no** ไม่ mî
**noisy** เสียงดัง sĕang•dang
**non-smoking** ห้ามสูบบุหรี่ hârm sòop•buh•rèe
**non-stop (flight)** เที่ยวบินตรง têaw•bihn trong
**noon** เที่ยง têang
**normal** ธรรมดา tahm•mah•dar
**north** เหนือ nŭea
**nose** จมูก jah•mòok
**not** ไม่ mî
**nothing** ไม่มีอะไร mî mee ah•ri
**notify** แจ้ง jâeng
**now** ตอนนี้ dtorn•née
**number** เบอร์ ber
**nurse** พยาบาล pah•yar•barn

# O

**office** ที่ทำงาน têe tahm•ngarn
**off-peak (ticket)** ช่วงออฟพีค chôarng órp•péek
**often** บ่อย bòhy

**OK** โอเค oe•ke

**old** เก่า gòu

**on** บน bon

**one-way ticket** เที่ยวเดียว têaw•deaw

**only** เท่านั้น tôu•náhn

**open** เปิด bpèrt

**opening hours** เวลาทำการ we•lar tahm•garn

**opera** โอเปร่า oo•bpe•râr

**operation** ผ่าตัด pàr•dtàht

**opposite** ตรงข้าม dtrong•kârm

**optician** ช่างตัดแว่น chârng dtàht•wǎen

**or** หรือ rǔee

**orchestra** วงออเคสตร้า wong or•kés•trâr

**order** สั่ง sàhng

**organize** จัดระบบ jàht rah•bòp

**original** ดั้งเดิม dâhng•derm

**out** ออก òrk

**outdoor** กลางแจ้ง glarng•jâeng

**outdoor pool** สระกลางแจ้ง sàh glarng•jâeng

**outside** ข้างนอก kârng•nôrk

**oven** เตาอบ dtou•òp

**over (more than)** มากกว่า mârk•gwàr

**overcharge** คิดเงินเกิน kíht•ngern gern

**overlook** จุดชมวิว jùht chom wihw

**overnight** ข้ามคืน kârm•kueen

**owe** เป็นหนี้ bpehn nêe

**own** เป็นเจ้าของ bpehn jôu•kǒrng

**owner** เจ้าของ jôu•kǒrng

**oxygen** ออกซิเจน óhk•sih•jêhn

## P

**pacifier** จุกนม jùhk•nom

**pack** ห่อ hòr

**package** พัสดุ páht•sah•dùh

**paddling pool [BE]** สระเด็ก sàh dèhk

**padlock** กุญแจคล้อง guhn•jae klórng

**pail** ถัง tǎhng

**pain** เจ็บ jèhp; **(muscle)** ปวด bpòart

**painting (picture)** ภาพวาด pârp•wârt

**pair** คู่ kôo

**pajamas** ชุดนอน chúht•norn

**palace** วัง wahng

**panorama** ภาพพาโนรามา pârp par•noe•rar•mâr

**pants** กางเกงขายาว garng•geng kǎr•yow

**panty hose** ถุงน่อง tǔhng•nôhng

**paper towel** กระดาษเช็ดมือ grah•dàrt chéht•muee

**paracetamol [BE]** พาราเซตามอล par•rar•séht•dtar•môhn

**parcel [BE]** พัสดุ páht•sah•dùh

**park** *n* สวนสาธารณะ sǒarn sǎr•tar•rah•náh; *v* จอดรถ jòrt•rót

**parking garage** อาคารจอดรถ ar•karn jòrt•rót

**parking lot** ที่จอดรถ têe jòrt•rót

**partner** หุ้นส่วน hûhn•sòarn

**party** งานปาร์ตี้ ngarn bpar•dtêe

**passport** หนังสือเดินทาง nǎhng•sǔee dern•tarng

**password** รหัส rah•hàht

**patient** คนไข้ kon kî

**pavement [BE]** ทางเท้า tarng•tów

**pay** จ่าย jie

**pay phone** โทรศัพท์สาธารณะ toe•rah•sàhp sǎr•tar•rah•náh

**payment** การจ่ายเงิน garn jie•ngern

**pedestrian** คนเดินถนน kon dern tah•nǒn

**pediatrician** หมอเด็ก mǒr•dèhk

**pedicure** ทำเล็บเท้า tahm léhp•tów

**pen** ปากกา bpàrk•gar

**penicillin** เพนิซิลลิน pe•nih•sih•lihn

**per** ต่อ dtòr

**performance** การแสดง garn sah•daeng

**perhaps** บางที barng•tee

**period (menstruation)** ประจำเดือน bprah•jahm•duean

**person** คน kon

**petrol** [BE] เบนซิน ben•sihn

**petrol station** [BE] ปั๊มน้ำมัน bpåhm náhm•mahn

**pharmacy** ร้านขายยา rárn kǐe yar

**phone** โทรศัพท์ toe•rah•sàhp

**phone call** โทรศัพท์ toe•rah•sàhp

**phone card** บัตรโทรศัพท์ bàht toe•rah•sàhp

**phone directory** สมุดโทรศัพท์ sah•mùht toe•rah•sàhp

**phone number** เบอร์โทรศัพท์ ber toe•rah•sàhp

**photocopy** ถ่ายเอกสาร tie èk•gah•sǎrn

**photograph** รูป rôop

**phrase** วลี wah•lee

**pick up** รับ ráhp

**picnic** ปิ๊คนิค bpíhk•níhk

**picnic area** ที่ปิ๊คนิค têe bpíhk•níhk

**piece** ชิ้น chíhn

**pill** ยา yar

**pillow** หมอน mǒrn

**PIN** รหัสพิน rah•hàht pihn

**place** สถานที่ sah•tǎrn•têe

**plan** แผน pǎen

**plane** เครื่องบิน krûeang•bihn

**plaster** [BE] เฝือก fùeak

**plastic** พลาสติก plárt•sah•dtìhk

**plastic wrap** ฟิล์มถนอมอาหาร feem tah•nǒrm ar•hǎrn

**plate** จาน jarn

**platform** ชานชาลา charn•char•lar

**play** v เล่น lêhn; (theater) ละคร lah•korn

**playground** สนามเด็กเล่น sah•nǎrm dèhk lêhn

**playpen** คอกเด็กเล่น kôrk dèhk lêhn

**please** กรุณา gah•rúh•nar

**plug** ปลั๊กไฟ bplåhk•fi

**plunger** ที่ดูดส้วม têe dòot sôarm

**pneumonia** ปอดบวม bpòrt•boarm

**poison** ยาพิษ yar•píht

**police** ตำรวจ dtahm•ròart

**police report** ใบแจ้งความ bi•jâeng•kwarm

**police station** สถานีตำรวจ sah•tǎr•nee dtahm•ròart

**pond** บ่อน้ำ bòr•nárm

**pool** สระว่ายน้ำ sàh wîe•nárm

**popular** เป็นที่นิยม bpehn•têe nih•yom

**port** ท่าเรือ târ•ruea

**porter** คนยกกระเป๋า kon yók grah•bpǒu

**portion** ขนาด kah•nàrt

**post** [BE] v ส่งจดหมาย sòng jòt•mǐe; n จดหมาย jòt•mǐe

**post office** ที่ทำการไปรษณีย์ têe tahm•garn bpri•sah•nee

**postage** ค่าแสตมป์ kâr sah•dtaem

**postbox** [BE] ตู้จดหมาย dtôo jòt•mǐe

**postcard** โปสการ์ด bpóet•sah•gárt

**pot** หม้อ môr

**pottery** เครื่องปั้นดินเผา krûeang•bpǎhn dihn•pǒu

**pound (weight)** ปอนด์ bporn

**pound sterling** เงินปอนด์ ngern•bporn

**practice** ฝึก fùek

**pregnant** ท้อง tórng

**prepaid phone card** บัตรโทรศัพท์ แบบเติมเงิน bàht toe•rah•sàhp bàep dterm•ngern

**prescription** ใบสั่งยา bi sàhng•yar

**present (time)** ปัจจุบัน bpàht•juh•bahn; n ของขวัญ kǒrng•kwǎhn

**press** v กด gòt

**price** ราคา rar•kar

**print** ปริ๊นท์ prihn

**prison** คุก kúhk

**private** ส่วนตัว sòarn•dtoar

**problem** ปัญหา bpahn•hǎr

**produce store** ร้านขายผักผลไม้ rárn kǐe pàhk pǒn•lah•mí

**profession** อาชีพ ar•chêep

**program** โปรแกรม bproe•graem
**prohibited** ห้าม hârm
**pronounce** ออกเสียง òrk•sĕang
**public** สาธารณะ săr•tar•rah•náh
**pull** ดึง dueng
**pump** ปั๊ม bpáhm
**pure** แท้ tâe
**purpose** วัตถุประสงค์ wáht•tùh•bprah•sŏng
**purse** กระเป๋าสตางค์ grah•bpŏu sah•tarng
**push** ผลัก plàhk
**push-chair [BE]** รถเข็นเด็ก rót•kĕhn dèhk
**put** ใส่ sì

## Q

**quality** คุณภาพ kuhn•nah•pârp
**queue [BE]** v เข้าคิว kôu•kihw;
  n คิว kihw
**quick** เร็ว rehw
**quiet** เงียบ ngêap

## R

**racetrack** ลู่แข่ง lôo•kàeng
**racket (tennis)** ไม้เทนนิส mí ten•níht
**railway station [BE]** สถานีรถไฟ
  sah•tăr•nee rót•fi
**rain** ฝนตก fŏn dtòk
**raincoat** เสื้อกันฝน sûea gahn fŏn
**rape** ข่มขืน kòm•kŭuen
**rapids** แก่ง gàeng
**rash** เป็นผื่น bpehn pùeen
**razor** มีดโกน mêet•goen
**razor blade** ใบมีดโกน bi mêet•goen
**reach** เอื้อม ûeam
**reaction** ปฏิกิริยา bpah•dtih•gih•rih•yar
**read** อ่าน àrn
**ready** พร้อม prórm
**real (genuine)** แท้ tâe

**receipt** ใบเสร็จ bi•sèht
**receive** ได้รับ dî•ráhp
**reception (desk)** แผนกต้อนรับ pah•nàek dtôrn•ráhp
**receptionist** พนักงานต้อนรับ pah•náhk•ngarn dtôrn•ráhp
**recommend** แนะนำ ná•nahm
**reduce** ลด lót
**reduction** ส่วนลด sùan•lót
**refrigerator** ตู้เย็น dtôo•yehn
**refund** v คืนเงิน kueen•ngern;
  n เงินคืน ngern•kueen
**region** เขต kèt
**regular** ธรรมดา tahm•mah•dar
**relationship** ความสัมพันธ์ kwarm săhm•pahn
**reliable** เชื่อถือได้ chûea•tŭee dîe
**religion** ศาสนา sàrt•sa•năr
**remember** จำได้ jahm•dîe
**remove** เอาออก ou•òrk
**renovation** ปรับปรุงใหม่ bpràhp•bpruhng mì
**rent** เช่า chôu
**rental car** รถเช่า rót•chôu
**repair** ซ่อม sôhm
**repeat** ซ้ำอีกที sáhm èek•tee
**replace** แทนที่ taen•têe
**report** แจ้งความ jâeng•kwarm
**reservation** การจอง garn•jorng
**reservation desk** แผนกรับจอง pah•nàek ráhp•jorng
**reserve** จอง jorng
**reservoir** อ่างเก็บน้ำ àrng•gèhp nárm
**responsibility** ความรับผิดชอบ kwarm ráhp•piht•chôrp
**rest** v พัก páhk
**rest area** ที่พักริมทาง têe•páhk rihm tarng
**restaurant** ร้านอาหาร rárn ar•hărn
**restroom** ห้องน้ำ hôhng•nárm
**retired** เกษียณ gah•sĕan

**return (come back)** กลับ glàhp; **(give back)** คืน kueen

**return ticket [BE]** ตั๋วขากลับ dtŏar kăr·glàhp

**right (correct)** ถูก tòok; **(direction)** ขวา kwăr

**ring** v กดกระดิ่ง gòt grah·dihng; **(jewelry)** n แหวน wăen

**river** แม่น้ำ mâe·nárm

**road** ถนน tah·nŏn

**robbery** การปล้น karn bplôn

**romantic** โรแมนติก roe·maen·dtihk

**roof** หลังคา lăhng·kar

**room** ห้อง hôhng

**room service** รูมเซอร์วิส room·ser·wiht

**rope** เชือก chûeak

**round** adj กลม glom; n **(golf)** รอบ rôrp

**round-trip ticket** ตั๋วไปกลับ dtŏar bpi·glàhp

**route** เส้นทาง sên·tarng

**row** v พาย pie; n แถว tăew

**rowboat** เรือพาย ruea·pie

**rubbish [BE]** n ขยะ kah·yàh

**rude** หยาบคาย yàrp·kie

**rush** เร่ง rêng

## S

**safe** n ตู้เซฟ dtôo·séf; adj ปลอดภัย bplòrt·pi

**safety** ความปลอดภัย kwarm bplòrt·pi

**safety pin** เข็มกลัด kĕhm·glàht

**sale [BE]** ลดราคา lót rar·kar

**sales tax** ภาษีมูลค่าเพิ่ม par·sĕe moon·kâr pêrm

**same** แบบเดียวกัน bàep·deaw·gahn

**sand** ทราย sie

**sandals** รองเท้าแตะ rorng·tów dtà

**sanitary napkin** ผ้าอนามัย pâr ah·nar·mai

**sanitary pad [BE]** ผ้าอนามัย pâr ah·nar·mai

**sauna** ซาวน่า sow·nâr

**save** เก็บรักษา gèhp ráhk·săr

**savings account** บัญชีออมทรัพย์ bahn·chee orm·sáhp

**say** พูด pôot

**scale** ตาชั่ง dtar·châhng

**scarf** ผ้าพันคอ pâr pahn kor

**schedule** ตาราง dtar·rarng

**scissors** กรรไกร gahn·gri

**screwdriver** ไขควง kĭ·koarng

**sea** ทะเล tah·le

**seafront** ติดทะเล dtiht tah·le

**seasickness** เมารือ mou ruea

**seat (on train, etc.)** ที่นั่ง têe nâhng

**seat belt** เข็มขัดนิรภัย kĕhm·kàht nih·ráh·pi

**sedative** ยาระงับประสาท yar rah·ngáhp bprah·sàrt

**see** เห็น hĕhn

**self-service** บริการตนเอง bor·rih·garn dton·eng

**sell** ขาย kĭe

**seminar** สัมมนา săhm·mah·nar

**send** ส่ง sòng

**senior citizen** ผู้สูงอายุ pôo sŏong ar·yúh

**separate** แยก yâek

**separated** แยกกันอยู่ yâek gahn yòo

**serious** จริงจัง jihng·jahng

**serve** เสิร์ฟ sèrp

**service (work)** บริการ bor·rih·garn; **(church)** สวดมนต์ sòart·mon

**service charge** ค่าบริการ kâr bor·rih·garn

**service included** รวมค่าบริการ roarm kâr bor·rih·garn

**set menu** อาหารชุด ar·hărn chúht

**sew** เย็บ yéhp

**sex (gender)** เพศ pêt; **(activity)** เซ็กซ์ séhk

shadow เงา ngou

shallow ตื้น dtûeen

shampoo แชมพู chaem·poo

shape รูปร่าง rôop·rârng

sharp คม kom

shave โกนหนวด goen·nòart

shaving cream ครีมโกนหนวด kreem goen·nòart

sheet (bed) ผ้าปูที่นอน pâr bpoo têe·norn

ship เรือ ruea

shock ช็อค chóhk

shoe รองเท้า rorng·tów

shoe repair ซ่อมรองเท้า sôhm rorng·tów

shoe store ร้านขายรองเท้า rárn kǐe rorng·tów

shop assistant พนักงานขาย pah·nák·ngarn kǐe

shopping ช็อปปิ้ง chóhp·bpîhng

shopping area ย่านช็อปปิ้ง yârn chóhp·bpîhng

shopping basket ตะกร้าช็อปปิ้ง dtah·grâr chóhp·bpîhng

shopping cart รถเข็น rót·kěhn

shopping centre [BE] ศูนย์การค้า sǒon·garn·kár

shopping mall ศูนย์การค้า sǒon·garn·kár

shopping trolley [BE] รถเข็น rót·kěhn

short สั้น sâhn

shorts กางเกงขาสั้น garng·geng kàr·sân

shoulder ไหล่ li

show n การแสดง garn sah·daeng; v แสดง sah·daeng

shower v อาบน้ำ àrp·nárm; n ห้องอาบน้ำ hôhng àrp·nárm

shut ปิด bpìht

sick ไม่สบาย mî sah·bie

side effect ผลข้างเคียง pǒn kârng·keang

sidewalk ทางเท้า tarng·tów

sight (attraction) สถานที่ท่องเที่ยว sah·tǎrn·têe tôhng·têaw

sightseeing tour ทัวร์ชมเมือง toar chom mueang

sign n ป้าย bpîe; v เซ็นชื่อ sehn·chûee

single (marital status) เป็นโสด bpehn·sòet

single room ห้องเดี่ยว hôhng·dèaw

sink อ่าง àrng

sit นั่ง nâhng

site สถานที่ sah·tǎrn·têe

size ขนาด kah·nàrt

skin ผิวหนัง pǐhw·nǎhng

skirt กระโปรง grah·bproeng

sleep นอน norn

sleeping bag ถุงนอน tǔhng·norn

sleeping car ตู้นอน dtôo·norn

sleeping pill ยานอนหลับ yar norn·làhp

sleeve แขนเสื้อ kǎen sûea

slice v ฝาน fàrn; n ชิ้น chíhn

slippers รองเท้าแตะ rorng·tów dtà

slow ช้า chár

small เล็ก léhk

smell n กลิ่น glìhn; v ได้กลิ่น dî·glìhn

smoke สูบบุหรี่ sòop·buh·rèe

smoking area บริเวณสูบบุหรี่ bor·rih·wen sòop·buh·rèe

snack อาหารว่าง ar·hǎrn wârng

snack bar สแน็คบาร์ sah·nák bar

sneakers รองเท้าผ้าใบ rorng·tów pâr·bi

snorkel สนอร์กเกิ้ล sah·nórk·gêrn

snow หิมะ hìh·máh

soap สบู่ sah·bòo

soccer ฟุตบอล fúht·bohn

sock ถุงเท้า tǔhng·tów

sold out ขายหมด kǐe mòt

some บาง barng

someone บางคน barng kon

something บางอย่าง barng yàrng

sometimes บางครั้ง barng kráhng

somewhere บางที่ barng têe

soon ในไม่ช้า ni·mî·chár

soother [BE] จุกนม jùhk·nom

sore ปวด bpòart

sore throat เจ็บคอ jèhp·kor

sorry ขอโทษ kŏr·tôet

sour เปรี้ยว bprêaw

south ทิศใต้ tíht·dtíe

souvenir ของที่ระลึก kŏrng·têe·rah·lúek

souvenir store ร้านขายของที่ระลึก rárn kĭe kŏrng·têe·rah·lúehk

spa สปา sah·bpar

space ที่ว่าง têe·wârng

spare สำรอง săhm·rorng

spatula ตะหลิว dtah·lĭhw

speak พูด pôot

special พิเศษ píh·sèt

specialist (doctor) หมอเฉพาะทาง mŏr chah·póh·tarng

spell สะกด sah·gòt

spend (money) ใช้จ่าย chí·jìe

sponge ฟองน้ำ forng·nárm

spoon ช้อน chórn

sport กีฬา gee·lar

sporting goods store ร้านขายเครื่อง กีฬา rárn kĭe krûeang·gee·lar

sports club สปอร์ตคลับ sah·bpòrt kláhp

spot (place, site) จุด jùht

spouse คู่สมรส kôo sŏm·rót

sprain แพลง plaeng

stadium สนามกีฬา sah·nărm gee·lar

staff พนักงาน pah·náhk·ngarn

stair บันได bahn·di

stamp แสตมป์ sah·dtam

stand ยืน yueen

standard มาตรฐาน mârt·dtah·tărn

standby ticket ตั๋วสำรอง dtŏar săhm·rorng

start เริ่ม rêrm

statue รูปปั้น rôop·bpăn

stay อยู่ yòo

steal ขโมย kah·moey

steep ชัน chahn

stiff (muscle) เมื่อย mûeay

stolen ถูกขโมย tòok kah·moey

stomach ท้อง tórng

stomachache ปวดท้อง bpòart·tórng

stop v จอด jòrt; (bus) n ป้ายรถเมล์ bpîe rót·me

store ร้านค้า rárn·kár

store directory [BE] รายการร้านค้า rie·garn rárn·kár

store guide รายการร้านค้า rie·garn rárn·kár

stove เตา dtou

straight (ahead) ตรงไป dtrong bpi

stream ลำธาร lahm·tarn

street ถนน tah·nŏn

stroller รถเข็นเด็ก rót·kĕhn dèhk

strong แข็งแรง kăng·raeng

student นักศึกษา náhk sùek·săr

study ศึกษา sùek·săr

style สไตล์ sah·tie

subtitled มีซับไตเติล mee sáhp·dti·dtêrn

subway รถไฟใต้ดิน rót·fi tí·dihn

subway map แผนที่รถไฟใต้ดิน păen·têe rót·fi tíe·dihn

subway station สถานีรถไฟใต้ดิน sah·tăr·nee rót·fi tíe·dihn

suggest แนะนำ ná·nahm

suit ชุดสูท chúht·sòot

suitable เหมาะสม mòh·sŏm

suitcase กระเป๋าเดินทาง grah·bpŏu dern·tarng

sun (light) แดด dàet

sunbathe อาบแดด àrp·dàet

sunblock ครีมกันแดด kreem gahn·dàet

sunburn แดดเผา dàet pŏu

sunglasses แว่นกันแดด wân·gahn·dàet

sunscreen ครีมกันแดด kreem gahn•dàet

sunstroke ลมแดด lom•dàet

suntan lotion โลชั่นอาบแดด loe•châhn àrp•dàet

superb เยี่ยมมาก yêam•mârk

supermarket ซุปเปอร์มาร์เก็ต súhp•bpêr•mar•gêht

supervision การดูแล garn doo•lae

supplement v เสริม sěrm

suppository ยาเหน็บ yar nèhp

sure แน่นอน nâe•norn

surfboard กระดานโต้คลื่น grah•darn dtôe•klûeen

swallow กลืน glueen

sweater เสื้อกันหนาว sûea gahn nǎrw

sweatshirt เสื้อสเวตเชิร์ต sûea sah•wéht•chért

sweep กวาด gwàrt

sweet adj หวาน wǎrn

swelling บวม boarm

swim ว่ายน้ำ wîe•nárm

swimming pool สระว่ายน้ำ sàh wîe•nárm

swimming trunks กางเกงว่ายน้ำ garng•geng wîe•nárm

swimsuit ชุดว่ายน้ำ chúht wîe•nárm

swollen บวม boarm

symbol สัญลักษณ์ sǎhn•yah•láhk

symptom อาการ ar•garn

synagogue โบสถ์ยิว bòet•yihw

## T

table โต๊ะ dtóh

take เอา ou

talk พูด pôot

tall สูง sǒong

tampon ผ้าอนามัยแบบสอด pâr ah•nar•mi bàep•sòrt

taste v ชิม chihm; n รสชาติ rót•chârt

taxi แท็กซี่ ták•sêe

taxi rank [BE] ที่จอดรถแท็กซี่ têe jòrt•rót ták•sêe

taxi stand ที่จอดรถแท็กซี่ têe jòrt•rót ták•sêe

team ทีม teem

telephone n โทรศัพท์ toe•rah•sàhp

telephone booth ตู้โทรศัพท์ dtôo toe•rah•sàhp

telephone call โทรศัพท์ toe•rah•sàhp

telephone number เบอร์โทรศัพท์ ber toe•rah•sàhp

tell บอก bòrk

temperature อุณหภูมิ uhn•hah•poom

tennis เทนนิส tehn•niht

tennis court สนามเทนนิส sah•nǎrm tehn•nít

tent เต็นท์ dtéhn

terminal เทอร์มินอล ter•mih•nôrn

text (SMS) v ส่งข้อความ sòng kôr•kwarm

Thai (language) ภาษาไทย par•sǎr ti; (person) คนไทย kon ti

Thailand ประเทศไทย bprah•têt ti

thank ขอบคุณ kòrp•kuhn

that นั่น nân

theater (movie) โรงหนัง roeng•nǎhng; (play) โรงละคร roeng•lah•korn

theft ขโมย kah•moey

then (afterwards) แล้วก็ láew•gôr

there ที่นั่น têe•nâhn

thermometer ปรอท bpah•ròrt

thick หนา nǎr

thief ขโมย kah•moey

thigh ต้นขา dtôn•kǎr

thin บาง barng

thing สิ่งของ sihng•kǒrng

think คิดว่า kiht•wâr

thirsty หิวน้ำ hǐhw•nárm

this นี่ nêe

throat คอ kor

through ผ่าน pàrn

ticket ตั๋ว dtŏar

ticket inspector คนตรวจตั๋ว kon dtròart dtŏar

ticket office แผนกจำหน่ายตั๋ว pah•nàek jahm•nie dtŏar

tie เนคไท nékh•tie

tight คับ káhp

tile กระเบื้อง grah•bûeang

time เวลา we•lar

timetable [BE] ตาราง dtar•rarng

tin opener [BE] ที่เปิดกระป๋อง têe bpèrt gra•bpŏhng

tip (service) v ทิป tihp

tire (vehicle) ยาง yarng

tired เหนื่อย nùeay

tissue กระดาษทิชชู่ grah•dàrt tiht•chôo

to (place) ถึง thŭeng

tobacco ยาสูบ yar•sòop

today วันนี้ wahn•née

toe นิ้วเท้า nihw•tóu

toilet [BE] ห้องน้ำ hôhng•nárm

toilet paper กระดาษชำระ grah•dàrt chahm•ráh

tomorrow พรุ่งนี้ prûhng•née

tongue ลิ้น lihn

tonight คืนนี้ kueen•née

too เกินไป gern•bpi; (also) เหมือนกัน mŭean•gahn

tooth ฟัน fahn

toothache ปวดฟัน bpòart fahn

toothbrush แปรงสีฟัน bpraeng sĕe•fahn

toothpaste ยาสีฟัน yar sĕe•fahn

torn ฉีก chèek

tough เหนียว nĕaw

tour ทัวร์ toar

tour guide ไกด์ทัวร์ gi toar

tourist นักท่องเที่ยว nákh•tôhng•têaw

tourist office สำนักงานท่องเที่ยว săhm•nákh•ngarn tôhng•têaw

tow truck รถลาก rót•lârk

towel ผ้าเช็ดตัว pâr•chéht•dtoar

tower หอคอย hŏr•kory

town เมือง mueang

toy ของเล่น kŏrng lên

toy store ร้านขายของเล่น rárn kĭe kŏrng•lên

traditional ดั้งเดิม dâhng•derm

traffic การจราจร garn jah•rar•jorn

trail เส้นทางเดินป่า sên tarng dern•bpàr

trailer รถพ่วง rót•pôarng

train รถไฟ rót•fi

train station สถานีรถไฟ sah•tăr•nee rót•fi

tram รถราง rót•rarng

transfer (finance) โอนเงิน oen•ngern

translate แปล bplae

translation คำแปล kahm•bplae

translator ผู้แปล poo•bplae

transport v ขนส่ง kŏn•sòng

trash ขยะ kah•yàh

trash can ถังขยะ tăhng kah•yàh

travel ท่องเที่ยว tôhng•têaw

travel agency บริษัททัวร์ bor•rih•sàht toar

travel sickness (by car) เมารถ mou rót; (by boat) เมาเรือ mou ruea

traveler's check เช็คเดินทาง chéhk dern•tarng

traveller's cheque [BE] เช็คเดินทาง chéhk dern•tarng

treatment การรักษา garn ráhk•săr

tree ต้นไม้ dtôn•mí

trim เล็ม lehm

trip การเดินทาง garn dern•tarng

trolley รถเข็น rót•kĕhn

trousers [BE] กางเกงขายาว garng•geng kăr•yow

truck รถบรรทุก rót bahn•túhk

true จริง jihng

T-shirt เสื้อยืด sûea•yûeet

tumor เนื้องอก núea·ngôrk
tunnel อุโมงค์ uh·moeng
turn เลี้ยว léaw
turn off ปิด bpiht
turn on เปิด bpèrt
TV ทีวี tee·wee
tweezers แหนบ nàep
twist บิด biht
type ชนิด chah·níht
typical ธรรมดา tahm·mah·dar

# U

ugly น่าเกลียด nâr·glèat
umbrella ร่ม rôm
unconscious หมดสติ mòt sah·dtih
under ใต้ dtie
underground station
  [BE] สถานีรถไฟใต้ดิน sah·tăr·nee rót·fi
  tîe·dihn
understand เข้าใจ kôu·ji
unit หน่วย nòary
United Kingdom สหราชอาณาจักร sah·hàh
  rârt·chah ar·nar·jàhk
United States สหรัฐอเมริกา sah·hàh·ráht
  ah·me·rih·gar
until กระทั่ง grah·tâhng
upstairs ชั้นบน cháhn·bon
urgent ด่วน dòarn
use ใช้ chí
username ชื่อผู้ใช้ chûee pôo·chí

# V

vacant ว่าง wârng
vacation วันหยุด wahn·yùht
vacuum cleaner เครื่องดูดฝุ่น krûeang
  dòot·fùhn
valet service บริการรับจอดรถ
  bor·rih·garn·ráhp jòrt·rót

valid ใช้ได้ chí·dîe
validate รับรอง ráp rorng
valuable มีค่า mee kâr
value มูลค่า moon·kâr
VAT [BE] ภาษีมูลค่าเพิ่ม par·sĕe moon·kâr
  pêrm
vehicle รถ rót
very มาก mârk
view วิว wihw
viewpoint จุดชมวิว jùht chom wihw
village หมู่บ้าน mòo·bârn
vineyard ไร่องุ่น rî àh·ngùhn
visa วีซ่า wee·sâr
visit เยี่ยม yêam
visiting hours เวลาเยี่ยม we·lar yêam
visually impaired พิการทางสายตา
  pih·garn tarng sǎry·dtar
volleyball วอลเล่ย์บอล wohn·lê·bohn
vomit อาเจียน ar·jean

# W

wait รอ ror
waiter พนักงานบริการชาย
  pah·náhk·ngarn·bor·garn chie
waiting room ห้องพักผู้โดยสาร
  hôhng·páhk pôo·doey·sǎrn
waitress พนักงานบริการหญิง
  pah·náhk·ngarn·bor·garn·yǐng
wake ปลุก bplùhk
wake-up call บริการโทรปลุก
  bor·rih·garn·toe bplùhk
walk เดิน dern
wall กำแพง gahm·paeng
wallet กระเป๋าเงิน grah·bpŏu ngern
ward (hospital) วอร์ดคนไข้ wòrt kon·kî
warm อุ่น ùhn
warning คำเตือน kahm·dtuean
washing machine เครื่องซักผ้า krûeang
  sáhk·pâr

watch นาฬิกาข้อมือ nar·lih·gar kôr·muee

water น้ำ nárm

water ski สกีน้ำ sah·gee nárm

waterfall น้ำตก náhm·dtòk

waterproof กันน้ำ gahn·nárm

wave คลื่น klûeen

way ทาง tarng

wear ใส่ sì

weather อากาศ ar·gàrt

weather forecast พยากรณ์อากาศ pah·yar·gorn ar·gàrt

wedding งานแต่งงาน ngarn dtàng·ngarn

week สัปดาห์ sàhp·dar

weekday วันธรรมดา wahn tahm·mah·dar

weekend วันเสาร์-อาทิตย์ wahn sŏu ar·tiht

weigh ชั่ง châhng

weight น้ำหนัก náhm·nàhk

welcome ยินดีต้อนรับ yihn·dee dtôrn·ráhp

west ทิศตะวันตก tiht dtah·wahn·dtòk

wetsuit เว็ทสูท wéht·sòot

what อะไร ah·ri

wheelchair รถเข็นคนพิการ rót kĕhn kon pih·garn

wheelchair ramp ทางขึ้นสำหรับรถเข็นคนพิการ tarng kûen săhm·ràhp rót kĕhn kon pih·garn

when เมื่อไหร่ mûea·rì

where ที่ไหน têe·nĭ

who ใคร kri

why ทำไม tahm·mi

wide กว้าง gwârng

wildlife สัตว์ป่า sàht bpàr

wind ลม lom

windbreaker เสื้อกันลม sûea gahn lom

window หน้าต่าง nâr·dtàrng

window seat ที่นั่งริมหน้าต่าง têe·nâhng rihm nâr·dtàrng

windsurfing เล่นวินด์เซิร์ฟ lêhn wihn·sérp

windy ลมแรง lom raeng

wipe เช็ด chéht

wireless ไร้สาย rí·sĭe

wish (bless) v อวยพร oary·porn

with กับ gàhp

withdraw (bank) ถอนเงิน tŏrn·ngern

withdrawal ถอน tŏrn

without ไม่ใส่ mî·sì

witness พยาน pah·yarn

wood (material) ไม้ mîe

wool ผ้าวูล pâr woon

work ทำงาน tahm·ngarn

wrap ห่อ hòr

write เขียน kĕan

wrong ผิด piht

# X

x-ray เอ็กซเรย์ éhk·sah·re

# Y

yacht เรือยอชท์ ruea yórt

year ปี bpee

yes ครับ♂ kráhp♂ ; ค่ะ♀ kâh♀

yesterday เมื่อวาน mûea·warn

young เด็ก dèhk

youth เด็ก dèhk

youth hostel ที่พักเยาวชน têe páhk you·wah·chon

# Z

zipper ซิป síhp

zoo สวนสัตว์ sŏarn·sàht

# Thai–English Dictionary

## ก

กงสุล **gong·sǔhn** consulate

กด **gòt** press; dial (phone)

กดกระดิ่ง **gòt grah·dìhng** v ring

กดชักโครก **gòt chák·krôek** flush (toilet)

กรรไกร **gahn·gri** scissors

กรอก **gròrk** fill out (form)

กรอบแว่น **gròrp wâen** frame (glasses)

กระจกเงา **gràh·jòk ngou** mirror

กระดาน **grah·darn** board

กระดานโต้คลื่น **grah·darn dtôe·klûeen** surfboard

กระดาษชำระ **grah·dàrt chahm·ráh** toilet paper

กระดาษเช็ดปาก **grah·dàrt chéht bpàrk** napkin

กระดาษเช็ดมือ **grah·dàrt chéht muee** paper towel

กระดาษทิชชู่ **grah·dàrt tíht·chôo** tissue

กระดาษฟอยล์ **grah·dàrt fory** aluminum [kitchen BE] foil

กระดุม **grah·duhm** button

กระดูก **grah·dòok** bone

กระท่อม **grah·tôhm** cottage

กระทะ **grah·táh** frying pan

กระทั่ง **grah·tâhng** until

กระเบื้อง **grah·bûeang** tile

กระป๋อง **grah·bpŏhng** n can

กระเป๋า **grah·bpǒu** luggage [baggage BE]; handbag

กระเป๋าเงิน **grah·bpǒu ngern** wallet

กระเป๋าเดินทาง **grah·bpǒu dern·tarng** suitcase

กระเป๋าถือขึ้นเครื่อง **grah·bpǒu tǔee kûen krûeang** carry-on [hand BE] luggage

กระเป๋ารถ **grah·bpǒu rót** (bus) fare collector

กระเป๋าสตางค์ **grah·bpǒu sah·tarng** purse

กระโปรง **gràh·bproeng** skirt

กระเพาะปัสสาวะ **grah·póh bpàht·sah·wáh** bladder

กรัม **grahm** gram

กรุณา **gah·rúh·nar** please

กลม **glom** adj round

กล่อง **glòhng** box

กล้องถ่ายรูป **glôhng tie·rôop** camera

กล้องส่องทางไกล **glôhng sòhng tarng gli** binoculars

กลับ **glàhp** return (come back)

กลางคืน **glarng·kueern** night

กลางแจ้ง **glarng·jâeng** outdoor

กล้าม **glârm** muscle

กลิ่น **glihn** n smell

กลืน **glueen** swallow

กลุ่ม **glùhm** group

กว้าง **gwârng** wide

กวาด **gwàrt** sweep

ก๊อกน้ำ **góhk·nárm** faucet

กอด **gòrt** hug

ก่อน **gòrn** before

กอล์ฟ **górp** golf

กัด **gàht** bite

กันน้ำ **gahn·nárm** waterproof

กับ **gàhp** with

กางเกงขายาว **garng·geng kǎr·yow** pants [trousers BE]

กางเกงขาสั้น **garng·geng kǎr·sâhn** shorts

กางเกงว่ายน้ำ **garng·geng wîe·nárm** swimming trunks

ก๊าซบิวเทน **gárt bihw·ten** butane gas

การขนส่ง **garn kŏn·sòng**
  *n* transport
การเคลมประกัน **garn klem
  bprah·gahn** insurance claim
การจราจร **garn jah·rar·jorn** traffic
การจอง **garn jorng** reservation
การจ่ายเงิน **garn joe·ngern** payment
การเชื่อมต่อ **garn chûeam·dtòr**
  connection
การใช้ยา **garn chí yar** medication
การดูแล **garn doo·lae** supervision
การเดินทาง **garn dern·tarng** journey; trip
การติดเชื้อ **garn dtìht·chúea**
  infection
การติดต่อ **garn dtìht·dtòr** *n* contact
การทำร้าย **garn tahm·ríe** *n* attack
การประชุม **garn bprah·chuhm**
  meeting
การประชุมเป็นทางการ **garn bprah·chuhm
  bpehn tarng·garn** convention
การประชุมสัมมนา **garn bprah·chuhm
  sǎhm·mah·nar** conference
การปล้น **karn bplôn** robbery
การรักษา **garn ráhk·sǎr** treatment
การวัด **garn wáht** measurement
การส่ง **garn sòng** delivery
การสอบ **garn sòrp** examination
การแสดง **garn sah·daeng**
  performance; *n* show
กำกับ **gahm·gàhp** *v* direct
กำแพง **gahm·paeng** wall
กิน **gihn** eat
กินอาหาร **gihn ar·hǎrn** dine
กิโลกรัม **gih·loe·grahm** kilogram
กิโลเมตร **gih·loe·mét** kilometer
กีตาร์ **gee·dtâr** guitar
กีฬา **gee·lar** sport
กุญแจ **guhn·jae** key; padlock
เก็บ **gèhp** keep

เก็บรักษา **gèhp ráhk·sǎr** save
เกม **gem** game
เกษียณ **gah·sěan** retired
เกสต์เฮาส์ **gét·hóu** guesthouse
เก่า **gòu** old
เก้าอี้เด็ก **gôu·êe dèhk** highchair
เก้าอี้ผ้าใบ **gôu·êe pâr·bi** deck chair
เกิด **gèrt** born
เกินไป **gern bpi** too (much)
เกียร์ **gear** gear
เกือบจะ **gùeap·jah** almost
แก้ไข **gâe·kǐ** alter (a garment)
แก่ง **gàng** rapids
แก้ว **gâew** glass
โกนหนวด **goen·nòart** shave (beard)
ใกล้ **glî** near
ใกล้ๆ **glî·glî** nearby
ไกด์(ทัวร์) **gí (toar)** *n* (tour) guide
ไกล **gli** far

ขนส่ง **kŏn·sòng** *v* transport
ขนาด **kah·nàrt** size; portion
ขนาดรับประทาน **kah·nàrt
  ráhp·bprah·tarn** dosage (medicine)
ขนาดสำหรับเด็ก **kah·nàrt sǎhm·ràhp
  dèhk** children's portion
ข่มขืน **kòm·kǔeen** rape
ขโมย **kah·moey** *v* steal; *n* theft, thief
ขยะ **kah·yàh** trash
ขยับ **kah·yàhp** move
ขยาย **kah·yǐe** enlarge
ขวด **kòart** bottle; jar
ขวดนมเด็ก **kòart·nom dèhk** baby bottle
ขวา **kwǎr** right (direction)
ขอโทษ **kǒr·tôet** apologize; sorry
ขอแสดงความยินดี **kǒr sah·daeng
  kwarm·yihn·dee** congratulations

ข้อกำหนดในการแต่งกาย **kôr gahm·nòt ni garn dtàeng·gie** dress code

ข้อความ **kôr·kwarm** message

ข้อผิดพลาด **kôr piht·plârt** error

ข้อมูล **kôr·moon** information

ของเก่า **kŏrng·gòu** antique

ของขวัญ **kŏrng·kwăhn** n present

ของที่ระลึก **kŏrng·têe·rah·lúek** souvenir

ของแท้ **kŏrng táe** authenticity

ของฝาก **kŏrng fàrk** gift

ของเล่น **kŏrng·lên** toy

ของเลียนแบบ **kŏrng lean·bàep** imitation

ขอบคุณ **kòrp·kuhn** thank

ขับ **kàhp** drive

ขา **kăr** leg

ขากรรไกร **kăr·gahn·gri** jaw

ขาเข้า **kăr·kôu** arrivals

ขาออก **kăr·òrk** departures

ข้างนอก **kârng·nôrk** outside

ข้างใน **kârng·ni** inside

ข้ามคืน **kârm kueen** overnight

ขาย **kĭe** sell

ขายหมด **kĭe mòt** sold out

ข่าว **kòw** news

ขี่ม้า **kèe már** horseback riding

ขึ้นเงิน **kûen·ngern** v cash

เขต **kèt** region

เขตคนเดินถนน **kèt kon dern tah·nŏn** pedestrian zone [precinct BE]

เขตอนุรักษ์ **kèt àh·núh·ráhk** conservation area

เขตอยู่อาศัย **kèt yòo·ar·sĭ** residential zone

เข็มขัด **kĕhm·kàht** belt

เข็มขัดนิรภัย **kĕhm·kàht níh·ráh·pi** seat belt

เขา **kŏu** horn (animal)

เข่า **kòu** knee

เข้า **kôu** v enter

เข้าใจ **kôu·ji** understand

เข้าถึง **kôu·tŭeng** v access

เข้าระบบ **kôu rah·bòp** log on

เขียน **kĕan** write

แข็ง **kăng** hard (solid)

แข็งแรง **kăng·raeng** strong (physical)

แข่งม้า **kàng már** horse racing

แขน **kăen** arm

แขนเสื้อ **kăen sûea** sleeve

ไขควง **kĭ·koarng** screwdriver

ไข่มุก **ki·múhk** pearl

ไข้ **kî** fever

ไข้หวัด **kî·wàht** n cold

ไข้หวัดใหญ่ **kî·wàht·yì** n flu

คงที่ **kong·têe** constant

คน **kon** person

คนขับ **kon kàhp** driver

คนไข้ **kon kî** patient

คนเดินถนน **kon dern tah·nŏn** pedestrian

คนตรวจตั๋ว **kon dtròart dtŏar** ticket inspector

คนเป็นโรคเบาหวาน **kon bpehn rôek·bou·wărn** n diabetic

คนพิการ **kon píh·garn** disabled (person)

คนยกกระเป๋า **kon yók grah·bpŏu** porter

คนอังกฤษ **kon ahng·griht** British (person)

คม **kom** sharp

ครอบครัว **krôrp·kroar** family

ครับ♂ **kráhp**♂ yes

คริสตัล **kríhs·dtâhn** crystal

ครีมกันแดด **kreem gahn·dàet** sunblock; sunscreen

ครีมแก้อักเสบ **kreem gâe àhk·sèp** antiseptic cream

ครีมโกนหนวด **kreem goen·nòart** shaving cream

ครีมนวดผม **kreem nôart·pŏm** conditioner (hair)

ครึ่ง **krûeng** half

คลอง **klorng** canal

คลับ **klàhp** club

คลับเต้นรำ **klàhp dtêhn·rahm** dance club

คลาสสิก **klárt·sihk** classical

คลีนิค **klee·nihk** clinic

คลื่น **klûeen** wave

คลื่นไส้ **klûeen·sî** nausea

ควบคุม **kôarp·kuhm** control

ควบคุมอาหาร **kôarp·kuhm ar·hǎrn** diet

ความช่วยเหลือ **kwarm chôarw·lǔea** assistance; help

ความดันเลือด **kwarm·dahn lûeat** blood pressure

ความปลอดภัย **kwarm bplòrt·pi** safety

ความยาว **kwarm yarw** length

ความร้อน **kwarm rórn** heat

ความรับผิดชอบ **kwarm ráhp·piht·chôrp** responsibility

ความเร็ว **kwarm·rehw** n speed

ความสนใจ **kwarm sŏn·ji** interest (hobby)

ความสัมพันธ์ **kwarm sǎhm·pahn** relationship

ความสูง **kwarm·sŏong** height

คอ **kor** neck

คอกเด็กเล่น **kôrk dèhk ·lêhn** playpen

คอนแท็คเลนส์ **kohn·tàk·lehn** contact lens

คอนเสิร์ต **kohn·sèrt** concert

คอมพิวเตอร์ **kohm·pihw·dtêr** computer

คอร์สภาษา **kórt par·sǎr** language course

ค่ะ ♀ **kâh** ♀ yes

คัน **kahn** itch

คับ **káhp** tight

ค่าเข้า **kâr kôu** admission charge

ค่าใช้จ่าย **kâr chí·jie** allowance; n cost

ค่าบริการ **kâr bor·rih·garn** service charge; commission

ค่าบริการต่อหัว **kâr bor·rih·garn dtòr·hǔa** cover charge

ค่าผ่านทาง **kâr pàrn·tarng** toll

ค่าผ่านประตู **kâr pàrn bprah·dtoo** entrance fee

ค่าแสตมป์ **kâr sah·dtaem** postage

คาสิโน **kar·sih·noe** casino

คำเตือน **kahm·dtuean** warning

คำแปล **kahm·bplae** translation

คำสั่ง **kahm·sàhng** instructions

คิดเงิน **kíht·ngern** v charge

คิดเงินเกิน **kíht·ngern gern** overcharge

คิดว่า **kíht wâr** think

คิว **kihw** n line [queue BE]

คิ้ว **kihw** eyebrow

คีม **keem** clamp

คีย์การ์ด **kee·gárt** key card

คืน **kueen** return; give back

คืนเงิน **kueen ngern** v refund

คืนนี้ **kueen·née** tonight

คือ **kuee** be

คุก **kúhk** prison

คุณ **kuhn** you

คุณภาพ **kuhn·nah·pârp** quality

คุมกำเนิด **kuhm·gahm·nèrt** contraceptive

คู่ **kôo** double; pair

คู่มือของที่ระลึก **kôo·muee kŏrng·têe·rah·lúek** souvenir guide

คู่มือแหล่งบันเทิง **kôo·muea làng bahn·terng** entertainment guide

คู่สมรส **kôo sŏm·rót** spouse

คู่หมั้น **kôo·mâhn** fiancé

เครือข่าย **kruea·kìe** network

เครื่องโกนหนวดไฟฟ้า **krûeang goen·nòart fi·fár** electric shaver

เครื่องคิดเงิน **krûeang kít·ngern** cash register

เครื่องช่วยฟัง **krûeang chôary·fahng** hearing aid

เครื่องซักผ้า **krûeang sáhk·pâr** washing machine

เครื่องดับเพลิง **krûeang dàhp·plerng** fire extinguisher

เครื่องดื่ม **krûeang·dùeem** n drink

เครื่องดูดฝุ่น **krûeang dòot·fùhn** vacuum cleaner

เครื่องนอน **krûeang·norn** bedding

เครื่องบิน **krûeang bihn** plane

เครื่องประดับ **krûeang bprah·dàhp** jewelry

เครื่องปั้นดินเผา **krûeang·bpâhn·dihn·pǒu** pottery

เครื่องแฟกซ์ **krûeang fàk** fax machine

เครื่องมือ **krûeang·muee** equipment

เครื่องยนต์ **krûeang·yon** motor

เครื่องล้างจาน **krûeang lárng·jarn** dishwasher

เครื่องลายคราม **krûeang lie·krarm** porcelain

เครื่องเล่นซีดี **krûeang lêhn see·dee** CD player

เครื่องสำอาง **krûeang sǎhm·arng** cosmetic

เคาน์เตอร์ **kóu·dtêr** counter

เคาะ **kóh** knock

แคชเชียร์ **káet·chea** cashier

แคลอรี่ **kae·lor·rêe** calorie

โคเชอร์ **koe·chêr** kosher

โคมไฟ **koem·fi** lamp

ใคร **kri** anyone; who

# ฆ

ฆ้อน **kórn** hammer

# ง

งดงามมาก **ngót·ngarm mârk** magnificent

ง่วง **ngôarng** drowsy

งาน **ngarn** job

งานแต่งงาน **ngarn dtàng·ngarn** wedding

งานทำถนน **ngarn tahm tah·nǒn** roadwork

งานปาร์ตี้ **ngarn bpar·dtêe** party

งานฝีมือ **ngarn fěe·muee** crafts

ง่าย **ngîe** easy

เงา **ngou** shadow

เงิน **ngern** currency; money; silver (metal)

เงินคืน **ngern·kueen** n refund

เงินบริจาค **ngern bor·rih·jàrk** donation

เงินปอนด์ **ngern·bporn** pound sterling

เงินมัดจำ **ngern máht·jahm** n deposit

เงินสด **ngern·sòt** n cash

เงินสเตอร์ลิง **ngern sah·dter·lihng** sterling silver

เงียบ **ngêap** quiet

# จ

จดหมาย **jòt·mǐe** n mail [post BE]; letter

จบ **jòp** v end

จมน้ำ **jom·nárm** drown

จมูก **jah·mòok** nose

จริง **jihng** true

จริงจัง **jihng·jahng** serious

จอง **jorng** reserve

จอด **jòrt** v stop

จอดรถ **jòrt·rót** v park

จักรยาน **jàhk·grah·yarn** bicycle

จักรยานยนต์ **jàhk·grah·yarn yon** motorcycle

จัดระบบ **jàht rah·bòp** organize

จับ **jàhp** catch

จาก **jàrk** depart; from

จาน **jarn** dish; plate

จ่าย **jie** pay

จำกัดความเร็ว **jahm·gàht kwarm·rehw** speed limit

จำได้ **jahm·dîe** remember

จำนวน **jahm·noarn** amount

จำเป็น **jahm·bpehn** essential; necessary

จี้ **jêe** mugging

จุกนม **jùhk·nom** pacifier [dummy BE]

จุด **jùht** spot (place; site)

จุดชมวิว **jùht chom wihw** viewpoint

จุดไฟ **jùht·fi** v light

จูบ **jòop** kiss

เจ **je** vegan

เจ็ทเล็ก **jéht·làk** jet lag

เจ็ทสกี **jéht sah·gee** jet-ski

เจ็บ **jèhp** pain; hurt

เจ็บคอ **jèhp·kor** sore throat

เจ้าของ **jôu·kǒrng** owner

แจ้ง **jâeng** notify

แจ้งความ **jâeng·kwarm** report (to police)

แจ๊ส **jáet** jazz

ใจดี **ji·dee** adj kind

ฉีก **chèek** torn

ฉีดยา **chèet·yar** inject

ฉุกเฉิน **chùhk·chěrn** emergency

ชกมวย **chók·moary** boxing

ชนิด **chah·níht** type

ช่วงออฟพีค **chôarng órp·péek** off-peak (ticket)

ช่วย **chôary** v help

ช่วยด้วย **chôary·dôary** help (command)

ช็อค **chókk** shock

ช่องคลอด **chông·klôrt** vagina

ช่องทำน้ำแข็ง **chôhng tahm náhm·kǎeng** freezer

ช้อน **chórn** spoon

ชอบ **chôrp** like

ช็อปปิ้ง **chóp·bpîhng** shopping

ชั่งน้ำหนัก **châhng náhm·nàhk** weigh

ชัน **chahn** steep

ชั้น **cháhn** floor (level)

ชั้นใต้ดิน **cháhn tîe·dihn** basement

ชั้นธุรกิจ **cháhn túh·ráh·gìht** business class

ชั้นบน **cháhn bon** upstairs

ชั้นประหยัด **cháhn bprah·yàht** economy class

ชั้นหนึ่ง **cháhn nùeng** first class

ชั่วโมง **chôar·moeng** hour

ช้า **chár** delay; slow

ช่าง **chârng** mechanic

ช่างตัดผม **chârng tàht·pǒm** barber

ช่างทำผม **chârng tahm·pǒm** hairdresser

ช่างทำแว่น **chârng tahm wân** optician

ชานชาลา **charn·char·lar** platform

ชาม **charm** bowl

ชายฝั่ง **chie·fàhng** coast

ชายหาด **chie·hàrt** beach

ชิ้น **chíhn** piece

ชิม **chihm** v taste

ชีวิต **chee·wìht** life

ชื้น **chúeen** damp

ชื่อ **chûee** name

ชื่อผู้ใช้ **chûee pôo·chí** username

ชุดกระโปรง **chúht grah·bproeng** dress

ชุดเป็นทางการ **chúht bpehn tarng·garn** formal dress

ชุดนอน **chúht·norn** pajamas
ชุดว่ายน้ำ **chút wîe·nárm** swimsuit
ชุดสูท **chúht sòot** suit
ชุน **chuhn** mend (clothes)
เช็ค **chéhk** *n* check [cheque BE]
เช็คเดินทาง **chéhk dern·tarng**
 traveller's check [traveller's cheque BE]
เช็คอิน **chéhk·ihn** check in
เช็คเอาท์ **chéhk·óu** check out
เช็ด **chéht** wipe
เช่า **chôu** hire; rent
เช้า **chów** morning
เชิญ **chern** invite
เชื่อถือได้ **chûea·tŭee·dîe** reliable
เชือก **chûeak** rope
เชื่อมต่อ **chûeam·dtòr** connect
แชมพู **chaem·poo** shampoo
ใช้ **chí** use
ใช้จ่าย **chí·jìe** spend
ใช้ได้ **chí·dîe** valid
ใช้แล้วทิ้ง **chí láew tíhng** disposable

ซ

ซองจดหมาย **sorng jòt·mĭe** envelope
ซ่อม **sôhm** repair
ซ่อมรองเท้า **sôhm rorng·tów** shoe repair
ซักแห้ง **sáhk·hâeng** dry clean
ซ้าย **sie** left
ซ้ำอีกที **sáhm èek·tee** repeat
ซิการ์ **síh·gâr** cigar
ซิป **síhp** zipper
ซีดี **see·dee** CD
ซื้อ **súee** buy
ซุปเปอร์ **súhp·bpêr** premium (fuel)
ซุปเปอร์มาร์เก็ต **súhp·bpêr·mar·gêht**
 supermarket
เซ็กซ์ **séhk** sex (activity)
เซ็นชื่อ **sehn·chûee** *v* sign
เซรามิก **se·rar·mìhk** ceramics

ด

ดนตรี **don·dtree** music
ด่วน **dòarn** urgent; express
ดอกไม้ **dòrk·mie** flower
ดอลลาร์ **dohn·lâr** dollar
ดัง **dahng** loud (noise); famous
ดั้งเดิม **dâhng·derm** original
ด่านเก็บค่าผ่านทาง **dàrn gèhp
 kâr·pàrn·tarng** toll booth
ด้านหน้า **dârn·nâr** front
ดำน้ำ **dahm·nárm** dive
ดิจิตอล **dih·jih·dtôhn** digital
ดี **dee** nice; good
ดีเซล **dee·sen** diesel
ดีมาก **dee mârk** great; very good
ดึง **dueng** pull
ดื่ม **dùeem** *v* drink
ดู **doo** look
เด็ก **dèhk** child
เด็กผู้ชาย **dèhk·pôo·chie** boy
เด็กผู้หญิง **dèhk·pôo·yĭhng** girl
เด็กอ่อน **dèhk·òrn** baby
เดิน **dern** walk
เดินป่า **dern bpàr** hike
เดินรถทางเดียว (วันเวย์) **dern·rót tarng
 deaw (wahn·we)** one-way (traffic)
เดือน **duean** month
แดด **dàet** sun (light)
แดดเผา **dàet pŏu** sunburn
โดย **doey** by
โดยประมาณ **doey bprah·marn**
 approximately
ได้กลิ่น **dî·glìhn** *v* smell
ได้รับ **dî·ráhp** receive
ได้ยิน **dî·yihn** hear

ตกแต่ง **dtòk·dtàng** decorative

ตกปลา **dtòk·bplar** fishing

ต้นขา **dtôn·kǎr** thigh

ต้นไม้ **dtôn·míe** tree

ตรง **dtrong** *adj* direct

ตรงข้าม **dtrong·kârm** across; opposite

ตรงไป **dtrong·bpi** straight (ahead)

ตรวจ **dtròart** *v* check

ตรวจสอบ **dtròart·sòrp** examine

ตลก **dtah·lòk** funny

ตลาด **dtah·làrt** market

ตลาดนัด **dtah·làrt náht** flea market

ต่อราคา **tòr rar·kar** bargain

ต่อสู้ **dtòr·sôo** fight

ต้อง **dtôhng** must

ต้องการ **dtôhng·garn** need

ตอนเช้า **dtorn·chów** morning

ตอนนี้ **dtorn·née** now

ตอนบ่าย **dtorn·bìe** afternoon

ตอนเย็น **dtorn·yehn** evening

ตะกร้า **dtah·grâr** basket

ตะกร้าช้อปปิ้ง **dtah·grâr
chóhp·bpîhng** shopping basket

ตะคริว **dtah·krihw** cramp (sports)

ตะไบขัดเล็บ **dtah·bi kàht léhp** nail file

ตะหลิว **dtah·lǐhw** spatula

ตั้งแคมป์ **dtâhng·káem** *v* camp

ตั้งท้อง **dtâhng·tórng** pregnant

ตัด **dtàht** *v* cut

ตัดการเชื่อมต่อ **dtàht garn
chûeam·dtòr** disconnect

ตัวกรอง **dtoar grong** filter

ตัวต่อ **dtoar·dtòr** wasp

ตั๋ว **dtǎar** ticket

ตั๋วขากลับ **dtǎar kǎr·glàhp** return ticket

ตั๋วขึ้นเครื่อง **dtǎar kûen krûeang** boarding
card

ตั๋วเที่ยวเดียว **dtǎar têaw·deaw**
one-way ticket

ตั๋วไปกลับ **dtǎar bpi·glàhp** round-trip
ticket

ตั๋วรถเมล์ **dtǎar rót·me** bus ticket

ตั๋วดูดู **dtǎar rúe·doo** season ticket

ตั๋วสำรอง **dtǎar sǎhm·rorng** standby
ticket

ตั๋วอิเล็กทรอนิกส์ **dtǎar
ee·léhk·tror·nihk** e-ticket

ตา **dtar** eye

ตาชั่ง **dtar·châhng** scale

ตารางเดินรถ **dtar·rarng dern rót** schedule
[timetable BE] (bus)

ต่างชาติ **dtàrng·chârt** foreign

ต่างประเทศ **dtàrng·bprah·têt** foreign;
abroad

ต่างหู **dtàrng·hǒo** earrings

ตาม **dtarm** follow

ตาย **dtie** dead

ต่ำ **dtàhm** low

ตำรวจ **dtahm·ròart** police

ติดกับ **dtit·gàhp** next to

ติดต่อ **dtìht·dtòr** contact

ติดต่อกันได้ **dtìht·dtòr gahn dîe**
contagious (disease)

ติดทะเล **dtìht tah·le** seafront

ตื้น **dtûeen** shallow

ตุ๊กตา **dtúhk·gah·dtar** doll

ตู้จดหมาย **dtôo jòt·mǐe** mailbox [postbox
BE]

ตู้เซฟ **dtôo·séf** *n* safe

ตู้โทรศัพท์ **dtôo toe·rah·sàhp**
telephone booth

ตู้นอน **dtôo·norn** sleeping car

ตู้เย็น **dtôo·yehn** refrigerator

เต้นรำ **dtêhn·rahm** dance

เต็นท์ **dtéhn** tent

เต็ม **dtehm** full

เตา **dtou** stove

เตารีด **dtou·rêet** *n* iron
เตาอบ **dtou·òp** oven
เติม **dterm** fill
เติมให้เต็ม **dterm hî dtehm** fill up
เตียง **dteang** bed
แต่ **dtàe** but
แตก **dtàek** break
แต่งงาน **dtàng·ngarn** marry
แต่งหน้า **dtàng·nâr** *v* make-up
แตร **dtrae** horn (car)
โต๊ะ **dtó** table
โต๊ะเช็คอิน **dtó chéhk·ihn** check-in desk
ใต้ **dtie** under
ไต **dti** kidney

ถนน **tah·nǒn** road; street
ถ้วย **tôary** cup
ถอน **tǒrn** withdrawal
ถอนเงิน **tǒrn·ngern** withdraw (bank)
ถัง **tǎhng** bucket
ถังขยะ **tǎhng kah·yàh** trash can
ถังน้ำมัน **tahng náhm·mahn** fuel tank
ถัดไป **tàht·bpi** next
ถ่าน **tàrn** charcoal
ถาม **tǎrm** ask
ถ่ายเอกสาร **tie èk·gah·sǎrn**
  photocopy
ถ้ำ **tâhm** cave
ถึง **tǔeng** to (place)
ถือ **tǔee** hold
ถุงขยะ **tǔhng kah·yàh** garbage bag
ถุงเท้า **tǔhng·tów** socks
ถุงน่อง **tǔhng·nôhng** panty hose
ถุงนอน **tǔhng·norn** sleeping bag
ถุงมือ **tǔhng·muee** gloves
ถุงยางอนามัย **tǔhng·yarng**
  **ah·nar·mi** condom

ถูก **tòok** cheap; right (correct)
ถูกกฎหมาย **tòok gòt·mǐe** legal
ถูกขโมย **took kah·moey** stolen
ถูกต้อง **tòok·dtôhng** correct
แถว **tǎew** *n* row

ทนายความ **tah·nie·kwarm** lawyer
ทราย **sie** sand
ทอง **torng** gold
ทองแดง **torng·daeng** copper
ท่องเที่ยว **tôhng·têaw** travel
ท้อง **tórng** stomach
ท้องถิ่น **tórng·tìhn** local
ท้องร่วง **tórng·rôarng** diarrhea
ทะเล **tah·le** sea
ทะเลสาบ **tah·le·sàrp** lake
ทั้งหมด **táhng·mòt** all
ทัวร์ชมเมือง **toar chom mueang**
  sightseeing tour
ทัวร์เดินนำเที่ยว **toar dern nahm**
  **têaw** guided walk
ทัวร์ทางเรือ **toar tarng ruea** boat trip
ทัวร์นำเที่ยว **toar nahm·têaw**
  guided tour
ทัวร์ระยะสั้น **toar rah·yáh sâhn** excursion
ทัวร์วันเดียว **toar wahn·deaw** day trip
ท่าเรือ **târ·ruea** harbor
ทาง **tarng** way
ทางขึ้นสำหรับรถเข็นคนพิการ **tarng kûen**
  **sǎhm·ràhp rót kěhn**
  **kon píh·garn** wheelchair ramp
ทางจักรยาน **tarng jàhk·grah·yarn**
  bike path; cycle route
ทางเดินชมธรรมชาติ **tarng dern chom**
  **tahm·mah·chárt** nature trail
ทางตัน **tarng·tahn** dead end
ทางเท้า **tarng·tów** sidewalk
  [pavement BE]

ทางเบี่ยง **tarng·bèang** detour

ทางม้าลาย **tarng·már·lie** pedestrian crossing [zebra crossing BE]

ทางหนีไฟ **tarng něe fi** fire escape; fire exit

ทางหลวง **tarng·lŏarng** highway [motorway BE]

ทางออก **tarng·òrk** *n* exit

ทางออกฉุกเฉิน **tarng·òrk chùk·chĕrn** emergency exit

ทำ **tahm** do

ทำความสะอาด **tahm kwarm·sah·àrt** *v* clean

ทำงาน **tahm·ngarn** work

ทำไม **tahm·mi** why

ทำร้าย **tahm·ríe** *v* attack

ทำเล็บเท้า **tahm léhp·tów** pedicure

ทำเล็บมือ **tahm léhp·muee** manicure

ทำสำเนา **tahm săhm·nou** copy

ทำอาหาร **tahm ar·hărn** *v* cook

ทำเอง **tahm·eng** homemade

ทิศ **tíht** direction

ทิศตะวันตก **tíht dtah·wahn·dtòk** west

ทิศตะวันออก **tíht dtah·wahn·òrk** east

ทิศใต้ **tíht·dtîe** south

ที่เขี่ยบุหรี่ **têe kèar·buh·rèe** ashtray

ที่จอดรถ **têe·jòrt·rót** parking lot [car park BE]

ที่จอดรถแท็กซี่ **têe jòrt rót ták·sêe** taxi stand [rank BE]

ที่ชอบ **têe chôrp** favorite

ที่ดิน **têe·dihn** land

ที่ดูดส้วม **têe dòot·sôarm** plunger

ที่ตั้งแคมป์ **têe dtăhng·káem** campsite

ที่ทำการไปรษณีย์ **têe·tahm·garn bpri·sah·nee** post office

ที่ทำงาน **têe·tahm·ngarn** office

ที่นอน **têe·norn** mattress

ที่นอนอัดลม **têe·norn àht·lom** air mattress

ที่นั่ง **têe·nâhng** seat (on train, etc.)

ที่นั่งเด็ก **têe·nâhng dèhk** child seat

ที่นั่งริมหน้าต่าง **têe·nâhng rihm nâr·dtàrng** window seat

ที่นั่น **têe·nâhn** there

ที่นี่ **têe·nêe** here

ที่ปิคนิค **têe bpíhk·níhk** picnic area

ที่เปิดกระป๋อง **têe bpèrt grah·bpŏhng** can [tin BE] opener

ที่เปิดขวด **têe bpèrt kòart** bottle opener

ที่เปิดจุกก๊อก **têe bpèr jùhk·góhk** corkscrew

ที่พัก **têe·páhk** accommodation

ที่พักเยาวชน **têe·páhk you·wah·chon** youth hostel

ที่พักริมทาง **têe·páhk rihm tarng** rest area

ที่รับกระเป๋า **têe ráhp grah·bpŏu** baggage claim

ที่รับฝากเสื้อโค้ท **têe ráhp·fàrk sûea·kóet** coat check

ที่รับแลกเงิน **têe ráhp lâek·ngern** currency exchange office

ที่แล้ว **têe·láew** last (previous)

ที่ว่าง **têe·wârng** space; room

ที่สูบบุหรี่ **têe sòop·buh·rèe** smoking area

ที่สูบลม **têe·sòop·lôm** air pump

ที่ใส่ของ **têe sì kŏrng** compartment

ที่หนึ่ง **têe·nùeng** first

ที่ไหน **têe·nĭ** where

ที่อยู่ **têe·yòo** address

ที่อุดฟัน **têe·ùht·fahn** filling (dental)

ทีม **teem** team

ทีวี **tee·wee** TV

ทุก **túhk** every

ทุ่ง **tûhng** field

เทนนิส **tehn·níht** tennis

เทปนำเที่ยว **tép nahm·têaw** audio guide

เทอร์มินอล **ter·mih·nôrn** terminal

เท่านั้น **tôu·náhn** only
เท่าไหร่ **tôu·rì** how much; how many
เท้า **tów** foot
เที่ยง **têang** noon [midday BE]
เที่ยงคืน **têang·kueen** midnight
เทียน **tean** candle
เที่ยว **têaw** tour
เที่ยวเดียว **têaw·deaw** one way
เที่ยวบิน **têaw·bihn** flight
เที่ยวบินตรง **têaw·bihn trong**
  non-stop flight
เที่ยวบินที่ **têaw·bhin têe** flight number
แท้ **táe** authentic; real; pure
แท็กซี่ **ták·sêe** taxi
แทนที่ **taen·têe** instead; replace
แทรก **sâek** insert
โทร **toe** v telephone
โทรศัพท์ **toe·rah·sàhp** call (phone);
  phone; phone call
โทรศัพท์มือถือ **toe·rah·sàhp**
  **muee·tŭee** cell [mobile BE] phone
โทรศัพท์สาธารณะ **toe·rah·sàhp**
  **săr·tar·rah·náh** pay phone
ไทย **ti** Thai

ธ

ธนาคาร **tah·nar·karn** bank
ธนาณัติ **tah·nar·náht** money order
ธรรมชาติ **tahm·mah·chârt** nature
ธรรมดา **tahm·mah·dar** normal; regular;
  typical
ธุรกิจ **túh·ráh·gìht** business

น

นก **nók** bird
นมผง (เด็ก) **nom·pŏng (dèhk)** formula
  (baby)
นวด **nôart** massage
นอน **norn** sleep

นอนไม่หลับ **norn mî làhp** insomnia
น้อย **nóry** little; few
น้อยกว่า **nóry·gwàr** less
นักท่องเที่ยว **náhk·tôhng·têaw** tourist
นักศึกษา **náhk·sùek·săr** student
นั่ง **nâhng** sit
นัด **náht** appointment
นั้น **nân** that
นา **nar** rice field
น่าเกลียด **nâr·glèat** ugly
นาง **narng** Mrs.
นาที **nar·tee** minute
นามบัตร **narm·bàht** business card
นาย **nie** Mr.
นาฬิกา **nar·lih·gar** clock
นาฬิกาข้อมือ **nar·lih·gar kôr·muee**
  watch
นาฬิกาปลุก **nar·li·gar bplùhk** alarm clock
นำ **nahm** lead
นำมา **nahm mar** bring
น้ำ **nárm** water
น้ำตก **náhm·dtòk** waterfall
น้ำพุ **náhm·púh** fountain
น้ำมัน **náhm·mahn** fuel
น้ำยาคอนแท็คเลนส์ **náhm·yar**
  **kohn·tàk·len** contact lens solution
น้ำยาล้างจาน **náhm·yar**
  **lárng·jarn** dishwashing liquid
น้ำหนัก **náhm·nàhk** weight
นิตยสาร **níht·tah·yah·sărn**
  magazine
นิ้ว **níhw** finger
นิ้วเท้า **níhw·tów** toe
นิ้วหัวแม่มือ **níhw hŏar·mâe·muee**
  thumb
นี่ **nêe** this
เนคไท **néhk·tie** tie
เนินเขา **nern·kŏu** hill
เนื้องอก **núea·ngôrk** tumor

เนื้อผ้า **núea·pâr** fabric
แน่นอน **nâe·norn** exact; sure
แนะนำ **ná·nahm** introduce; recommend; suggest
ใน **ni** in
ในประเทศ **ni bprah·têt** domestic
ในไม่ช้า **ni·mî·chár** soon
ไนท์คลับ **ní·klàp** night club
ไนลอน **ni·lôhn** nylon

## บ

บกพร่อง **bòk·prôhng** faulty
บทเรียน **bòt·rean** lesson
บน **bon** on
บริการ **bor·rih·garn** service (work)
บริการฉุกเฉิน **bor·rih·garn chùk·chěrn** emergency service
บริการซักรีด **bor·rih·garn sáhk·rêet** laundry service
บริการตนเอง **bor·rih·garn dton·eng** self-service
บริการโทรปลุก **bor·rih·garn toe bplùhk** wake-up call
บริการรับจอดรถ **bor·rih·garn ráhp jòrt·rót** valet service
บริการลูกค้า **bor·rih·garn lôok·kár** customer service
บริการอินเตอร์เน็ต **bor·rih·garn ihn·dter·nèht** internet service
บริษัท **bor·rih·sàht** company
บริษัททัวร์ **bor·rih·sàht toar** travel agency
บริสุทธิ์ **bor·rih·sùht** innocent; pure
บวม **boarm** swelling
บ่อน้ำ **bòr·nárm** pond
บอก **bòrk** tell
บ่อย **bòhy** frequent; often
บ๋อย **bǒhy** waiter
บังคับ **bahng·káhp** mandatory
บัญชีกระแสรายวัน **bahn·chee grah·sǎe rie·wahn** checking account

บัญชีออมทรัพย์ **bahn·chee orm·sáhp** savings account
บัตร **bàht** card
บัตรเครดิต **bàht kre·dìht** credit card
บัตรจอดรถ **bàht jòrt·rót** parking ticket
บัตรโทรศัพท์ **bàht toe·rah·sàhp** phone card
บัตรโทรศัพท์แบบเติมเงิน **bàht toe·rah·sàhp bàep dterm·ngern** prepaid phone card
บัตรนักศึกษาสากล **bàht náhk·sùek·sǎr·sǎr·gon** International Student Card
บัตรประจำตัว **bàht·bprah·jahm·dtoar** identification
บัตรประจำตัวผู้เอาประกัน **bàht·bprah·jahm·dtoar pôo·ou·bprah·gahn** insurance card
บันได **bahn·di** ladder; stairs
บันไดเลื่อน **bahn·di·lûean** escalator
บัลเลต์ **bahn·lê** ballet
บาง **barng** some; thin
บางคน **barng·kon** someone
บางครั้ง **barng·kráhng** sometimes
บางที **barng·tee** perhaps
บางที่ **barng·têe** somewhere
บางอย่าง **barng·yàrng** something
บาดเจ็บ **bàrt·jèhp** injure
บาดแผล **bàrt·plǎe** *n* cut
บ้าน **bârn** house
บาร์ **bar** bar
บาสเก็ตบอล **bárt·sah·gêht bohn** basketball
บิกินี่ **bih·gih·nêe** bikini
บิด **biht** twist
บิน **bihn** fly
บิล **bihn** bill
บุหรี่ **buh·rèe** cigarette
เบนซิน **ben·sihn** gas [petrol BE]
เบรก **brèk** *n* brake

เบรคฉุกเฉิน **brèk chùhk·chěrn**
emergency brake

เบอร์ต่อ **ber dtòr** extension (phone)

เบอร์โทรศัพท์ **ber toe·rah·sàhp**
phone number

เบอร์แฟ็กซ์ **ber fàk** fax number

เบา **bou** *adj* light (weight)

เบาหวาน *n* diabetic

แบบเดียวกัน **bàep deaw·gahn** same

แบบฟอร์ม **bàep·form** form

โบสถ์ **bòet** church

ใบขับขี่ **bi kàhp·kèe** driver's license

ใบแจ้งความ **bi jâeng·kwarm** police report

ใบมีดโกน **bi mêet·goen** razor blade

ใบรับรอง **bi ráhp·rorng** certificate

ใบสั่งยา **bi sàhng·yar** prescription

ใบเสร็จ(รับเงิน) **bi·sèht (ráhp·ngern)**
receipt

ปฏิกิริยา **bpah·dtih·gih·rih·yar**
reaction

ปฏิทิน **bpah·dtih·tihn** calendar

ปรอท **bpah·ròrt** thermometer

ประกันภัย **bprah·gahn·pi** insurance

ประกันสุขภาพ **bprah·gahn
sùhk·kah·pârp** health insurance

ประจำเดือน **bpràh·jahm·duean**
period (menstrual)

ประชาสัมพันธ์ **bprah·char·sǎhm·pahn**
information desk

ประตู **bprah·dtoo** gate; door

ประตูทางออกขึ้นเครื่อง **bprah·dtoo
tarng·òrk kûen krûeang** departure gate

ประเทศ **bprah·têt** country

ประภาคาร **bprah·par·karn**
lighthouse

ประเภท **bprah·pêt** kind (type)

ประมาณ **bprah·marn** about

ประหลาด **bprah·làrt** bizarre

ปรับปรุง **bpràhp·bpruhng** improve

ปรับปรุงใหม่ **bpràhp·bpruhng mì**
renovation

ปรึกษา **bprùek·sǎr** consult

ปลอดภัย **bplòrt·pi** *adj* safe

ปล่อย **bplòhy** let

ปลั๊กแปลงไฟฟ้า **bpláhk bplaeng
fi·fár** adapter

ปลาย **bplie** *n* end

ปลายทาง **bplie·tarng** destination

ปลุก **bplùhk** wake

ปวด **bpòart** sore

ปวดท้อง **bpòart·tórng** stomachache

ปวดประจำเดือน **bpòart
bprah·jahm·duean** menstrual cramps

ปวดฟัน **bpòart·fahn** toothache

ปวดหลัง **bpòart·lǎhng** backache

ปวดหัว **bpòart·hǔa** headache

ปวดหู **bpòart·hǒo** earache

ปอด **bpòrt** lung

ปอดบวม **bpòrt·boarm** pneumonia

ป้อน **bpôrn** feed

ปอนด์ **bporn** pound (weight)

ปัจจุบัน **bpàht·juh·bahn** present (time)

ปัญหา **bpahn·hǎr** problem

ปั๊ม **bpáhm** pump

ปั๊มน้ำมัน **bpáhm náhm·mahn** gas [petrol
BE] station

ป่า **bpàr** forest

ปาก **bpàrk** mouth

ปากกา **bpàrk·gar** pen

ป้าย **bpîe** label; *n* sign

ป้ายรถเมล์ **bpîe rót·me** bus stop

ปิคนิค **bpíhk·níhk** picnic

ปิด **bpìht** *v* close; turn off; shut

ปี **bpee** year

เป้สะพายหลัง **bpê sah·pie lǎhng**
backpack

เป็น **bpehn** be
เป็นของ **bpehn·kǒhng** belong
เป็นเจ้าของ **bpehn jôu·kǒrng** own
เป็นที่นิยม **bpehn têe·níh·yom** popular
เป็นผื่นคัน **bpehn pùeen·kahn** rash
เป็นลม **bpehn·lom** faint
เป็นโสด **bpehn·sòet** single (unmarried)
เป็นหนี้ **bpehn·nêe** owe
เปรี้ยว **bprêaw** sour
เปลเด็ก **bple·dèhk** crib
เปลี่ยน **bplèan** v change
เปิด **bpèrt** turn on; open
เปิดดู **bpèrt·doo** browse
แปรงแปรงผม **bpraeng bpraeng·pǒm** hairbrush
แปรงสีฟัน **bpraeng sěe·fahn** toothbrush
แปล **bplae** translate
โปรแกรม **bproe·graem** program
โปรแกรมส่งข้อความ **bproe·graem sòng kôr·kwarm** instant messenger
โปสการ์ด **bpóet·sah·gárt** postcard
ไป **bpi** go
ไปรษณีย์ด่วน **bpri·sah·nee dòarn** express mail
ไปรษณีย์อากาศ **bpri·sah·nee ar·gàrt** airmail

ผงซักฟอก **pǒng sáhk·fôrk** detergent
ผม **pǒm** hair
ผลข้างเคียง **pǒn·kârng·keang** side effect
ผลัก **plàhk** push
ผ่าตัด **pàr·dtàht** operation
ผ้าก็อซ **pâr·górt** gauze
ผ้าซาติน **pâr sar·dtin** satin
ผ้าปูที่นอน **pâr bpoo têe·norn** sheet (bed)

ผ้าฝ้าย **pâr·fíe** cotton
ผ้าพันคอ **pâr·pahn·kor** scarf
ผ้าพันแผล **pâr·pahn·plǎe** bandage [plaster BE]
ผ้าม่าน **pâr·mârn** curtain
ผ้าลูกไม้ **pâr lôok·mí** lace
ผ้าห่ม **pâr·hòm** blanket
ผ้าอนามัยแบบสอด **pâr ah·nar·mi bàep·sòrt** tampon
ผ้าอ้อม **pâr·ôrm** diaper [nappy BE]
ผ่าน **pàrn** through
ผิด **piht** wrong
ผิดกฎหมาย **piht gòt·mǐe** illegal
ผิดพลาด **piht·plârt** mistake
ผิวหนัง **pǐhw·nǎhng** skin
ผู้จัดการ **pôo·jàht·garn** manager
ผู้ชาย **pôo·chie** man
ผู้โดยสาร **pôo·doey·sǎrn** passenger
ผู้นำ **pôo·nahm** leader (group)
ผู้แปล **poo·bplae** translator
ผู้สอน **pôo·sǒrn** instructor
ผู้สูงอายุ **pôo·sǒong·ar·yúh** senior citizen
ผู้ใหญ่ **pôo·yì** adult
ผู้อำนวยการ **pôo·ahm·noary·garn** director (company)
ผ้าเช็ดตัว **pâr·chéht·dtoar** towel
ผ้ายีนส์ **pâr·yeen** denim
ผ้าวูล **pâr woon** wool
ผ้าไหม **pâr·mǐ** silk
ผ้าอนามัย **pâr ah·nar·mi** sanitary napkin [pad BE]
ผ่าน **pàrn** v pass (drive)
เผ็ด **pèht** hot (spicy)
แผงขายหนังสือพิมพ์ **pǎeng kǐe nǎhng·sǔee·pihm** newsstand
แผน **pǎen** plan
แผนที่ **pǎen·têe** map
แผนที่ถนน **pǎen·têe tah·nǒn** road map

แผนที่รถไฟใต้ดิน **păen·têe rót·fi ti·dihn** subway [underground BE] map

แผ่นพับ **pàen·páhp** brochure

แผนกของหาย **pah·nàek kŏrng hĭe** lost and found [lost-property office BE]

แผนกจำหน่ายตั๋ว **pah·nàek jahm·nìe dtŏar** ticket office

แผนกต้อนรับ **pah·nàek dtôrn·ráhp** reception (desk)

แผนกรับจอง **pah·nàek ráhp·jorng** reservation desk

แผลพุพอง **plăe púh·porng** blister

ฝ

ฝน **fŏn** *n* rain

ฝนตก **fŏn·dtòk** *v* rain

ฝังเข็ม **făhng·kĕhm** acupuncture

ฝาครอบเลนส์ **făr·krôrp·lehn** lens cap

ฝากกระเป๋า **fàrk grah·bpŏu** *v* check (luggage)

ฝากเงิน **fàrk·ngern** *v* deposit (bank)

ฝากไว้ **fàrk·wí** leave (deposit)

ฝาน **fărn** *v* slice

ฝึก **fùek** practice

ฝูงคน **fŏong·kon** crowd

พ

พจนานุกรม **pót·jah·nar·núh·grom** dictionary

พนักงาน **pah·náhk·ngarn** staff

พนักงานขาย **pah·náhk·ngarn kĭe** shop assistant

พนักงานดับเพลิง **pah·náhk·ngarn dàhp·plerng** fire department [brigade BE]

พนักงานต้อนรับ **pah·náhk·ngarn dtôrn·ráhp** receptionist

พนักงานต้อนรับบนเครื่องบิน **pah·náhk·ngarn dtôrn·ráhp bon krûeang bihn** flight attendant

พนัน **pah·nahn** bet

พบ **póp** meet

พยากรณ์อากาศ **pah·yar·gorn ar·gàrt** weather forecast

พยาน **pah·yarn** witness

พยาบาล **pah·yar·barn** nurse

พรม **prom** carpet

พร้อม **prórm** ready

พระพุทธรูป **práh·púht·tah·rôop** Buddha image

พลั่ว **plôar** shovel

พลาสติก **plárt·sah·dtihk** plastic

พวงกุญแจ **poarng guhn·jae** key ring

พอ **por** enough

พอดี **por·dee** fit

พ่อแม่ **pôr·mâe** parents

พัก **páhk** *v* rest; stay

พัฒนา **páht·tah·nar** develop

พัดลม **páht·lom** fan

พัสดุ **páht·sah·dùh** package [parcel BE]

พาโนรามา **par·noe·rar·mâr** panorama

พาราเซตตามอล **par·rar·séht·dtar·môhn** acetaminophen [paracetamol BE]

พาย **pie** *v* row

พาสปอร์ต **párs·sàh·bpòrt** passport

พิการ **píh·garn** *adj* handicapped

พิการทางสายตา **píh·garn tarng sáry·dtar** visually impaired

พิการทางหู **píh·garn tarng hŏo** hearing impaired

พิพิธภัณฑ์ **píh·píht·tah·pahn** museum

พิมพ์ **pihm** print

พิเศษ **píh·sèt** special

พิวเตอร์ **pihw·dtêr** pewter

พี่เลี้ยงเด็ก **pêe·léang dèhk** babysitter

พื้นเมือง **púeen·mueang** native

พูด **pôot** talk; say; speak

เพชร **péht** diamond

เพนิซิลลิน **pe·níh·sih·lihn** penicillin

เพราะว่า **próh·wâr** because
เพศชาย **pêt·chie** male
เพศหญิง **pêt·yǐhng** female
เพิ่ม **pêrm** extra
เพิ่มเติม **pêrm·dterm** additional
เพื่อ **pêua** for
เพื่อน **pûean** friend
เพื่อนร่วมงาน **pûean·rôarm·ngarn**
colleague
แพง **paeng** expensive
แพลง **plaeng** sprain
แพลตตินั่ม **pláet·dtih·nâhm** platinum
โพลีเยสเตอร์ **poe·lee·yét·dtêr** polyester

ฟองน้ำ **forng·nárm** sponge
ฟัน **fahn** tooth
ฟันปลอม **fahn·bplorm** denture
ฟิล์มถนอมอาหาร **feem tah·nŏrm
ar·hǎrn** plastic wrap [cling film BE]
ฟุตบอล **fúht·bohn** soccer [football BE]
เฟอร์นิเจอร์ **fer·nih·jêr** furniture
แฟกซ์ **fàk** fax
แฟลต **flàt** apartment [flat BE]
ไฟ **fi** fire; *n* light
ไฟฉาย **fi·chǐe** flashlight
ไฟแช็ก **fi·chák** lighter
ไฟฟ้า **fi·fár** electronic

ภรรยา **pahn·rah·yar** wife
ภาพวาด **pârp·wârt** painting (picture)
ภาษาไทย **par·sǎr ti** Thai (language)
ภาษาอังกฤษ **par·sǎr ahng·grìht**
English (language)
ภาษีมูลค่าเพิ่ม **par·sěe moon·kâr
pêrm** sales tax [VAT BE]
ภาษีศุลกากร **par·sěe
sǔhn·lah·gar·gorn** duty (tax)

ภูเขา **poo·kǒu** mountain
ภูมิแพ้ **poom·páe** allergy

มรกต **mor·rah·gòt** emerald
มรสุม **mor·rah·sǔhm** monsoon
มอเตอร์ไซค์ **mor·dter·si** moped;
motorcycle
มะเร็ง **mah·rehng** cancer
มังสวิรัติ **mahng·sàh·wíh·ráht**
vegetarian
มัสยิด **máht·sah·yíht** mosque
มา **mar** come
มาถึง **mar·těung** arrive
มาเยี่ยม **mar·yêam** *v* visit
ม้า **már** horse
มาก **mârk** much; very
มากกว่า **mârk·gwàr** over (more than);
more
มาตรฐาน **mârt·dtah·tǎrn** standard
มาสคารา **márs·kar·râr** mascara
มินิบาร์ **míh·níh bar** mini-bar
มิสซา **míht·sar** mass (church)
มี **mee** have; contain
มีความสุข **mee kwarm·sùhk** happy
มีค่า **mee·kâr** valuable
มีชื่อเสียง **mee chûee·sěang** famous
มีซับไตเติล **mee sáhp·dti·dtêrn**
subtitled
มีเสน่ห์ **mee sah·nè** attractive
มีด **mêet** knife
มีดโกน **mêet·goen** razor
มืด **mûeet** dark
มือ **muee** hand
มือสอง **muee·sŏrng** secondhand
มุม **muhm** corner
มูลค่า **moon·kâr** value
เมนู **me·noo** menu
เมนูเด็ก **me·noo dèhk** children's menu

เมมโมรี่การ์ด **mem·moe·rêe gárt**
memory card

เมาเครื่องบิน **mou krûeang·bihn**
airsickness

เมารถ **mou rót** motion sickness

เมาเรือ **mou ruea** seasickness

เมื่อวาน **mûea·warn** yesterday

เมื่อไหร่ **mûea·rì** when

เมือง **mueang** town

เมื่อย **mûeay** stiff (muscle)

แม่น้ำ **mâe·nárm** river

แมลง **mah·laeng** bug; insect

แมลงกัดต่อย **mah·laeng gàht·dtòry**
insect bite

แมลงสาบ **mah·laeng·sàrp** cockroach

โมง **moeng** o'clock

ไม่ **mî** no; not

ไม่กี่ **mî·gèe** a few

ไม่เคย **mî·kery** never

ไม่แพง **mî paeng** inexpensive

ไม่มีอะไร **mî mee ah·ri** nothing

ไม่สบาย **mî sah·bie** sick [ill BE]

ไม่ใส่ **mî sì** without

ไม้ **míe** wood (material)

ไม้กวาด **míe·gwart** broom

ไม้กอล์ฟ **míe·górf** golf club

ไม้แขวนเสื้อ **míe·kwăen·sûea**
hanger; coat hanger

ไม้ถูพื้น **míe tŏo·púeen** mop

ไม้เทนนิส **míe tehn·níht** racket (tennis)

ไมเกรน **mi·gren** migraine

ไมโครเวฟ **mi·kroe·wép** microwave
(oven)

## ย

ยกเลิก **yók·lêrk** cancel

ยกเว้น **yók·wéhn** except

ยอมรับ **yorm·ráhp** accept; approve

ย่อยนมไม่ได้ **yôry nom mî·dîe**
lactose intolerant

ยังไง **yahng·ngi** how

ยา **yar** medicine

ยากันแมลง **yar gahn mah·laeng**
insect repellent

ยาชา **yar·char** anesthetic

ยานอนหลับ **yar norn·làhp** sleeping pill

ยาปฏิชีวนะ **yar bpah·dtih·chee·wah·náh**
antibiotics

ยาพิษ **yar·píht** poison

ยาระงับกลิ่นตัว **yar rah·ngáhp
glihn·dtoar** deodorant

ยาระงับประสาท **yar rah·ngáhp
bprah·sàrt** sedative

ยาระบาย **yar rah·bie** laxative

ยาลดกรด **yar lót·gròt** antacid

ยาสีฟัน **yar sĕe·fahn** toothpaste

ยาเส้น **yar·sên** tobacco

ยาเหน็บ **yar·nèhp** suppository

ยาก **yârk** difficult

ยาง **yarng** tire

ย่านใจกลางเมือง **yârn ji·glarng mueang**
downtown

ย่านช็อปปิ้ง **yârn chóhp·bpîhng**
shopping area

ย่านธุรกิจ **yârn túh·ráh·gìht** business
district

ยามไลฟ์การ์ด **yarm lí·gàrt** lifeguard

ยาว **yow** long

ยินดีต้อนรับ **yihn·dee dtôrn·ráhp**
welcome

ยีนส์ **yeen** jeans

ยืน **yueen** stand

ยืนกราน **yueen·grarn** insist

ยืนยัน **yueen·yahn** confirm

ยืม **yueem** borrow

ยุงกัด **yuhng·gàht** mosquito bite

ยุ่ง **yûhng** busy

ยูโรเช็ค **yoo·roe·chéhk** Eurocheque

เย็น **yehn** cool

เย็บ **yéhp** sew

เยี่ยมมาก **yêam·mârk** superb

แยก **yâek** separate

แยกกันอยู่ **yâek gahn yòo** separated (marital status)

แยกตามรายการ **yâek dtarm rie·garn** itemized

## ร

รถ **rót** vehicle

รถเข็น **rót·kěhn** cart [trolley BE]

รถเข็นกระเป๋า **rót·kěhn grah·bpǒu** luggage cart [trolley BE]

รถเข็นคนพิการ **rót·kěhn kon píh·garn** wheelchair

รถเข็นเด็ก **rót·kěhn dèhk** stroller [push-chair BE]

รถเช่า **rót·chôu** car rental [hire BE]

รถบรรทุก **rót bahn·túhk** truck [lorry BE]

รถบัสทางไกล **rót báht tarng gli** long-distance bus

รถพยาบาล **rót pah·yar·barn** ambulance

รถพ่วง **rót·pôarng** trailer

รถไฟ **rót·fi** train

รถไฟใต้ดิน **rót·fi tîe·dihn** subway [underground BE]

รถเมล์ **rót·me** bus

รถยนต์ **rót·yon** car

รถราง **rót·rarng** tram

รถลาก **rót·lârk** tow truck

รถเสบียง **rót sah·beang** dining car

รบกวน **róp·goarn** bother; disturb

ร่ม **rôm** umbrella

รวม **roarm** merge; include

รวมค่าบริการ **roarm kâr·bor·rih·garn** service included

รสชาติ **rót·chârt** flavor; taste

รหัส **rah·hàht** code; password

รหัสประเทศ **rah·hàht bprah·têt** country code

รหัสพื้นที่ **rah·hàht púeen·têe** area code

รอ **ror** wait

รองเท้า **rorng·tów** shoe

รองเท้าแตะ **rorng·tów dtà** slippers; sandals

รองเท้าบู๊ท **rorng·tów bóot** boots

รองเท้าผ้าใบ **rorng·tów pâr·bi** sneakers

ร้อน **rórn** *adj* hot

รอบ **rôrp** *n* round (golf)

รอบๆ **rôrp·rôrp** around

รอบกลางวัน **rôrp glarng·wahn** matinée

รอยฟกช้ำ **rory fók·cháhm** bruise

ระเบียง **rah·beang** balcony

ระมัดระวัง **rah·máht·rah·wahng** caution

ระยะทาง **rah·yáh·tarng** distance

ระวัง **rah·wahng** beware; careful

ระหว่าง **rah·wàrng** between; during

ระหว่างประเทศ **rah·wàrng bprah·têt** international

รัก **ráhk** love

รับ **ráhp** pick up

รับประกัน **ráhp·bprah·gahn** guarantee

ราคา **rar·kar** price; *v* cost

ร้านกาแฟ **rárn gar·fae** cafe

ร้านกิฟต์ช็อป **rárn gíp·chòhp** gift store

ร้านขายขนม **rárn kǐe kah·nǒm** candy store

ร้านขายของชำ **rárn kǐe kǒrng·chahm** grocery store

ร้านขายของที่ระลึก **rárn kǐe kǒrng têe·rah·lúehk** souvenir store

ร้านขายของเล่น **rárn kǐe kǒrng·lên**
  toy store

ร้านขายเครื่องกีฬา **rárn kǐe**
  **krûeang·gee·lar** sporting goods store

ร้านขายเครื่องมืออุปกรณ์
  **rárn kǐe krûeang·muee**
  **ùhp·bpah·gorn** hardware store

ร้านขายงานฝีมือ **rárn kǐe**
  **ngarn·fěe·muee** craft shop

ร้านขายดอกไม้ **rárn kǐe dòrk·míe**
  florist

ร้านขายผักผลไม้ **rárn kǐe pàhk**
  **pǒn·lah·míe** produce store

ร้านขายยา **rárn kǐe yar** pharmacy
  [chemist BE]

ร้านขายยาเปิด 24 ชั่วโมง **rárn kǐe yar bpèrt**
  **yêe·sìhp·sèe chôar·moeng**
  all-night pharmacy [chemist BE]

ร้านขายรองเท้า **rárn kǐe rorng·tów**
  shoe store

ร้านขายเสื้อผ้า **rárn kǐe sûea·pâr**
  clothing store [clothes shop BE]

ร้านขายเหล้า **rárn kǐe lôu** liquor store

ร้านขายอาหารสุขภาพ **rárn kǐe ar·hǎrn**
  **sùhk·kah·pârp** health food store

ร้านค้า **rárn·kár** store

ร้านค้าปลอดภาษี **rárn·kár bplòrt**
  **par·sěe** duty-free

ร้านเครื่องประดับ **rárn**
  **krûeang·bprah·dàhp** jeweler

ร้านซักรีด **rárn sáhk·rêet**
  laundromat [launderette BE]

ร้านซักแห้ง **rárn sáhk·hâeng** dry cleaner

ร้านทำเล็บ **rárn tahm·léhp** nail salon

ร้านเบเกอรี่ **rárn be·ger·rêe** bakery

ร้านหนังสือ **rárn nǎhng·sǔee**
  bookstore

ร้านอาหาร **rárn ar·hǎrn** restaurant

รายการ **rie·garn** *n* list

รายการร้านค้า **rie·garn rárn·kár** store
  guide [directory BE]

รายละเอียด **rie·lah·èat** detail

รายวัน **rie·wahn** daily

ร้าว **róarw** fracture

ริมฝีปาก **rihm·fěe·bpàrk** lip

รีด **rêet** *v* iron

รีบ **rêep** hurry

รู **roo** hole

รู้จัก **róo·jàhk** know

รู้สึก **róo·sùek** feel

รู้สึกตัว **róo·sùek·dtoar** conscious

รู้สึกสนุก **róo·sùek sah·nùhk** enjoy

รูป **rôop** photograph

รูปแบบ **rôop·bàep** feature

รูปปั้น **rôop·bpâhn** statue

รูปร่าง **rôop·rârng** shape

รูมเซอร์วิส **room ser·wìht** room service

เร่ง **rêhng** rush

เร่งความเร็ว **rêhng kwarm·rehw**
  *v* speed

เร็ว **rehw** quick; fast

เริ่ม **rêrm** start; begin

เรียก **rêak** call (summon)

เรียนรู้ **rean·róo** learn

เรือข้ามฟาก **ruea kârm·fârk** ferry

เรือแคนู **ruea kae·noo** canoe

เรือชูชีพ **ruea choo·chêep** life boat

เรือเดินทะเล **ruea dern tah·le** ship

เรือพาย **ruea·pie** rowboat

เรือยนต์ **ruea·yon** motorboat

เรือยอชต์ **ruea·yórt** yacht

เรื่องตลก **rûeang dtah·lòk** joke

โรคไขข้อเสื่อม **rôek kǐ·kôr sùeam**
  arthritis

โรคเบาหวาน **rôek bou·wǎrn** diabetes

โรคแพ้อากาศ **rôek páe ar·gàrt** hay fever

โรคโลหิตจาง **rôek loe·hìht jarng**
  anemia

โรคหอบหืด **rôek hòrp·hùeet** asthma

โรคหัวใจ **rôek hǒar·ji** heart condition

โรงพยาบาล **roeng pah·yar·barn** hospital

โรงยิม **roeng yihm** gym

โรงรถ **roeng·rót** garage

โรงแรม **roeng·raem** hotel

โรงละคร **roeng lah·korn** theater (play)

โรงหนัง **roeng·năhng** movie theater [cinema BE]

โรแมนติก **roe·maen·dtìhk** romantic

ไร่องุ่น **rî àh·ngùhn** vineyard

ไร้สาย **rí·sǐe** wireless

## ล

ลง **long** get off (bus, etc.)

ลด **lót** reduce

ลดราคา **lót rar·kar** clearance; sale

ลบ **lóp** delete

ลม **lom** air (tire); wind

ลมแดด **lom·dàet** sunstroke

ลมแรง **lom raeng** windy

ล้มลง **lóm·long** collapse

ล็อค **lóhk** lock

ล่องเรือ **lôhng·ruea** cruise

ล็อตเตอรี่ **lóht·dter·rêe** lottery

ล็อบบี้ **lóhp·bêe** lobby (theater, hotel)

ละคร **lah·korn** *n* play

ละลาย **lah·lie** dissolve

ล่า **lâr** hunt

ล่าม **lârm** interpreter

ลำคอ **lahm·kor** throat

ลำธาร **lahm·tarn** stream

ลำไส้ **lahm·sî** bowel

ลิตร **líht** liter

ลิ้น **líhn** tongue

ลินิน **lih·nihn** linen

ลิปสติก **líhp·sah·dtìhk** lipstick

ลิฟต์ **líhp** elevator [lift BE]

ลึก **lúek** deep

ลืม **lueem** forget

ลู่ม้าวิ่ง **lôo már wîhng** horsetrack

ลู่วิ่ง **lôo wîhng** racetrack

ลูกเต๋า **lôok·dtǒu** *n* dice

ลูกบอล **lôok·bohn** ball

เล็ก **léhk** small

เลน **len** lane

เล่น **lêhn** *v* play

เล่นวินด์เซิร์ฟ **lêhn wihn·sérp** windsurfing

เลนส์ **lehn** lens

เล็บ **léhp** nail

เล็ม **lehm** trim

เลว **lew** bad

เลี้ยว **léaw** turn

เลือก **lûeak** choose

เลือด **lûeat** blood

เลือดออก **lûeat·òrk** bleed

แลกเงิน **lâek·ngern** *v/n* change (money)

แลกเปลี่ยน **lâek·bplìean** exchange

แล้ว **láew** already

แล้วก็ **láew·gôr** then (afterwards)

และ **lá** and

โลชั่นหลังโกนหนวด **loe·châhn lǎhng goen·nòart** aftershave

โลชั่นอาบแดด **loe·châhn àrp·dàet** suntan lotion

โลหะ **loe·hàh** metal

## ง

วง (ดนตรี) **wong (don dtree)** band (music)

วลี **wah·lee** phrase

วอร์ดคนไข้ **wòrt kon·kî** ward (hospital)

วอลเล่ย์บอล **wohn·lê·bohn** volleyball

วัง **wahng** palace

วัดขนาด **wáht kah·nàrt** *v* measure

วัตถุประสงค์ **wáht·tùh bprah·sŏng** purpose

วัน **wahn** day

วันเกิด **wahn·gèrt** birthday

วันธรรมดา **wahn tahm·mah·dar** weekday

วันนี้ **wahn·née** today

วันพรุ่งนี้ **wahn prûhng·née** tomorrow

วันสุดสัปดาห์ **wahn sùht·sàhp·dar** weekend

วันหยุด **wahn·yùht** vacation [holiday BE]

ว่าง **wârng** available; empty, free, vacant

วาดภาพ **wârt·pârp** v paint (picture)

ว่ายน้ำ **wîe·nárm** swim

วาล์ว **wow** valve

วิชา **wíh·char** course

วิดีโอเกม **wih·dee·oe·gem** video game

วิว **wihw** view

วีซ่า **wee·sâr** visa

วีซ่าเข้าประเทศ **wee·sâr kôu bprah·têt** entry visa

เว็ตสูท **wét·sòot** wetsuit

เวลา **we·lar** time

เวลาทำการ **we·lar tahm·garn** opening hours

เวลาเยี่ยม **we·lar yêam** visiting hours

เวียนศีรษะ **wean sĕe·sàh** dizzy

แว่นกันแดด **wân gahn·dàet** sunglasses

แว่นตา **wân·dtar** glasses (optical)

ศาสนา **sàrt·sa·nǎr** religion

ศึกษา **sùek·sǎr** study

ศุลกากร **sǔhn·lah·gar·gorn** customs

ศูนย์การค้า **sǒon·garn·kár** shopping mall [centre BE]

ศูนย์บริการทางธุรกิจ **sǒon bor·rih·garn tarng túh·ráh·gìht** business center

สกปรก **sòk·grah·bpròk** dirty

สกีน้ำ **sah·gee nárm** water skis

ส่ง **sòng** deliver; drop off; send

ส่งข้อความ **sòng kôr·kwarm** v text (SMS)

ส่งจดหมาย **sòng jòt·mǐe** v mail [post BE]

สด **sòt** fresh

สเตนเลส **sah·dten·lèt** stainless steel

สไตล์ **sah·dtie** style

สถานที่ **sah·tǎrn·têe** site; place

สถานที่ท่องเที่ยว **sah·tǎrn·têe tôhng·têaw** sight (attraction)

สถานที่นัดพบ **sah·tǎrn·têe náht·póp** meeting place

สถานทูต **sah·tǎrn·tôot** embassy

สถานีขนส่ง **sah·tǎr·nee kǒn·sòng** bus station

สถานีตำรวจ **sah·tǎr·nee dtahm·ròart** police station

สถานีรถไฟ **sah·tǎr·nee rót·fi** train [railway BE] station

สถานีรถไฟใต้ดิน **sah·tǎr·nee rót·fi tîe dihn** subway [underground BE] station

ส้น **sôn** heels

สนอร์เกิ้ล **sah·nórk·gêrn** snorkel

สนามกอล์ฟ **sah·nǎrm górp** golf course

สนามกีฬา **sah·nǎrm gee·lar** stadium

สนามเด็กเล่น **sah·nǎrm dèhk lên** playground

สนามเทนนิส **sah·nǎrm tehn·níht** tennis court

สนามบิน **sah·nǎrm·bihn** airport

สนุก **sah·nùhk** fun

สแน็คบาร์ **sah·nák bar** snack bar

สบายดี **sah·bie dee** fine (health)

สบู่ **sah·bòo** soap

สปอร์ตคลับ **sah·bpòrt kláhp** sports club

สปา **sah·bpar** spa

สมรภูมิ **sah·mŏr·rah·poom** battleground

สมาชิก **sah·mar·chíhk** member

สมุดโทรศัพท์ **sah·mùht toe·rah·sàhp** phone directory

สร้อยข้อมือ **sôry kôr·muee** bracelet

สร้อยคอ **sôry kor** necklace

สระกลางแจ้ง **sàh glarng·jâeng** outdoor pool

สระเด็ก **sàh dèhk** kiddie [paddling BE] pool

สระว่ายน้ำ **sàh wîe·nárm** swimming pool

สระว่ายน้ำในร่ม **sàh wîe·nárm ni rôm** indoor pool

สร้าง **sârng** build

สลัก **sah·làhk** engrave

สวดมนต์ **sòart·mon** prayer

สวน **sŏarn** garden

สวนพฤกษศาสตร์ **sŏarn prúek·sah·sàrt** botanical garden

สวนสนุก **sŏarn sah·nùhk** amusement park; theme park

สวนสัตว์ **sŏarn sàht** zoo

สวนสาธารณะ **sùan sǎr·tar·rah·náh** *n* park

ส่วนตัว **sòarn·dtoar** private

ส่วนลด **sòarn·lót** discount; (price) reduction

สวม **sŏarm** wear

ส้วมเคมี **sôarm ke·mee** chemical toilet

สวย **sŏary** beautiful

สหรัฐอเมริกา **sah·hàh·ráht ah·me·rih·gar** United States

สหราชอาณาจักร **sah·hàh rârt·chah·ar·nar·jàhk** United Kingdom

ส้อม **sôrm** fork

สะกด **sah·gòt** spell

สะพาน **sah·parn** bridge

สะอาด **sah·àrt** *adj* clean

สั่ง **sàhng** order

สังเคราะห์ **sǎhng·króh** synthetic

สัญชาติ **sǎn·chârt** nationality

สัญญาณไฟไหม้ **sǎhn·yarn fi·mî** fire alarm

สัญลักษณ์ **sǎhn·yah·láhk** symbol

สัตว์ **sàht** animal

สัตว์ป่า **sàht·bpàr** wildlife

สั้น **sâhn** short

สัปดาห์ **sàhp·dar** week

สัมมนา **sǎhm·mah·nar** seminar

สาธารณะ **sǎr·tar·rah·náh** public

สามี **sǎr·mee** husband

สาย **sǐe** late

สายการบิน **sǐe·garn·bihn** airline

สายตายาว **sǐe·dtar yow** far-sighted [long-sighted BE]

สายตาสั้น **sǐe·dtar sâhn** near-sighted [short-sighted BE]

สำคัญ **sǎhm·kahn** important; main

สำนักงานท่องเที่ยว **sǎhm·náhk·ngarn tôhng·têaw** tourist office

สำรอง **sǎhm·rorng** spare

สำหรับขาย **sǎhm·ràhp kǐe** for sale

สิ่งของ **sihng·kŏrng** thing

สี **sěe** color; paint

สี่แยก **sèe·yâek** intersection

สุขภาพ **sùhk·kah·pârp** health

สุดท้าย **sùht·tíe** last

สุนัข **suh·náhk** dog

สุนัขนำทาง **suh·náhk nahm·tarng** guide dog

สุสาน **sùh·sǎrn** cemetery

สุเหร่า **suh·ròu** mosque

สุเหร่ายิว **suh·ròu yihw** synagogue

สูง **sŏong** tall; high

สูตินรีแพทย์ **sŏo·dtih·nah·ree·pâet** gynecologist

สูบบุหรี่ **sòop buh·rèe** smoke

เส้น **sêhn** line

เส้นทาง **sêhn·tarng** route

เส้นทางเดินป่า **sêhn·tarng dern·bpàr** trail

เสาเต็นท์ **sŏu dtéhn** tent pole

เสิร์ฟ **sèrp** serve

เสีย **sĕa** break down; broken

เสียหาย **sĕa·hĭe** damage

เสียงดัง **sĕarng dahng** noisy

เสื้อกันฝน **sûea gahn fŏn** raincoat

เสื้อกันลม **sûea gahn lom** windbreaker

เสื้อกันหนาว **sûea gahn nŏw** sweater

เสื้อโค้ท **sûea·kóet** coat

เสื้อเจ็กแก็ต **sûea ják·gèht** jacket

เสื้อชูชีพ **sûea choo·chêep** lifejacket

เสื้อผู้หญิง **sûea pôo·yĭhng** blouse

เสื้อยกทรง **sûea yók·song** bra

เสื้อยืด **sûea yûeet** T-shirt

แสดง **sah·daeng** *v* show

แสดงรายการสิ่งของ **sah·daeng rie·garn sihng·kŏrng** declare

แสตมป์ **sah·dtaem** stamp

ใส่ **sì** put

ห

หญ้า **yâr** grass

หน่วย **nòary** units

หนัก **nàhk** heavy

หนัง **năhng** movie [film BE]; leather, skin

หนังสือ **năhng·sŭee** book

หนังสือนำเที่ยว **năhng·sŭee nahm·têaw** guide book

หนังสือพิมพ์ **năhng·sŭee·pihm** newspaper

หนา **năr** thick

หน้า **nâr** face

หน้ากาก **nâr·gàrk** mask

หน้าต่าง **nâr·dtàrng** window

หน้าผา **nâr·păr** cliff

หน้าอก **nâr·òk** breast; chest

หนาว **nŏw** *adj* cold

หมดแรง **mòt·raeng** exhausted

หมดสติ **mòt sah·dtìh** unconscious

หมวก **mòark** hat

หมวกแก๊ป **mòark gáp** cap

หมวกนิรภัย **mòark níh·ráh·pi** helmet

หมอ **mŏr** doctor

หมอเฉพาะทาง **mŏr chah·póh·tarng** specialist (doctor)

หมอเด็ก **mŏr dèhk** pediatrician

หมอฟัน **mŏr·fahn** dentist

หมอก **mòrk** fog

หมอน **mŏrn** pillow

หมั้น **mâhn** engaged

หมุด **mùht** peg

หมุดปักเต็นท์ **mùht bpàhk dtéhn** tent peg

หมู่บ้าน **mòo·bârn** village

หยด **yòt** drip

หย่า **yàr** divorce

หยาบคาย **yàrp·kie** rude

หยุด **yùht** *v* brake; stop

หรือ **rŭee** or

หลงทาง **lŏng·tarng** lost

หลวม **lŏarm** loose

หลอดไฟ **lòrt·fi** lightbulb

หลัง **lăhng** back; behind

หลังคา **lăhng·kar** roof

หลังจาก **lăhng·jàrk** after

หลาย **lĭe** many

หวัด **wàht** *n* cold

หวาน **wărn** *adj* sweet

หวี **wĕe** comb

หอคอย **hŏr·kory** tower

หอศิลป์ **hŏr·sĭhn** gallery

ห่อ **hòr** pack; wrap

ห่อไป **hòr bpi** to go [take away BE] (food)

ห้อง **hôhng** room

ห้องครัว **hôhng·kroar** kitchen

ห้องคอนเวนชั่น **hôhng kohn·wehn·châhn** convention hall

ห้องคู่ **hôhng·kôo** double room

ห้องเดี่ยว **hôhng·dèaw** single room

ห้องนอน **hôhng·norn** bedroom

ห้องน้ำ **hôhng·nárm** bathroom; restroom [toilet BE]

ห้องประชุม **hôhng bprah·chuhm** meeting room

ห้องพักผู้โดยสาร **hôhng páhk pôo·doey·sărn** waiting room

ห้องพักผู้โดยสารขาออก **hôhng páhk pôo·doey·sărn kǎr·òrk** departure lounge

ห้องลองเสื้อผ้า **hôhng lorng sûea·pâr** fitting room

ห้องสมุด **hôhng sah·mùht** library

ห้องอาบน้ำ **hôhng àrp·nárm** n shower

ห้องอาหาร **hôhng ar·hǎrn** dining room

หัตถกรรม **hàht·tah·gahm** handicraft

หั่น **hàhn** v dice

หัว **hǔa** head

หัวใจ **hǔa·ji** heart

หัวใจวาย **hǔa·ji wie** heart attack

หา **hǎr** find

ห่าง **hàrng** away

ห้างสรรพสินค้า **hârng sàhp·pah·sǐhn·kár** department store

ห้าม **hârm** prohibited

ห้ามสูบบุหรี่ **hârm sòop buh·rèe** no smoking

หาย **hǐe** missing; lose (item)

หายใจ **hǎi·ji** breathe

หิมะ **hìh·máh** snow

หิว **hǐhw** hungry

หิวน้ำ **hǐhw·nárm** thirsty

หุ้นส่วน **hûhn·sòarn** partner

หู **hǒo** ear

หูหนวก **hǒo·nòark** deaf

เหตุการณ์ **hèt·garn** event

เห็น **hěhn** see

เห็นด้วย **hěhn·dôary** agree

เหนียว **něaw** tough (texture)

เหนือ **něua** north

เหนื่อย **nùeay** tired

เหมาะสม **mòh·sǒm** suitable

เหมือนกัน **mǔean·gahn** also; too

เหมือนกับ **mǔean·gàhp** v like (same)

เหรียญ **rěan** coin

เหล็ก **lèhk** iron (metal)

เหล็กกล้า **lèhk·glâr** steel

แห้ง **hâeng** adj dry (clothes)

แหนบ **nàep** tweezers

แหวน **wǎen** n ring (jewelry)

โหล **lòe** dozen

ให้ **hî** give

ให้นม **hî·nom** breastfeed

ให้ยืม **hî yueem** lend

ใหญ่ **yì** big; large

ใหม่ **mì** new

ไหมขัดฟัน **mǐ kàht·fahn** dental floss

ไหม้ **mî** burn

ไหล่ **lì** shoulder

## อ

องศา **ong·sǎr** degree (weather)

อธิบาย **ah·tíh·bie** describe

อนุญาต **ah·núh·yârt** allow

อนุสาวรีย์ **ah·núh·sǎr·wah·ree** memorial

อนุสาวรีย์สงคราม **ah·núh·sǎr·wah·ree sŏng·krarm** war memorial

อบซาวน่า **òp sow·nâr** v sauna

อพาร์ตเมนต์ **ah·párt·méhn** apartment

อเมริกัน **ah·me·rih·gahn** American

อยากได้ **yàrk·dîe** want

อย่างไม่เป็นทางการ **yàrng mî·bpehn tarng·garn** informal

อยู่ **yòo** stay; live

อร่อย **ah·ròhy** delicious

อโรมาเทราปี **ah·roe·mâr te·rar·pêe** aromatherapy

อวยพร **oary·porn** v wish (bless)

ออก **òrk** out

ออกจาก **òrk·jàrk** v leave

ออกจากระบบ **òrk·jark rah·bòp** log off

ออกเสียง **òrk·sěang** pronounce

ออกซิเจน **óhk·sih·jên** oxygen

ออเคสตร้า **or·két·trâr** orchestra

อ่อน **òrn** light (color)

อะไร **ah·ri** what

อะไหล่ **ah·lì** replacement part

อัตโนมัติ **àht·tah·noe·máht** automatic

อัตราแลกเปลี่ยน **àht·dtrar lǎek·bplèarn** exchange rate

อันตราย **ahn·dtah·rie** dangerous

อาการ **ar·garn** symptom

อาการท้องผูก **ar·garn tórng·pòok** constipation

อาการอักเสบ **ar·garn àhk·sèp** inflammation

อากาศ **ar·gàrt** weather

อาคาร **ar·karn** building

อาคารจอดรถ **ar·karn jòrt·rót** parking garage

อ่าง **àrng** sink

อ่างเก็บน้ำ **àrng·gèhp·nárm** reservoir

อาจจะ **àrt·jah** maybe

อาเจียน **ar·jean** vomit

อาชีพ **ar·chêep** profession

อ่าน **àrn** read

อาบแดด **àrp·dàet** sunbathe

อาบน้ำ **àrp·nárm** v bath

อาบน้ำฝักบัว **àrp·nárm fàhk·boar** v shower

อาหาร **ar·hǎrn** food; meal

อาหารกลางวัน **ar·hǎrn glarng·wahn** lunch

อาหารจานด่วน **ar·hǎrn jarn·dòarn** fast food

อาหารชุด **ar·hǎrn chúht** set menu

อาหารเช้า **ar·hǎrn chóu** breakfast

อาหารเด็ก **ar·hǎrn dèhk** baby food

อาหารเป็นพิษ **ar·hǎrn bpehn·píht** food poisoning

อาหารไม่ย่อย **ar·hǎrn mî yôry** indigestion

อาหารเย็น **ar·hǎrn yehn** dinner

อาหารว่าง **ar·hǎrn wârng** snack

อินซูลิน **ihn·soo·lihn** insulin

อินเตอร์เน็ต **ihn·dter·nèht** internet

อินเตอร์เน็ตคาเฟ่ **ihn·dter·nèht kar·fê** internet cafe

อีบูโปรเฟน **ee·boo·bproe·fen** ibuprofen

อีเมล์ **ee·mew** e-mail

อีเมล์แอดเดรส **ee·mew át·drét** e-mail address

อุณหภูมิ **uhn·hah·poom** temperature

อุดฟัน **ùht·fahn** filling (dental)

อุ่น **ùhn** warm

อุบัติเหตุ **uh·bàht·tih·hèt** accident

อุปกรณ์ดำน้ำ **ùhp·bpah·gorn dahm·nárm** diving equipment

อุปกรณ์เดินป่า **ùhp·bpah·gorn dern·bpàr** hiking gear

อุปรากร **ùhp·bpah·rar·gorn** opera

อุโมงค์ **uh·moeng** tunnel

อู่เรือ **òo ruea** dock

เอ็กซเรย์ **éhk·sah·re** x-ray

เอกอัครราชทูต **èk·àhk·kah·rârt·chah·tôot** ambassador

เอทีเอ็ม **e·tee·ehm** ATM

แอร์ **ae** air conditioning

แอสไพริน **áes·pi·rihn** aspirin

เอา **ou** take
เอาออก **ou òrk** remove
เอื้อม **ûeam** reach
โอเค **oe·ke** OK
โอนเงิน **oen·ngern** transfer (finance)
ไอ **i** cough
ไอโอดีน **i·oe·deen** iodine

## ฮ

ฮันนีมูน **hahn·nee·moon** honeymoon
ฮัลโหล **hahn·lŏe** hello (phone)
ฮาลาล **har·larn** halal